The Bradford Pals

The author wishes to express his grateful thanks to Mr. George Sassoon for allowing him to use verses written by his father, Siegfried Sassoon, and to the family of Eric Kennington for permission to reproduce "The Infantryman".

The author acknowledges his debt to the Imperial War Museum for allowing photographs and pictures from its collection to be reproduced, to the Ministry of Defence and the Prince of Wales's Own Regiment of Yorkshire for permission to reproduce their Crown Copyright MOD listings of officers and men killed in the War, to the MOD Pattern Room, Nottingham, to the Public Record Office, and to the Telegraph and Argus for permission to reproduce their photographs.

I would also like to thank the following Bradford Libraries' staff: Bob Duckett and Elvira Willmott for the Reading List, Peter Arendt for the design work and Robert Walters for putting it all together.

Cover based on "Oppy Wood, 1917" by John Nash. Imperial War Museum, catalogue No. 2243. It is reproduced with their kind permission.

I dedicate this book to the late George Morgan of Bradford, a former Sergeant in 'B' Company, the 16th Battalion, the West Yorkshire Regiment, without whose assistance it would never have been written: as were his comrades, a brave and patriotic man, the like of whom we may never see again.

A short history of the 16th and 18th battalions of the Prince of Wales Own West Yorkshire Regiment; based on the war diaries of the battalions and the experiences of the men who served in them from August 1914 to February 1918.

The Bradford Pals

by

Ralph N. Hudson

4th edition

© Ralph N. Hudson, 2013
The moral right of the author has been asserted.

1st edition published by the author in 1977.
2rd edition published by Bradford Libraries, ©1993
3rd edition (revised) published by Bradford Libraries, © 2000
4th edition published by Ralph N. Hudson, © 2013

All rights reserved.

TABLE OF CONTENTS

CHAPTER 1: IN THE BEGINNING: 1

CHAPTER 2: EARLY DAYS IN FRANCE: 13

CHAPTER 3: THE SOMME: 25

CHAPTER 4: NEUVE CHAPELLE, FESTUBERT, GIVENCHY: 50

CHAPTER 5: HEBUTERNE: 57

CHAPTER 6: GOMMECOURT PARK AND ROSSIGNOL WOOD: 62

CHAPTER 7: GAVRELLE AND OPPY WOOD: 73

CHAPTER 8: ARLEUX AND MERICOURT: 89

CHAPTER 9: AND IN THE END: 101

APPENDIX 1: THE TYKE, NO. 2: 108

APPENDIX 2: DOCUMENTS RELATING TO THE COURTS MARTIAL OF HERBERT CRIMMINS AND ARTHUR WILD: 130

APPENDIX 3: MAPS: 137

APPENDIX 4: OFFICERS & MEN WHO DIED IN THE GREAT WAR: 146

APPENDIX 5: FIRST COMPLETE ROLL CALL: 166

APPENDIX 6: READING LIST: 181

INDEX OF MEN AND PLACES MENTIONED IN THE TEXT: 184

ADDENDUM: BATTLE ORDER 1/7/16: 191

LIST OF ILLUSTRATIONS

1: Sergeant Albert Edward Sands, 16th Bn., served 1914-1919, page xi
2: George Morgan, page xii
3: Physical training, Manningham Park, 1914, page 1
4: Bradford Recruting Headquaters, page 2
5: Captain Blagbrough and Lieutenant Robinson instructing recruits, page 3
6: Rifle drill in Manningham Park, 1914, page 5
7: Pals marching into Ripon, May 1915, page 5
8: Young recruits, three still in their blue uniforms, page 6
9: Off Duty - Bradford Officers "Somewhere in the east", page 8
10: Pals enamel lapel badge, page 9
11: Captain Donald G Smith, page 11
12: .303 Vickers Mk 1 machine gun, page 11
13: The Infantryman, by Eric Henn Kennington, page 12
14: Very lights over the Somme, page 13
15: Private Jimmy F. Hogson, killed by sniper in 1916, page 15
16: Grave Marker, Private James Frederick Hodgson, page 16
17: Layout for Kit Inspection, page 17
18: George Morgan, the young recruit, page 19
19: Cyril Tetlow, page 20
20: Private F. Slingsby, page 22
21: 7.92 mm MG'08 Spandau machine gun, page 23
22: A Listening-post, by Arthur Bradbury, page 24
24: A battalion of the 31st Division marching to the front line, page 25
25: Captain C. S. Duckitt, page 29
26: Private Dawson Horne, page 31
27: Sappers installing assault ladders in assembly trench, page 32
28: Private Norman Waddilove, page 35
29: Corporal Squire Clough, page 36
30: Lieutenant Colonel H. F. G. Carter, page 41
31: Walking wounded 1, page 42
32: Facsimile of letter from Stuart Cloete, page 43
33: Advanced dressing station, Somme, 1916, page 44
34: Walking wounded 2, page 45
35: Percy Bateman, page 47

36: Private Harry Redman, page 48
37: Lieutennant Robert Sutcliffe, page 48
38: Frank Burn with Fred Hall and Frank Booth standing in the remains of the British Front Line facing Serre, July 1st., 1966, page 49
39: Shrapnel balls from the fields of the Somme, page 50
40: Captain Harry H. Dalley, page 52
41: 31st Division Men in a SAP-Head, Givenchy, page 54
42: Captain Alan Clough, page 55
43: Captain Harry Dalley with his wife, page 56
44: .303" Short Magazine Lee Enfield rifle, pages 57 and 62
45: Certificate of Merit, page 58
46: .303" Lewis machine gun, page 61
47: 2nd Lieutenant O. H. Staff, page 64
48: 2nd Lieutenant N. H. Priday, page 65
49: Major Robinson, page 69
50: Frank Burn, September 1916, page 70
51: Gavrell Trench, 1917, by Adrian Hill, page 72
52: No-Man's Land, Serre, 1916, page 73 and 89
53: 2nd Lieutenant R. W. Clarkson, page 74
54: Corporal W. Palframan, page 76
55: Lieutenant-Colonel A. C. Croydon, page 81
56: Albert and Mabel Hanson, page 85
57: Lieutenant-Colonel H. F. G. Carter with sergeants, page 87
58: The Interior of a Dug-out, by Adrian Hill, page 88
59: Frank James Symonds, page 100
60: Major G. S. Guyon, page 49
61: Bradford Pals Comradeship Association Headquarters name-plate, page 101
62: George Taylor at Serre Cemetery in 1974 , page 104
63: The Prince of Wales inspects Old Comrades in the Twenties, page 106
64: Survivors of the Pals at Bradford Cenotaph, July ist, 1977, page 106
65: The Tyke, No. 2, pages 108 to 129
66: Facsimiles from the trial transcripts, page 130
59: The father of Pte. Frederick Rowland Wade in a Somme cemetery, page 146
67. George William Broadhead, page 61

AUTHOR'S PREFACE:

I grew up in the shadow of two battalions. In an age when many young women did not marry because there were not enough men to go round. People spoke of the 'Pals', almost in a whisper.

I grew up in a town, like many other northern towns in that time, which had lost its best young men.

When I was younger, I was too busy with my own affairs to worry myself too much with the dying of these young men, probably even more interested in another war of my own time. As I approached an age when I would be too old to fight, but my son approached an age when he would, I became appalled by the implications of war and particularly the destruction of these two battalions. I resolved to find out what had really happened to them.

This short book is an attempt to record their story.

FOREWORD BY LESLIE SANDS

In that grim autumn of 1914, the young men came from everywhere to take the King's shilling and to offer him their dedicated services. From mills and mines, from office chairs and civic departments, from loom and bench and lathe and counter, they flooded the recruiting centres in answer to the nation's call for young manhood. With a patriotic fervour rarely equalled in the annals of our history, these lads turned themselves from a citizens' army into a highly skilled professional fighting force whose determination and fortitude would earn them the admiration of the world. The Pals' Battalions, in Bradford and elsewhere, gave all their physical and mental energies in a total commitment to the preservation of the homeland and the defence of assaulted freedom. In the case of the Bradford Pals, the majority also gave their lives. Those few who came back (for the two battalions of volunteers were "thrice decimated in battle") rarely talked to outsiders about their part in what came to be known as "The Great War". They had seen what was left of their youth and their ideals destroyed in the mud and filth of Flanders; and disillusion and moral betrayal are not favoured topics of conversation among war veterans because they represent a waste of precious time.

No 16/568 Sgt. Albert Edward Sands, 16th Bn., served 1914-1919, father of Leslie Sands.

One thing stayed intact for these survivors, one single factor that had sustained them all through the horrors of the Western Front and remained with them now, to give some consolation in the post-war days of bitter recrimination and reassessment. The Pals were a close circle that denied all intrusion, but there was a bond between each and every one of them that would never be severed. They treasured - and guarded jealously - the golden bond of comradeship. They had been aptly named.

Bradford has always honoured the First and Second Pals Battalions. It owes a debt of gratitude now to the author of this book, Mr. Ralph Hudson, who has worked tirelessly with application, understanding and compassion, to ensure that their glory and their tragedy are kept vividly alive for us nearly eighty years later. We who came after must revere them, for we inherited the privilege of their memory and the freedom that meant the sacrifice of an entire generation - the day before yesterday.

Leslie Sands, 1993.

George Morgan

Phyical training, Manningham Park, 1914

CHAPTER 1: IN THE BEGINNING

War is endemic,
and governments are carriers.
Martha Gellhorn. BBCTV circa 1990

Much has been written about the flood of volunteers who, in a mood of crusading idealism, answered Field-Marshal Kitchener's call to arms in 1914. So overwhelming was their response that the Regular Army, until then of small establishment, approximately 125,000 men, was completely unable to absorb the numbers involved. To resolve this problem and to satisfy the zeal of the would-be volunteers, who felt unable to accept long delays before they joined the colours, many towns formed 'Citizens' Army Leagues'. These leagues, on obtaining the approval of the War Office, raised their own battalions and bore the cost of clothing, feeding and training them until such time as the War Office could absorb them into regular formations. A leading Bradfordian, Sir W. E. B. Priestly, M.P., led a group of prominent Bradford businessmen to seek permission of Field-Marshal Kitchener to form such a league. Permission being granted, the Bradford Citizens' Army League was formed on the 20th September, 1914, with its depot at 23 Bridge Street and the Lord Mayor as Chairman.

Volunteers rushed to enlist. Men of all ages from mid-teens to mid-forties besieged the recruiting office, established at the Mechanics Institute, where the band of the 2nd 6th (Reserve) Battalion of the West Yorkshire Regiment played patriotic tunes and marching music, and where a Sergeant Major besported himself in full 'Regimentals'.

The Bradford Telegraph told its readers "The special inducement of the new Bradford Service battalion is that young men shall be enrolled to serve, shoulder to shoulder, with their friends and colleagues in civil life". Standards in physique and intelligence were set very high. Men were rejected for the slightest physical defect. Mr. George Morgan, one of the first to volunteer, was asked his age by a Recruiting Sergeant. When he replied that he was sixteen the Sergeant advised him "You had better go outside, come back again and tell me something different". He recalled "I came back in and told him that I was nineteen and I was in. When I told my mother that I had joined up, she said that I was a fool and she'd give me a good hiding, but I said 'I'm a man now and you can't hit a man'". Mr. Arthur Wadsworth was so disgusted at being rejected because of his age - he was also sixteen - that he walked to Leeds and joined the 'Leeds Pals', this time suitably revising his age. Within a week 1,000 volunteers had been accepted into the battalion.

However, a battalion cannot be formed from raw recruits alone, it needs officers and N.C.O.s. These positions were, in the main, filled by retired officers and reservists known as 'Dug-outs', together with what the War Office chose to describe as 'suitably qualified young men'. The latter were usually young volunteers whose sole experience of the martial arts had been one afternoon per week with the 'Officer Cadet Corps' of the local grammar school, shy young men in new, well-cut clothes, spiral puttees, stiff new Sam Brown belts and brown boots. Officers' breeches cost £2.12s.6d. a pair, a tunic £3.7s.6d., from Pope & Bradley, the gentlemen's outfitters.

Some of the 'Dug-outs' appear to have had difficulty in ridding these young Bradfordians of what was seen as a rather casual attitude towards military etiquette. A soldier rebuked for not saluting an officer is said to have replied "but I know him!" Other 'Dug-outs' had trouble with local dialect. An officer who asked a soldier why he was not wearing his cap on parade was rather perplexed by the reply: "Arz bart".

Bradford Recruiting Headquaters, The Yorkshire Observer, 9 February 1915

IN THE BEGINNING

The battalion was to be known, officially, as the 16th Battalion, the Prince of Wales Own West Yorkshire Regiment. Locally it was known as 'The Bradford Pals' and later, when the Citizens' Army League were able to cope with the organisation of a second battalion, as the 'First Bradford Pals'.

For the first three months the battalion made its Headquarters at the skating rink which, until recent years, stood on Manningham Lane, drilled in the local parks with obsolescent Long Lee-Enfield rifles, but returned home each evening to sleep. For this they were paid a food and lodging allowance of 21 shillings per week (£1.05 in decimal currency). A private soldier's pay was 7 shillings per week (approximately 35 pence). From this he would be expected to make an allotment of 3 shillings and 6 pence (about 17 pence) to his next of kin. This would be made up in the case of an allotment to a mother to 10 shillings and two pence (approximately 51 pence) by the Army. Thus, the spending power of the private soldier was 3 shillings and 6 pence per week (17 pence), from which he would be expected to supply such needs as soap, shaving materials, toothpaste, boot polish and metal polish (for cleaning buttons and cap badges, etc.). Each man was issued with two blue uniforms of the best worsted which Bradford's looms could weave, one of which had silver buttons bearing the city's coat of arms. As with other Citizens' Army Leagues throughout the country, the citizens of Bradford bore the total costs and expenses of the battalion.

On January 14th, 1915, the 'First Pals' marched to Skipton where they were to be accommodated in a purpose-built camp. The Bradford Daily Telegraph commented on the prevailing weather, "A more unpropitious day for the Bradord Pals to march to their new quarters in Skipton could not have happened", being a day of high winds and heavy showers. Their march began from the Town Hall Square where

Captain Blagbrough and Lieutenant Robinson instructing recruits, Manningham Park, 1914

they were inspected by the Lord Mayor. The 'ARGUS', describing the scene, said they had "displayed themselves as a body of fit, smart, purposeful manhood". When all farewells were said, the order rang out from their commanding officer, Colonel G. H. Muller, seated on his white charger, and they marched off in style. Their route took them via Blubberhouses Moor, where they spent the night in improvised accommodation. 'B' Company bedded down in the local church hall where George Morgan, now a member of this company, had to sleep on top of the piano, such was the shortage of space.

The 'League' now felt sufficiently confident to contemplate a second battalion, and in February, 1915, the 'Second Bradford Pals' was formed. This battalion was officially designated the 18th (Service) Battalion, the Prince of Wales Own West Yorkshire Regiment. The 'Second Pals' established themselves under canvas in Bowling Park. Alfred Scott had joined the First Pals in September, 1914, and was training with them at Skipton.

However, Alfred Scott had a elder brother, a former regular in the Coldstream Guards and a reservist who had been called to the colours. When he was posted to the Second Pals as Regimental Sergeant Major he 'claimed' his younger brother, and had him transferred to his own battalion, presumably to be able to "keep an eye own him!!" Thus Alfred Scott had the distinction of serving both battalions. It was said that, when R.S.M. Scott took the parade in Bradford, his voice could be heard in Wigan! The career of Sergeant Major H. Scott is described in some detail in Richard Alford's book "On the Word of Command".

Gilbert Isles was employed by a Thomas Whitley, an astute business man. Mr Whitley announced to his staff that anyone who volunteered for military service was assured of a job on his return from the war. Gilbert recalled "I thought I ought to go. Some of my school friends had already joined." So, just before the Whitsuntide holiday in May, he walked into Bradford to enlist. Stripped naked he appeared before the doctor for his medical examination. Now Gilbert was a very fit young man. He was a keen cross country runner and had been a member of the Airedale Harriers since he was fifteen. The doctor looked at him and remarked, "I wish they were all like you!" So Gilbert took the King's Shilling and was enlisted into the 18th Battalion the West Yorkshire Regiment. When he returned home wearing his Bradford Pals broach his mother said "Aye Lad, Ah thowt thee would!"

The doctor who examined Tony Miller told him that his chest was too narrow and referred him to a Mr Crawshaw, manager of Salmon Glucksteins. Mr Crawshaw, a keen member of the All Saints Gymnastic Club, gave him a crash course of body building which lasted several weeks. When Tony returned to the recruiting office he was passed fit into "D" Company of the 18th Battalion. On hearing the news his mother rushed to seek the advice of the family General Practitioner, one Doctor Woodroofe, saying "our Anthony has joined the Army, the 18th West Yorks. Do you think he will be alright?" Doctor Woodroofe is said to have replied: "Well, it will either cure or kill him!" Of what the good doctor thought Tony needing curing,

IN THE BEGINNING

Rifle drill in Manningham Park, 1914. Albert Sands, front row on the left

we will never know, but events were to show that there was a good chance of it killing him.

The reserves of the two battalions were brought together at the Bowling Park camp towards the end of May and, by process of evolution, they progressed towards indpendent status. In July they moved to Colsterdale to join the reserves of the two battalions, which had been raised in Leeds, to form the 19th (Local Reserve) Battalion West Yorkshire Regiment. However, the reserves of these four battalions became too bulky to handle as one unit so the reserves of the 16th and 18th battalions were moved to Clipstone in Nottinghamshire where they became the

Pals marching into Ripon, May 1915. The photograph was provided by Dudley Wilcock, whose father, Herbert, is in the second column from the men's right, third row from the front of the rows were all men are visible.

20th Battalion West Yorkshire Regiment. These reserve companies were, initially, made up of men from serving battalions who were seen as unfit for foreign service. Later some of these men were discharged whilst others were transferred to the 1st Yorkshire Garrison Regiment for home service. The remainder formed the actual reserves who would be drafted as replacements for casualties in the service battalions.

The Citizens' Army League was, in fact, pressured by the War Office in January 1915 to raise another battalion of men qualified to perform a dual role of Pioneers and Infantry. Initially the League took the view that the Bradford area was not suitable for this purpose. When the request was repeated in August the League agreed to combine with other West Riding authorities to raise such a battalion. This was to be known as the 21st Service (Pioneer) Battalion West Yorkshire Regiment.

In May, 1915, the 16th and 18th Battalions marched to Ripon, and, swapping their blue uniforms for regulation khaki, were absorbed into the Regular Army.

Initially both battalions formed part of the original 31st Division which included the 12th Battalion the York and Lancaster Regiment (known as the Sheffield City Battalion as featured in J. Harris's book, "Covenant with Death"), the 13th and 14th Battalions the York and Lancaster Regiment (the 1st and 2nd Barnsley Pals), the 11th Battalion the East Lancashire Regiment (the Accrington Pals) and the 12th Battalion the King's Own Yorkshire Light Infantry (the Halifax Pals). However, in the early part of the war, Lord Kitchener seems to have looked upon his 'New Army' divisions as a source of replacement brigades and not to have seriously considered training them as fully operational formations.

Young recruits, three still in their blue uniforms, Harry Severn on the left.

IN THE BEGINNING

In April, 1915, the original 31st Division was broken up into independent brigades for draft-finding purposes. Subsequently in September, 1915, both battalions moved, as part of the 93rd Infantry Brigade, to Fovant in Wiltshire where they were issued with tropical kit which included pith helmets, lengths of muslin called 'pugarees' (to be wound around the helmet as an insulator) and grey flannel body belts. They also exchanged their Long Lee-Enfields with short bayonets for the current active service rifle, the Mark 3 short Lee-Enfield with its 18" bayonet, although they still retained their obsolete leather belts with leather ammunition pouches worn on each side. Each pouch could contain a bandolier of fifty rounds and two clips each of five rounds.

The 93rd Infantry Brigade was composed of the 15th (Leeds Pals), the 16th and 18th Battalions of the West Yorkshire Regiment, and the 18th Battalion of the Durham Light Infantry (Durham Pals). Before leaving Fovant they were inspected by a ruddy faced General, a 'Dug-out',who advised, with tears in his eyes, that they should "Trust in God and keep your rifles clean".

On December 6th they entrained for a destination kept secret at the time from 'other ranks' which proved to be Liverpool Docks. They embarked on the Canadian Pacific steamship Empress of Britain, a vessel of some 14,000 tons displacement, designed to carry 1,550 passengers in peacetime. The ship had been converted to a trooper by removing most of its passenger cabins which opened up large areas between decks where hammocks could be slung from the deckhead. Beneath the hammocks were tables and bench seats where meals were to be taken. When not in use enamel mugs and plates were stored on the tables. Troops were only to be allowed on deck barefoot, as it was considered that Army boots in such numbers would not be conducive to the care of the wooden decks. Additional lavatory accommodation, which had been installed in the well decks, was to prove woefully inadequate with results that can only be left to the imagination.

They left the Mersey accompanied by two Royal Navy destroyers, but by the next morning these escorts had disappeared. By the afternoon of the fourth day The Empress was steaming in wide circles to the west of Gibraltar, waiting for nightfall before passing through the Straits.

Soon after midnight with Gibraltar safely behind them the Empress proceeded at her normal speed. All was quiet below decks save for the throb of the engines and the creaking of the hull, when suddenly men were aroused from their sleep by a loud, high-pitched mechanical screech coming from the bowels of the ship. Almost simultaneously there was the sensation of the hull colliding, bows on, with a large obstacle. For a moment the Empress rocked violently from side to side, mugs and other loose objects cascading from the tables and clattering on to the decks. Then all was silence, not even the throb of the engines to be heard. The silence between decks was soon broken as men fumbled for clothes and life jackets in the semi-darkness, the only illumination being provided by the low power electric 'night lights' which were mounted on the bulkheads.

After a few moments two officers came down the companion ways to reassure everyone that all was well, saying that the ship had been in collision with a fishing boat. In view of the violence of the impact, many thought this an unlikely story. However, about 30 minutes later the welcome throb of the engines was heard again and the ship proceeded on its way. It was learned the next day that the so-called fishing boat had, in fact, been the French steamer Djingjurd with some sixty souls on board, two of whom were killed. All the rest were safely taken on board the Empress. The Djingjurd sank within twenty minutes of the collision.

The Empress proceeded to Malta for a short stay while the damaged bows were inspected, and then resumed her journey east. None of the 'other ranks' had been told of her destination, prompting much speculation whether they were heading for Gallipoli, where fighting still raged, or perhaps India?

On December 18th, off Cyprus, a U-boat was sighted some miles to starboard. Two shots were fired from the ship's gun, causing the U-boat to dive. Almost immediately another U-boat was sighted some two thousand yards to port. This boat followed the example of its companion, without attempting any warlike act. Each of these incidents, had fate decreed, could have proved more catastrophic than the fate which awaited them in the crater fields of France.

On December 21st they sailed into the wide expanse of Alexandria harbour, and anchored for the night. From thence there only remained the short voyage to Port Said where both battalions finally disembarked on December 22nd, 1915. The following day the 16th Battalion despatched 'C' Company, under the command of Captain Blagbrough, to an outpost at Ras-el-Aish. The rest of the Battalion, together with the 18th, remained in Port Said until January 1st, 1916. These first few days in Egypt were spent in a tented camp a short distance outside Port Said, near

' OFF DUTY' -BRADFORD OFFICERS "SOMEWHERE IN THE EAST"
Appeared in The Yorkshire Observer, 18 February 1916

enough for the men to explore the sights and shops of the town. Bathing parades were especially enjoyed when the battalions were marched to the nearby beaches to plunge into the inviting waters of the Mediterranean, needless to say, without bothering too much about the lack of bathing costumes.

Their next destination was Kantara, a small town on the east bank of the Suez Canal, in those days little more than a railway station and a few other buildings. From here they moved into the desert to a location known as 'Point 70' where they were employed on outpost duties and the construction of defences. The purpose of these was to protect the northern caravan routes from the Turks. The day after their arrival, a 'Drum Head' service was conducted for the 18th Battalion by their chaplain, the Reverend Thornton who, in peacetime, was a curate at Bradford Parish Church (now Bradford Cathedral). He told the men that they were standing on the

Enamel lapel badge which was given to volunteers when they enlisted before they were issued with their blue uniforms.

caravan route from Palestine to Egypt, probably the route which Christ took on his journey into Egypt.

Life here was tedious and uncomfortable. The Pals learned to suffer heat, dirt, flies, scorpions and camel spiders. Water was strictly rationed, being brought in by camel train. Each man received one gallon a day which had to suffice for cooking and washing as well as for drinking.

Food was monotonous, if not poor. Normal army rations of that time were converted to 'desert rations' at the following scale:

Standard army rations	Desert rations
1lb of meat	1lb of preserved meat (bully beef)
1lb of fresh bread	1lb of biscits or 3/4lb of flour
1/50lb of mustard	1/8lb of curry powder
4oz of fresh vegetables	2oz of rice or 3oz of potatoes or
Cheese	4oz of onions
	Condensed milk at the rate of 1 tin per 16 men

The biscuits were approximately round in shape, about three inches in diameter and about a half inch thick. They were so hard that it was impossible to eat them unless they were first soaked in tea or stew. The general opinion was that they had been stored as surplus from some long-forgotten colonial war.

At Point 70 the Pals became acquainted with the members of a British India Army Regiment, namely the Mysore Lancers who were camped near by. Writing to his wife, John Will of the 16th Battalion described these professional soldiers as 'fine reliable and honourable fighting men who were totally loyal to the British crown.' John and his friends were so overwhelmed by the warm and hearty welcome they received on their first social call that it became a custom for them to pay a visit most evenings. The Mysores were largely responsible for their own catering and were always ready to exchange a bowl of curry for a packet of English cigarettes. This was a welcome supplement to the boring diet that the Pals were receiving.

One day the Divisional Commander paid them a visit. George Morgan was on a trench digging detail when he arrived. He approached the detail, mounted on his horse, dressed in immaculately laundered and pressed khaki and gleaming riding boots, and asked: 'Have you any complaints?' Lance Corporal Gee spoke up, saying 'We don't get enough to eat, Sir'. The Divisional Commander glared down at the Lance Corporal and said, in a sarcastic tone: "Well, you certainly look very well on it." Life in George Morgan's platoon was made more bearable by the presence of Private George Harrison who seemed able to turn his hand to anything. When sand storms blew down other tents, their's would stand. George would have gone out and driven in the pegs before the storm struck. The platoon motto became 'leave it to George'. Other characters in the platoon were Owen Moor who was always to be found 'doing someone a favour'; Bill Kenny, a Roman Catholic, who had studied for the priesthood - he was regarded as the platoon philosopher; Squire Clough, a quiet young man from a wealthy family - he became engaged to the Mayor of Pudsey's daughter before leaving England; Billy Booth, a close friend of

George Morgan, and Dawson Horne, the platoon comedian, who entertained everyone with stories of how he intended to rout the enemy single handed.

Private J. Patchet of 'A' Company was caught after lights out in his tent writing a letter by candlelight. He was ordered to extinguish the light and turn in. Feeling this to be unreasonable, he continued to write. Private Patchet therefore found himself on a charge and up before the Colonel. Now Private Patchet was, in civilian life, a solicitor and, in this instance, considered the charge to be unreasonable and himself innocent. Therefore when asked if he would accept the Colonel's punishment he demanded a court martial. The Army granted his request. Later a field-court martial awarded him two years hard labour.

Captain Donald G Smith

Captain Smith of 'B' Company rebuked one of his men for writing an 'indecent letter' which the Captain had to censor. Surprised at this accusation the soldier asked what part of his letter, written to a workmate, was offensive. Captain Smith sternly pointed to a paragraph in which the soldier had written: "Since I've been in Egypt, I've had some forbidden fruit!!!"

The activity which, after digging trenches, more frequently absorbed the rest of the battalion's time was to prevent local Arabs stealing their kit, a task to which they applied themselves with zeal.

.303" Vickers Mk I machine gun. MOD Pattern Room, Nottingham

The Infantryman, by Eric Henn Kennington. This appeared as the frontispiece of Tempest's " History of the Sixth Battalion West Yorkshire Regiment", 1921. It gives a good impression of what the ordinary soldier had to carry into battle. Reproduced here courtesy of the family of the artist.

Very lights over the Somme. Imperial War Museum, Negative Q1208.

CHAPTER 2: EARLY DAYS IN FRANCE

I cannot hear their voices, but I see
Dim candles in the barn: they gulp their tea,
And soon they'll sleep like logs. Ten miles away
The battle winks and thuds in blundering strife.
And I must lead them nearer, day by day,
To the foul beast of war that bludgeons life.

Siegfried Sassoon.

At the beginning of 1916, Field-Marshal Haig's plans for a grand offensive by the British on the western front were nearing completion. The 93rd Infantry Brigade was ordered to France to join, as part of the new 31st Division, the largest army ever fielded by Great Britain, an army composed entirely of volunteers.

The Brigade sailed from Port Said on February 29th, 1916, aboard the S.S. Minneapolis, a vessel fated to be lost to a U-boat attack on its return voyage. They disembarked in Marseilles on March 6th and marched from the docks to railway sidings where they boarded some ramshackle wagons marked 'Quarante Hommes ou Huit Chevaux'. The train began its journey north at a leisurely pace, the weather becoming bitterly cold as time passed. So recently accustomed to sunny climes the men had only iron rations and the contents of their water bottles to sustain them. From time to time they passed French ambulance trains carrying wounded from Verdun to hospitals in the South.

On March 9th, they reached their destination, Pont Remy, a railhead near Abbeville. The following day the 16th Battalion marched to Merelessart, the 18th Battalion to Citerne, where they were to remain for two weeks. The march was not to be recalled with pleasure by anyone. The weather was still bitterly cold and, added to this, it began to snow as the battalions marched off. The marching was hard going over the rough road cobble pave. Fifty minutes of marching would be followed by ten minutes rest. Covering nine to twelve miles a day, they slept at night in barns on filthy straw with the smell of open middens. As they got closer to the forward areas, night illuminations held their gaze; in their ears was the sound of heavy detonations.

There followed a period of training and general familiarization. During this period a party of officers and N.C.O.'s of the 16th Battalion were attached to units in the front line to gain first hand experience in the trenches. These were:

Captain F. Holmes	Captain G. S. Blagbrough
Captain A. Clough	Captain R. W. A. Pringle
Captain H. Russell	Lieutenant S. L. F. Hoffman
Lieutenant R. Sutcliffe	Lieutenant C. T. Ransome
2nd Lieut. J.M.H. Hoffman	2nd Lieutenant F. 0. Brumley
2nd Lieutenant P. C. Parker	2nd Lieutenant C. F. Claxton
Company Q. M. S. Hicks	Corporal Moor
Sergeant Watson	Corporal Flood
Sergeant Binclark	Corporal McConnel
Sergeant Ambler	Corporal Newton
Sergeant W. Morgan	Corporal Nelson
Sergeant Sowden	Corporal Owen
Sergeant Buttler	Lance Corporal Woodhouse
Sergeant Saville	Lance Corporal Burgoyne
Sergeant Dodsworth	Lance Corporal Shackleton
Sergeant Pullen	Lance Corporal Corless
Sergeant Manley	

To gain experience in trench work 'half companies' of the 18th Battalion were attached to the 18th Battalion of the Durham Light Infantry who were in the front line at that time.

On March 25th, both battalions began a march towards the Beaumont-Hamel area, resting each night in villages en route. They finally went into billets in Bus-les-Artois at the beginning of April. Here the rolling plains of Picardy reminded many of the 'Pals' of their native Yorkshire.

The 18th Battalion lost their Commanding Officer, Lieutenant-Colonel E. C. H. Kennard, when he departed for England on April 18th. His place was taken by Major, acting Lieutenant-Colonel, M. N. Kennard. Captain, acting Major, Carter was second-in-command of the Battalion. The 16th Battalion was, at that time, commanded by Major E. C. Kennedy.

At this point it is well worth considering the comments of Mr. George Taylor, then a private soldier in the 18th Battalion and later a recipient of a 'Field Commission', regarding the standard of training. Both battalions had been taught 'magazine rapid

Private Jimmy F. Hodgson, killed by sniper in 1916.

fire', each man being able to put fifteen aimed shots in one minute on to a four foot square target at three hundred yards range. At this they had reached a very high standard. Their route-marching was also second to none. Unfortunately route marching was to prove of little use in the coming holocaust whilst 'magazine rapid fire' was only of use in defence. All the junior officers were completely inexperienced. But both battalions did now enjoy the atmosphere of a somewhat exclusive club. An example of the prevailing spirit is to be found in the case of Private Jimmy Hodgson, George Morgan's cousin. Jimmy Hodgson ruptured himself during training but refused an offer of a discharge and demanded an operation so that he could "stay with the battalion." Knowing this, his comrades would insist that the heavier parts of his equipment were "shared amongst the platoon" when route marching, etc. In point of fact, George Morgan helped to carry his equipment into the line on June 30th, the night before the beginning of the Somme offensive. Jimmy Hodgson was killed by a sniper after July 1st. The Bradford-born author, Mr. J. B. Priestley, was later to describe these men, and those of other 'New Army' battalions, as the intellectual and physical elite of the nation.

On April 20th, at 5.00 p.m., the 16th Battalion marched from Bus-les-Artois and relieved the 10th Battalion, the East Yorkshire Regiment, in the trenches near Colin Camps. 'A', 'C' and 'D' Companies, under Captains Pringle and Blagbrough and Major Moor, occupied the front line. 'B' company, under Captain Holmes formed the reserve. The 18th Battalion had, on the previous day, occupied the right sub-sector south of the Serre Road, facing Redan Ridge and the Quadrilateral Redoubt.

Now began their apprenticeship in the art of war. Tours of duty usually consisted of four days in the front line, followed by four days in the support trenches, followed by a spell in reserve.

The front line here was well dug in hard ground and divided into short bays as protection against enfilade fire, with fire steps for manning the parapet. It was well protected by belts of barbed wire along the front a few yards into No-Man's Land, which was about 200 yards wide hereabouts. They were cold and wet, and smelt of poisonous gas, from gas shells, of explosives, and of the latrines. Ever present was the sickly sweet smell of decaying human flesh coming from the corpses which lay unburied in No-Man's Land. During the day front line duty consisted primarily in maintaining a watch by periscope for enemy activity, in carrying out any necessary repairs to the trench, and in weapon cleaning. The main activities on both sides took place at night when wiring parties were sent out with appropriate covering

Grave Marker, Private James Frederick Hodgson. Le Touret Military Cemetery.

arrangements by more men further out. Patrols were despatched to investigate the enemy barbed wire defences, to gather intelligence and to be alert to the presence of enemy patrols. For those taking part in these activities feelings varied depending on individual strength of nerve when approaching the German wire, but to some extent these were replaced by the sheer exasperation of having to manipulate coils of barbed wire and corkscrew stakes over churned up ground in darkness whilst making futile efforts not to make a noise. Not surprisingly, in total contrast to the apprehension felt marching towards the front line to take over, would be the sensation of the return to security once the trench was regained after the uncertainties of No-Man's Land. Out there was always the possibility of being stalked, like game, by an enemy patrol, or of a machine gun opening up in the vicinity.

Both sides used Very lights at night, apart from when they had patrols or working parties out in front. As a result, with experience, the amount of activity taking place in one's vicinity could be judged by the presence, or otherwise, of Very lights overhead. The Germans also used parachute flares which illuminated the ground underneath, and hung in the air much longer than did the Very lights. Both sides also used coloured rockets to signal emergencies. The sensation of being clearly exposed to view when standing upright in No-man's land was almost overwhelming at first. Complete immobility was found to be the best protection. But there was always the chance that one of these flares might fall, still glowing, at your feet, or right on to you, if you were on the ground.

By dawn everyone would have returned to the trenches and the order "STAND TO (ARMS)" would be given. Then every man had to be alert with rifle loaded and bayonet fixed. As dawn broke the periscope watch of 'No-Man's Land' was resumed. To keep eyes and senses alert, after days and nights with practically no sleep, strained will power to the limit, but to be caught asleep at "STAND TO" was a very serious offence which could result in court martial. However, the arrival of a cup of tea laced with rum at "STAND DOWN" served as a reviver. Stew (skilly) and tea would be fetched up by the orderly men for the day from the field cookers located just behind the lines. These supplies were transported in large cylinders which had an outer annular space filled with hot water. This device was supposed to keep the inner, consumable contents warm. As can be imagined, by the time the orderlies had struggled along communication trenches which were often deep in mud, the container's hot fare was no longer very hot.

It was not possible to remove or change any item of clothing while in the trenches.

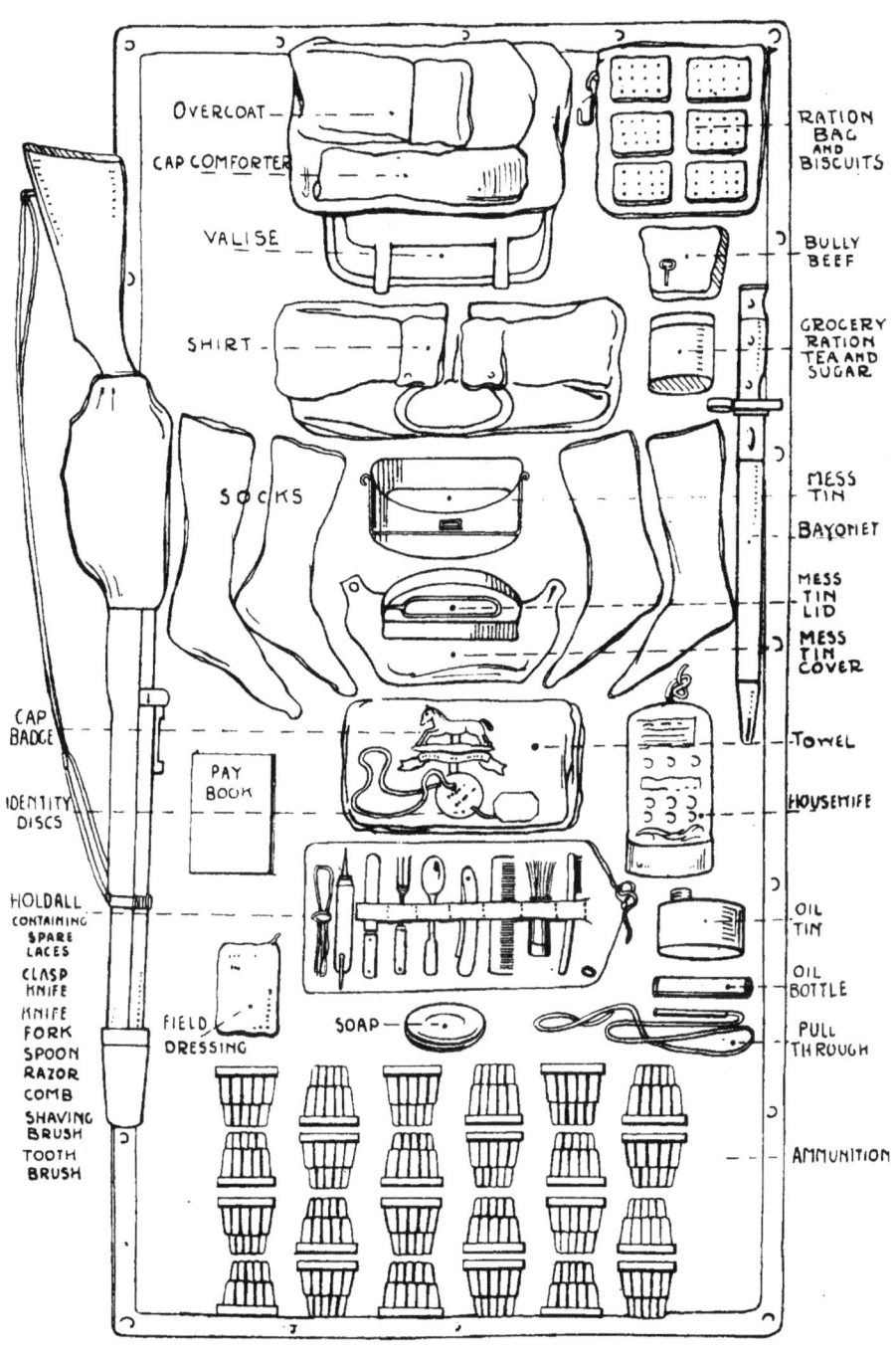

Layout for Kit Inspection from 'The History of the 6th Batallion, Wesy Yorkshire Regiment', by Tempest and Gregory.

There were no facilities for ablutions, and elementary arrangements to serve as latrines were usually excavated out of the side of the trench. In such mole-like-conditions uniforms, even in spells of dry weather, soon became soiled, and in wet weather, caked in mud. It can hardly be surprising then that a missile causing the simplest injury could carry dirt into the wound and the threat of gangrene. In the heavily manured soil of Belgium this was to cause a condition previously unknown to the medical profession, gas gangrene. Evacuating the wounded from the front line was another problem, the trenches often being too narrow to allow a stretcher to be manoeuvred around the corners of the bays, etc. A wounded man would therefore be made as comfortable as possible on a stretcher in a dug-out or rough shelter cut into the side of the trench until he could be carried out over the top after dark. In the meantime he would be given First Aid, using the field dressing sewn into the lower right flap of his tunic. This consisted of a waterproof cover containing a phial of iodine, which would first be poured into the wound, and a two and a half yard bandage with a gauze pad stitched eighteen inches from one end, with which to cover the wound. Only a reader old enough to have had a cut or graze painted with iodine will be able to imagine the effect of a phial of iodine being poured into an open and, probably deep, wound. Less seriously wounded men who were mobile would have their wounds dressed, and be told to make their own way back to the line as Walking Wounded. However, it was not unknown for apparently lightly wounded men, making their own way to a Casualty Clearing Station, to suddenly fall down dead. We now know that these men had died of shock caused by their wounds.

These conditions led to another landmark of which all the men soon became aware. This was the discovery of body lice in underwear. It should be explained that spare underwear, except socks, was not included in a soldier's kit. It is well to remember that a soldier carried everything he owned on his back when he moved. Exchange underwear was supplied from a common stock of used garments which, after the indescribably squalid conditions of the trenches, would all have been infested with body lice. These exchange garments would be issued, supposedly cleaned and fumigated, when soldiers came out of the line to rest. However, once donned, the heat of the body would hatch the eggs in the seams, and the itching would return.

The men were soon able to identify the sound and results of the more common types of projectile. *Whizzbangs*, small, low trajectory, high velocity shells, were most likely to be aimed at forward positions. High trajectory 5.9's usually were used to knock out mine heads and trench mortar positions. *Minenwerfers* or *Minnies*, were enormous 110 lbs cigar-shaped mortar bombs, standing 3 foot 6 inches, which gave a 'pop' as they left the mortar. The Minnie was the largest projectile of its kind used by the German Army. They were said to wobble their way across No-Man's Land making a distinctive "Whoosh, Whoosh" sound whilst airborne, and on such an uncertain trajectory that the recipients were never sure where the projectile would land. However, a few yards either way made little difference, so enormous was the

EARLY DAYS IN FRANCE

destruction they caused. Men caught by this weapon simply disappeared. It was often necessary to parade a platoon to establish who had been killed. Rifle grenades were a particularly nasty device which, giving no warning of their approach, simply 'arrived' on the parapet. These were about the size of a Mills grenade. Snipers in Hides in No-Man's Land would fire with great accuracy at anything which moved above the parapet, so "Keeping your head down" was literally a matter of life or death.

The 16th Battalion suffered its first casualty on April 22nd when Private E. MacKay, the C.O.'s servant, was seriously wounded by a whizz-bang splinter. The following day Privates Smith, Slingsby and Bannister, all of "C" Company, were killed by shell fire. They were buried that night near Sucrerie. On June 4th, shell fire blew in 'C' Company Headquarters, killing Lieutenant R. E. Laxton and burying Captain H. Russell, who subsequently died. One morning at daybreak in early June a large notice appeared in front of the German line, somewhere near Redan. It read:

HAMPSHIRE SUNK
KITCHENER DEAD

On his first day in the front line, George Morgan found himself on duty in a 'listening post' some way in front of his own parapet. A listening post may have been a "sap head" reached via a narrow trench dug out from the front line, but, more usually, was an isolated shell hole, heavily wired in. Their purpose was to provide early warning of enemy activity. He later admitted to being more afraid of the huge brown rats that thrived on the dead in No-Mans Land, than he was of the Germans. Later, while he slept in a dug-out, one of these foul scavengers ate its way through the side of his haversack to steal his cheese ration. He never lost his loathing of these creatures and, in later months, waged a personal war against them. His ploy was to fix a piece of cheese to the tip of his bayonet. He would then place his rifle across the parapet, his finger on the trigger, taking up the first pressure. The first rat to nibble at his cheese promptly received a round of ball and was despatched to its "happy hunting ground".

George Morgan, the young recruit

George well remembered his feelings on their first relief from trench duty. They were met a short distance behind the line by the Battalion cooks with field cookers, brought up as near as they dared. He huddled up to the side of a field cooker, enjoying its radiated heat, sipped strong hot tea which tasted of wood smoke, munched a cold bacon sandwich in thick slices of bread, and listened to the dull, ever-present, rumble of artillery which was to form the backdrop to his life for the next two years. His feelings were a combination of relief and just a little self satisfaction. Had he not survived, passed his own, self-set test? Perhaps it would not be so bad, after all.

One of the differences the Pals experienced in France was the much harsher application of the British Army disciplinary code compared with their earlier experiences in the Middle East. For example, it is said that Field-Marshal Haig considered an occasional execution by firing squad of anyone who could be accused of cowardice or desertion to be 'good for discipline'. This was brought home to the Pals at an early date when two young soldiers from one of the battalions, out on an evening spree

Cyril Tetlow

in a local estaminet, drank rather too much wine and, as a result, were unable to find their way back to their camp. They were picked up by the Military Police and subsequently brought before a Court Martial charged with being absent from their place of duty while on active service. The Court found them guilty and sentenced them to Death by Firing Squad. Everyone in their Battalion was convinced that they would be reprieved. The punishment for the offence when in England would have been ten days confined to barracks and, after all, this was an all volunteer battalion - desertion was unthinkable. However, this was not to be. The Battalion was confined to camp for two days, after which they were paraded and told of the Court's finding, of the sentence and that "the sentence has been duly carried out." One thousand young volunteers stood on parade in a bewildered silence.

The families of these two unfortunate young Bradfordians were advised that the two had been killed in action. It was the wish of the members of the Bradford Pals Old Comrades' Association, who told the writer this story in 1976, that any surviving next of kin should be allowed to continue to believe that this was how those two young men met their deaths. However, now that the identities of these two young men is widely known it seems appropriate that their names are included here. The transcript of their trial appears as Appendix 2. The author leaves it to readers to draw their own conclusions.

Mr Cyril Tetlow, who lived in Heaton until his death in 1961 and who served with the 21st Battalion, West Yorkshire Regiment, once recalled how, whilst working as a clerk in his Company Office, he took notes from the Company Sergeant Major on the items required for a forthcoming execution which his battalion had been selected to carry out. The C.S.M. listed the following items:

1. A wooden chair to sit the condemned on.
2. Sandbags with which to weigh down the chair so as to prevent the condemned kicking it over in a bid to save himself.

3. Sufficient rope to tie the arms and legs of the condemned to the chair.
4. A hood-type gas helmet to put over the head of the condemned (put on backwards so that the eye pieces were at the rear).
5. A disc of white paper or cloth of about six inches diameter, together with a pin to fix to the tunic over the heart of the condemned as an aiming point.
6. A firing squad of twelve men would need to be selected. They would be handed previously loaded rifles, a proportion of which would be loaded with blank cartridges.
7. A suitable spot would need to be selected for the execution.

Cyril Tetlow also recalled another occasion when, visiting a local estaminet to enjoy the luxury of a plate of egg and chips, he met a friend from civilian life who was serving with another battalion. His friend, normally abstemious, ordered a large brandy and, ashen faced and visibly shaken, said to him: "This morning I was on a firing party, we shot a lad from another battalion. I feel terrible."

During the First World War some 346 British soldiers were executed for desertion or cowardice, 10% of them officers, although ten times that number were sentenced to death but had their sentences commuted. Battle fatigue was recognised as a sickness by the Americans long before the British.

One family who discovered the fate of their son, Private A. Ingham of the Manchester Regiment, a boy of seventeen who was charged with deserting a front line trench, had his gravestone inscribed:

SHOT AT DAWN
ONE OF THE FIRST TO ENLIST
A WORTHY SON OF HIS FATHER

When Mr Bill Hughes, the then Prime Minister of Australia, heard of this incentive for good discipline he warned the Field-Marshal that if he allowed the execution of just one Australian soldier then the ANZACs would be removed from his command. It is interesting to note that, in two world wars, Australian and New Zealand soldiers proved to be some of the most ferocious shock troops in the allied armies, even without the Field-Marshal's incentive.

The whole brigade moved to Gezaincourt on June 19th. Here they began a special course of training to prepare them for the coming offensive. Here they practised going over the top, leaving trenches by way of assault ladders, the principle of attacking in wave formations, that is, advancing in open order while maintaining spacing and direction, and attacking their objective - trenches dug to represent those of the enemy.

When their training was complete they were addressed by the Corps Commander, Lieutenant-General Sir A.G. Hunter-Weston, who was not liked by the Pals because of, in their view, his superior attitude, and known by them as 'Bunter-Weston'. He told them that, having watched them in training, he was delighted with all he had seen, that all they would have to do was "walk into Serre" as all the Germans would be dead, a view which they were not inclined to share.

Pte F. Slingsby, 16th Batt. One of the first "Pals" to be killed in action, 23/4/16

This was to be the Big Push which would end the war. Reserves of men, including the Cavalry Divisions, were waiting to stream through the gap they were to make in the German lines, etc., etc. This was to be, for the Pals, a marvellous chance to finish the war.

They were told that "even if your brother or your friend falls wounded, do not stop for him. He will be tended to by the stretcher bearers." They were also told that there would be so-called Battle Police in the trenches, armed with revolvers, who would shoot dead anyone who refused to 'go over the top'. They were bewildered by this, even angry. At that date, June 30th 1916, the strength of the British Army in France was 1,426,000 men, all of whom were volunteers.

While at Gezaincourt Major G. S. Guyon of the Royal Fusiliers arrived to command the 16th Battalion.

7.92mm MG'08 Spandau machine gun. MOD Pattern Room, Nottingham.

A Listening-post, Thiepval Somme, 1916, By Arthur Bradbury.
Imperial War Museum, picture No. 1661.

A battalion of the 31st Division marching to the front line before the attack on July 1st, 1916. Imperial War Museum, Negative Q 743.

CHAPTER 3: THE SOMME

"Good morning, good morning," the General said
When we met him last week on our way to the line.
Now the soldiers he smiled at are most of 'em dead,
And we're cursing his staff for incompetent swine.
"He's a cheery old card," grunted Harry to Jack
As they slogged up to Arras with rifle and pack.
. . . .
But he did for them both with his plan of attack.

Siegfried Sassoon

The valley of the Somme at the end of June was the place and time selected by General Joffre and Field-Marshal Douglas Haig for their combined offensive of 1916. Their objectives were threefold:

    1: To relieve the pressure on Verdun;
    2: To assist the Allies in other theatres of the war by stopping the transfer of any enemy troops from the western front;
    3: To wear down the strength of the enemy forces facing them.

It is beyond the scope of this book to attempt an analysis of the execution of this plan. Let the words of Sir Winston Churchill in his book 'World Crises' suffice:

The military conceptions underlaying the scheme of attack were characterised by simplicity. The policy of the French and British commanders had selected, as a point for their offensive, what was undoubtably the strongest and most perfectly defended position in the world.

The 31st Division formed part of Lieutenant-General Sir A.G. Hunter-Weston's VIII Corps on the British left. The role allocated to the Division in the assault was to attack on a 'two-brigade' front, with the 94th Brigade on the left and the 93rd Brigade on the right, take Serre and then to swing left, thus closing the left flank and protecting the advance of the 4th and 29th Divisions, fighting on their right.

Each brigade was to attack on a 'two company front', that is, each battalion advancing in two waves, each of two companies. The 92nd Brigade formed the divisional reserve.

The 93rd Infantry Brigade was to complete its task in four 'bounds'. The troops in each 'bound' were to hold the ground they had taken, whilst the troops in the next 'bound' leap-frogged through them.

The First Bound:

The object of the first bound for the 93rd Brigade was the German trench K30c 2.6 to the junction of the trenches at K36a 1.9. This trench was to be taken by the 15th West Yorkshire Regiment (the 'Leeds Pals') and then consolidated and garrisoned by two companies of that battalion. The line was to be known as the GREEN LINE.

The Second Bound:

The 16th West Yorks were to leap-frog through the GREEN LINE and take the German trenches K36a 8.7. This was to be consolidated and garrisoned by the two remaining companies of the 15th West Yorks and was to be known as the RED LINE.

The Third Bound:

The objective of this bound was to be the German trench running from the South East corner of the orchard at L23a 2.6 to L25a 7.4 and then to Pendant Copse. This line was to be taken by the 16th Battalion with one company of the Durham Light Infantry on their right. This line was to be consolidated and
garrisoned by the 16th Battalion together with their Durham Light Infantry comrades and was to be known as the BROWN LINE.

The Fourth Bound:

The fourth and final objective was to take the German trench from point L25a 7.4 to the crossroads at L26a 5.6 and thence the junction of Pendant Alley East and Puiseux trench. This task was allocated to the 18th Battalion, who were also to consolidate and garrison it, and was to be known as the BLUE LINE. This final bound would have swung the line left and sealed the flank, the British now occupying a line running from John Copse to Puiseux trench.

The actual attack on each line was to be carried out by waves of troops at distances from fifty to two hundred yards apart. The confidence, which the staff planners placed in the effectiveness of the five-day bombardment of the German lines preceding the assault, is reflected by the stores and equipment which the battle order required to be carried by troops completing each 'bound forward'. These were as follows:

By all N.C.O.'s and other ranks:

> Waterproof sheet and cardigan
> 3 sandbags
> 170 rounds small arms ammunition
> Full water bottle
> I extra day's rations
> 2 mills bombs

By all men: 1 pick or shovel in the proportion of 2 shovels to 1 pick.

Added to this, of course, was a rifle, with fully charged magazine, and bayonet weighing about 10 lbs. Gas masks were to be carried by all ranks. In addition the brigade battle order required that wire cutters should be carried by each section according to the number available. These were attached by a lanyard to the shoulder strap and carried in the belt. Men carrying wire cutters were required to wear a yellow arm band, this apparently to facilitate the salvaging of cutters from the dead. Two mallets were required to be carried in a similar manner by each platoon and to be used in the removal of enemy wire entanglements in order to 'use them for our own purposes'. Each platoon was also required to carry six rolls of barbed wire, each roll being carried on stakes between two men. The total load carried by each man was probably in the order of 90 lbs.

With the foregoing in mind the battle order instructions under the heading of "Discipline" is most illuminating, and reads:

> "When advancing to the attack, cheering and doubling should not be allowed. The former advertises the fact that troops are attacking and the latter is too great an effort to men carrying heavy weights."

One of the lessons learnt by the British Army at the Battle of Loos the previous year was that German snipers were trained to select as priority targets British officers, easily identified by their distinctive tunics with 'Sam Brown' belts, riding breeches and brown boots. As a result, casualties among officers had been high. Therefore officers were instructed to dress "as nearly as possible like their men. Puttees must be worn, if necessary over their trench boots. Badges of rank will be worn on the shoulder straps, not on the sleeve." However this order was ignored by most officers, one of whom carried only a walking stick when he 'went over the top', which may account for the repeated experience of high casualties amongst the officers.

During the preliminary bombardment of the enemy front, one which began on June 25th, a lull was arranged each night at varying times to allow British patrols to examine the enemy's wire. On the night of June 29th at approximately 11.30 p.m. Lieutenant Clough of the 18th Battalion led a fighting patrol, consisting of four officers and 25 other ranks, towards the German front. However, when some 25 yards from the enemy line, they came under a heavy bomb attack and suffered heavy casualties.

Two officers and nine other ranks were killed and 18 other ranks wounded, two of whom later died of their wounds. Lieutenant Clough, himself wounded, reported the enemy trenches to be deep and well manned.

His report reads as follows

> "Party left our front line trenches as scheduled 12.28 p.m., 30th June, 1916. Advance was slow owing to numerous shell holes and flares. Apparently our party was seen as soon as we had left our own trenches for they seemed prepared for us and we were met by bombs when between 25 and 30 yards from their trenches. They sent up a single green rocket and formed a barrage of hand grenades in front of us and trench mortars and artillery behind us. The trenches seemed fairly knocked about and the wire was cut, where we were, in sufficient quantity to allow the passage of troops. Their trenches seemed very full of men and apparently are very deep.
>
> Finding we could not get forward, I brought my party back as well and as soon as I possibly could. This took some two hours. As far as I can judge, my casualties at present are about ten killed and 12 wounded, out of 38 men and four officers. At present two officers, Lieutenant F. Watson and 2nd Lieutenant J. W. Worsnop, are missing. I have been slightly wounded myself in two places. Our H. E. shells were all dropping a little over half way between our line and the German line and quite 20 yards short of their wire, and this was taking place during our scheduled hour for the raid. My watch, sent by Colonel Craven, was synchronized with our artillery officers."

Other patrols on VIII Corps front were reporting 'not much damage to wire' and 'not a sign of a gap anywhere'. Whether the General Staff disbelieved these reports or merely chose to ignore them, sticking to their belief that 'no one could remain alive after this, the heaviest bombardment in history' it is not possible to say.

After a meeting with Lieutenant-General Sir A. G. Hunter-Weston, the Brigadier Major wrote, "The Corps Commander was extremely optimistic, telling everyone that the wire had been blown away, although we could see it standing strong and well: that there would be no German trenches and all we had to do was walk into Serre". Nevertheless General Sir Henry Rawlinson, commanding the Fourth Army, wrote in his diary on the evening of June 30th: " . . . the artillery work during the bombardment and the wire cutting had been done well, except in VIII Corps which is somewhat behind." On June 30th, both battalions received instructions to move up to the trenches that night. Most ranks spent the afternoon writing letters and 'putting one's affairs in order'. Sergeant H. Drake was to remember a friend who spent the time writing a lengthy and detailed will. His friend was shot through the head while climbing over the parapet a few hours later. In a letter which later appeared in the Bradford Daily Mail, Lieutenant R. Sutcliff wrote: "Just a line to say I go 'over the lid' tomorrow. My company are in the first line of attack and hope to do great things. Naturally we hope to come through alright but someone's bound to go under and it's the only way to end the war. It's a great thing to be in and I'm glad our division is one of the first chosen to go over."

George Morgan spent the afternoon with his friends, Billy Booth, Bill Kenny and Dawson Horne. Bill Kenny expressed the view that "in this attack some of us are going to be killed." He asked George to exchange home addresses with him and to agree that, should one of them not survive, then the other would write to next of kin.

Captain C. S. Duckitt

A reserve of 10% of all ranks was selected to remain behind to form the nucleus of new battalions, should casualties prove heavy. In the early evening the battalions marched out of Bus-les-Artois, moving off in half companies, the 16th Battalion at 6.35 p.m. and the 18th Battalion at 8.45 p.m., and made towards the sound of the guns. A sound which had been heard distinctly at a distance of 12 miles for the last five days. As they marched out of the village they passed on the roadside their Divisional Commander, Major General R. Wanless O'Gowan and some of his staff sitting astride beautifully groomed horses. He called out: "Good luck, men, there is not a German left in their trenches. Our guns have blown them to Hell!" They marched with a great clatter of studded boots on the pave, weapons and equipment jangling and rattling. After watching his comrades swing past, whistling and singing, full of youthful confidence, Fred Rawlings, who stayed behind with the 16th Battalion's reserve, wrote in his diary: "Battalion set off in good spirits. Wish I was going with them."

In an orchard a little to the north west of Colincamps, they ate a meal of bully beef stew and then, at 10.00 p.m., moved on. As they passed through Colincamps the villagers lined the street and stood in silent salute as their allies marched by, even though the village was subjected to shelling, being only two kilometres behind the line. It was here that the 18th Battalion suffered their first casualty, Captain Duckitt of 'D' Company, who was wounded by a shell splinter. Cross country tracks, marked by tapes led them to the communication trenches, Southern Avenue and Sackville Street, and thence to the assembly trenches (see map 2). Men glanced in awe towards the barrage which thundered and flashed in the eastern sky. As they approached the forward trenches the sense of comradeship seemed to grow stronger. Behind Sackville Street, conveniently near the casualty clearing station in Basin Wood, the pioneer Battalion, the 12th King's Own Yorkshire Light Infantry, had dug a large common grave around which there already lay a number of blanket draped bodies, evidence of the pounding the 92nd Brigade had been receiving whilst holding the line. This was underlined as they entered the communication trench by stretcher bearers having to manoeuvre their loads around the incoming troops.

Both battalions were now taking casualties from shell fire. It was in Sackville Street that George Morgan's cousin, Sergeant Bill Morgan, was killed, his head shattered by a shell splinter. Word reached George Morgan, "Billy Morgan's got it" but there was no time for sentiment in the war and George had to go on. Sergeant Morgan had been in the battalion from the beginning, his battalion number was "8".

By 3.00 a.m. all companies were in the positions allocated to them. 'A' and 'C' Companies of the 16th Battalion, together with the Company of the Durham Light Infantry, occupied North and South Monk trenches whilst the remaining two companies were situated in Bradford trench, 'B' Company on the right and 'D' Company on the left. The two leading Companies of the 18th Battalion 'A' and 'D' occupied Dunmow trench, whilst 'C' and 'B' Companies assembled in Languard trench.

It was a clear starlit night, the main hostile activity seemingly being indicated by the drone of shells passing overhead in both directions. Putting his spade across the trench George Morgan formed a makeshift seat. Carefully he applied his weight and, finding it hold, leaned his back against the trench wall, grateful for a chance to rest his aching limbs. Looking around his new surroundings his eyes fell on the corpse of a young soldier, probably killed by a shell burst. Thrown on to the parados, a hand hung back into the trench, the fingers clawed in final agony. The head lolled back, jaw sagging in a stupid expression, the sightless eyes staring at the night sky. In his mind's eye George saw a small child looking up into the face of a young woman, asking:

> "Does everyone die, Mummy?"
> "Yes, they do," replied the young woman.
> "Will I die, Mummy?"
> "Yes," replied the young woman, "but not for a long time."

Tony Miller sat on the fire step of Dunmow trench, thinking to himself "Well, whatever is the matter with me? I'm stuck here and I'm a bit scared!" Everyone was too keyed up to sleep but there was very little talking now, everyone sat alone with his own thoughts, thinking of home and family. Apprehension must have played its part, too, but George remembered being more afraid of showing his fear and 'letting the side down'. The one exception was Dawson Horne who, even at that hour, never lost his cheerfulness and his ability to make a joke. He called to George "When we get into the German trenches, if I can find a little German without his

Private Dawson Horne

rifle, won't I chase the bugger round!!"

Whilst they awaited zero hour, all ranks received an issue of rum. The men in George Morgan's section registered their disgust when Captain Smith, a strict teetotaller who commanded 'B' Company, poured the surplus down a sump hole. Dawson Horne refused his ration, saying, "I prefer to 'go over' right in the head." George Morgan was to be the third man to go up his particular assault ladder; as they waited for zero hour with hearts thumping, stomachs twisting into knots, mouths dry, he could still hear the voice of Dawson Horne, joking, "I can't wait to get at 'em."

As Dick Collins waited with Dickie Bond, the Bradford City international outside right, to go over the top together as part of a Lewis gun section of four men, he was hit on the back by a spent shrapnel ball. Dickie Bond said to him, "You've got yours. You won't get another now", but Dickie Bond was to be proved wrong.

The men were told that 'battle police' had been ordered to shoot anyone who refused to leave the trench at zero hour. George Morgan remembered the anger of the men of the all-volunteer battalion at such a suggestion, and the words just quoted of Dawson Horne, which were to prove the last he ever heard from his friend.
On the opposite side of No-Man's Land, knee high with summer grass, awaited the highly professional and battle hardened troops of the 169th Regiment. Crouched in their deep shelters, they waited for the barrage to lift. This, they knew, would be the moment to haul machine guns and ammunition up dug-out steps and into position.

At 6.25am the bombardment, by 18 pounders, 4.5 inch howitzers and 2 inch trench mortars concentrated on the enemy's front line and assembly trenches but, at 7.30am lifted onto the enemy support lines. After a 10 minute pause, an intense bombardment of his front line by trench mortars began. Thus warned that the assault was imminent, enemy artillery retaliated with a surprisingly accurate triple wall deluge of explosives and shrapnel. Much of the British front line and assembly trenches and the lead Battalions in them simply disappeared.

At 7.21am the leading platoons of the 15th Battalion (the 'Leeds Pals') went over the parapet and lined up on previously laid tapes. Immediately enemy machine guns began firing at them and German troops were seen manning and firing from

Sappers installing assault ladders in assembly trench. Imperial War Museum. Negative Q 6229.

their parapet. Private R. N. Bell of "B" Company recalled:

"As daylight came with the promise of a fine and warm day and as the hours passed, the enemy turned his attention to the front line trenches on which shrapnel shells and whizz-bangs were now being directed all along the front line leaving us with no doubt about the awareness of the Germans of the imminence of the coming attack. As zero hour drew near the hail of shellbursts overhead and on the front line, where volumes of earth were being thrown up, seemed to increase and the noise was such as to mask the sound of our own artillery. As regards the intended contribution by the Stokes trench mortars operating in or near our own front line in the final stage, there is no knowing whether it had any effect. On the other hand, to quote the official history of the war, the enemy barrage on our lines at this point was described as so constant and severe that the cones of the explosions gave the impression of a thick belt of poplar trees. Just before 7.30 came the shrill sound of the platoon officers' whistles signalling the order to rise from the trenches and move forward. For a fleeting moment this seemed almost welcome but, almost simultaneously with the sound of the whistles, a new sound joined the din from shell fire, and that was the rattle of machine gun fire directly on our front, soon to be joined by others, the significance of which could not have been lost to any of us. Despite all this those still unwounded scrambled out of the Assembly trench, dug a short distance behind the front line, as best they could, "A" Company into no-man's land and "B" Company a short distance behind. For my part, almost immediately on reaching the surface, my foot caught on a projecting piece of wire and I sprawled full length on the ground. Picking myself up I moved forward with the rest, that is those who had not already been hit, until we were able to drop into the shell torn front line. In front of me at this time was my platoon commander on the point of climbing out again from the fire step, when he fell back having been hit in the face. At the same time a call came from the right to 'move to the left', as the well-known figure of the Grenadier Guards Sergeant, attached to the Battalion since its formation, his face now covered with blood, appeared from the right moving towards me. The trench was now almost blocked with dead and wounded, all of whom I knew well and had served with for over a year. Having made my way a little further along leftwards, as instructed, I realised that I was entirely alone, the rest of the company seemingly having melted away and, although a momentary glance to the rear had shown waves of men inopen order - the 16th Battalion West Yorks., presumably - nothing more was seen of them. All this took place in less time than it takes to write about and the parapet was still being swept by machine gun fire."

Private Bell remembered that, later in the day when survivors of the battalion assembled in a support trench, only 49 uninjured men answered a roll call.

The 15th Battalion had lost all its officers almost at once. Eleven were killed and eleven were wounded, including their Commanding Officer, Major R. B. Neill, who was wounded, and the Adjutant, Captain Stanley T. A. Neil, who was killed. Of those who left the front line trench, few advanced more than a hundred yards beyond the British wire. Of those who left Leeds trench in the second wave, few advanced more than forty yards from the parapet.

At 7.30am in response to the shrill call of officers' whistles, the leading platoons of the 16th Battalion's 'A' and 'C' Companies and 'D' Company of the 18th Durhams, climbed out of North and South Monk trenches. They stepped into a nightmare of exploding shells and machine gun fire. To help maintain direction everyone had been instructed to 'make straight for Serre Church steeple'. The fact that five days of heavy bombardment would probably have reduced the church to a heap of rubble, as indeed it had, seems to have escaped the attention of the planners. By the time they had advanced as far as Leeds trench they had suffered heavily. By 8.35am most of the officers, including the Commanding Officer, Major Guyon, were killed or wounded, and the advance was held up. Let 2nd Lieutenant C.F.Laxton, the Battalion Intelligence Officer, take up the story:

"...at five minutes to zero Major Guyon, Ransome and myself left our headquarters for the front line. We had only been in SAP A about two minutes when Major Guyon was struck through the helmet by a bullet. Ransome and I were alongside at the time, and bandaged him up, though unconscious and apparently dying, the wound being in the temple. We were obliged to leave as things did not appear to be going well. We urged the men on, and saw the columns advancing over Leeds trench, one being led by Captain Pringle. Things seemed to stop, men were falling and no one advancing over our front line. Stead was in the front line with a few men, which we scraped together for a rush. Stead and I scrambled out and the men tried to follow, but were mown down by machine gun fire, I got about 15 yards before being hit by a bullet in the left knee and a piece of shrapnel in the right thigh and managed to crawl to a shell hole about 5 yards in front, where I found Stead shot dead. After staying there for about 15 minutes, I tried to regain our trenches, leaving all surplus kit, and gained a shell hole a few yards nearer. Ransome evidently saw me and came out to my assistance. I sent him back to find the nearest place where I could crawl into the trench, this he did and I followed him. This was the last I saw of him but afterwards I heard he was suffering from shell shock with Lieutenant Hoffman."

Private Harry Severn of "A" Company had hardly stepped off the parapet when he was struck by fragments from a German shell which exploded close by. He lay on the ground for some time, in great pain, passing in and out of consciousness with his right arm shattered and his left arm also badly injured. Some time after dusk he heard a stretcher bearer say "don't bother with him, he's had it."

Determined to prove them wrong, willing himself back into consciousness, he somehow got to his feet and staggered, crawled and dragged himself back to the relative safety of the trench which he had recently left. From there he was taken to a Casualty Clearing Station.

In a letter to his parents Private George Gransbury of the 16th Battalion wrote:

"Over we went and, as we were the first the fireworks started. The Bosche meant keeping us at long range, and, not caring to be gun fodder, we knocked on and got about 100 yards, and only about 25 of us left in our Company. Our officer was wounded and a corporal was in charge. Still, on we went and began to miss each other. I dropped on Captain Pringle, who was wounded, and dragged him to a shell hole in which were Captain D. Smith (wounded in the back), and Lieutenant R. Sutcliffe, also wounded. A few privates filled up the spare places. I was creeping up the side of the crater to see what was going on when a high explosive dropped right on top of us. How I escaped, God alone knows. Captain Pringle was blown from the opposite side on to the top of me and I was buried but could breathe. A lad came along and helped me out."

As the first platoons of 'B' and 'D' Companies clambered over the parapet of

Bradford trench, they too came under a heavy fire from high explosives, shrapnel and machine guns. 'B' Company began to take casualties, although 'D' Company did not suffer heavily until they came up to, and over, the front line. Heavy machine gun fire then took a dreadful toll.

Number 7 Platoon, 'B' Company, was led 'over the lid' by 2nd Lieutenant Frank Symonds, a debonair young man lately at grammar school. He sprang up the assault ladder and over the parapet, calling to his men to follow him. He was very calm and smoking a cigarette, revolver in hand, in the best tradition of a British officer. His men clambered out after him, although George Morgan nearly fell backwards off the assault ladder, such was the weight of his equipment. As he stepped over the parapet he was almost knocked back into the trench by Private Norman Illingworth, his hands covering his face, blood streaming through his fingers, who blundered into him, and then fell headlong into the trench. As he lined up on the starting tape, a ruddy complexioned man to his left, who had only recently arrived in a draft from England, screamed, fell against him and crumpled up - his complexion drained to chalk as his life blood spilled out. Over on his right a man, hit in the crotch, was writhing on the ground, clutching his wound, screaming in agony. Looking half towards the left he could see the village of Puisieux blazing, set alight by British shelling.

They moved off from the starting tape as if on parade, rifles held at the port. After a few paces his friend, Billy Booth, fell badly wounded, crying out "Oh God! Help me, do help me". Corporal Harry Metcalf called out: 'Leave him, George, we must go on. He'll be seen to by the stretcher bearers". Another few paces and Harry Metcalf was hit and fell, calling out: "Go on, George, the second wave will be along any minute". George was now completely alone, his section having melted away.

Private Norman Waddilove

A shell splinter sliced off one of his ammunition pouches and knocked him on to his back. Deciding that he 'could not fight the war alone' he took shelter in a shell hole to await the next wave, the 18th Battalion, intending to go on with them, but the 18th Battalion never reached him. He was, in fact, the only member of his section to survive the battle unhurt. Some time later he was able to regain Bradford trench where he stumbled over the body of Private Norman Waddilove, only son of the Bradford industrialist. He had been shot dead whilst climbing the assault ladder and had fallen back into the trench. Death must have been instantaneous, he looked as if he had fallen asleep. Near the parapet he saw the body of Corporal Squire

Clough. His back had been torn open by wounds so numerous that it was impossible to estimate their number. An exploding shell threw George Rockliff into the air, peppering his leg with splinters. He fell back to earth, only to be impaled by the thigh on the bayonet of a comrade.

Many of those who witnessed the assault could not initially understand why so many of the advancing men were doubling up and falling on to their knees in such odd postures. It was only when they became able to distinguish the screams of the wounded above the noise of battle that they realised these men had been hit.

Sergeant Major G. Cussons, who left Bradford trench with 'B' Company head-quarters, is recorded as saying:

Corporal Squire Clough

"At 7.25, five minutes before zero, the enemy machine guns, rifle fire and shrapnel were directed against the parapet of our assembly trench, the southern half of Bradford trench, causing us to suffer considerably. A lot of men never got off the ladder but fell back from the parapet. On getting out of the trenches to take up our positions in front, we lost heavily through the line to shrapnel, machine gun and rapid rifle fire. By the time we attained our position in front of Bradford trench most of the officers and N.C.O.'s and many men had been knocked out. At zero we advanced and continued to advance until the company head-quarters with which I was, found ourselves in front of the battalion - all in front having been hit. We found ourselves then half way between Leeds trench and the front line. At this point I continued to advance, Captain D. Smith having been knocked out. (Captain Smith's last message to 'Battalion,' brought in. by his runner, read 'Company advancing steadily') and I carried on until I reached the front line. In our advance we passed the majority of 'A' Company, laying killed or wounded, halfway between Leeds trench and the front line. I found in the front line a good many men of the 15th Battalion West Yorks and what was left of the Durham Light Infantry Company who were attached to us. Also a few of the King's Own Yorkshire Light Infantry. I found no officers or N.C.O.'s of these Regiments or of my own Regiment. The order came to 'ease off to the left'. I proceeded to do this and found Lieutenant Jowett of my Regiment, who ordered me to try to collect and organise the few men who were left with a view to advancing again. At this moment the enemy stared shelling our front line very heavily, with shrapnel and high explosives. This would be nearly one hour after zero, but of course I cannot give the correct time. Within a very short time, all the men we had collected were knocked out including Mr. Jowett, who gave me instructions to make my way back to Battalion Headquarters and report that there were no men left. He told me that he had already sent back to Battalion Headquarters three or four times but with out success. This would be about one hour and a half after zero, and I could make out that some of our men were then advancing towards the enemy lines and must have been quite close up to the German parapet. I saw some of the Germans show themselves over the parapet, shoot at and throw bombs at what must have been some of our men who were still advancing."

The last message received from 'D' Company, brought in by Private Drake, the company runner, read:

TO:	O/C 16th West Yorks
FROM:	O/C 'D' Company
	'D' Company advancing. Casualties unknown. (Sgd.) Alan Clough, Captain
PLACE:	In front of Bradford trench
TIME:	8.00 a.m., 1.7.16

Private Price (Machine Gun Section) whose gun was carried behind the last line (the last platoon) with orders to follow up 'D' Company, later recorded:

". . . my own section was wiped out as we went into No- Man's Land. We were 70 yards out and I saw Captain Clough on our left and further left our other gun. We went out and over the parapet at a slow double. Met a man of the 15th West Yorks, he said that no one had passed him advancing - the rest dropped through travasing machine gun fire. I looked at the front line but could see no Germans. We stayed there for some time - until about 2.00 p.m. In the meantime my No. 1 had crawled back (I hear he is still alive). I crawled out and got into Sackville trench and finally reported to Battalion Headquarters. I saw Captain Clough wounded in No-Man's Land, probably in the left wrist, he appeared to try to move backwards and I think he was hit again. Of the machine gun section to which I was attached, five of the six got into No-Man's Land before being hit."

At 8.20 am the 18th Battalion Headquarters received a message from 'Brigade' that the 16th Battalion was held up and ordering the commanding officer to go forward to SAP "A" to investigate. Having assessed the situation the Colonel rejoined his leading companies in Dunmow trench. Here Private Frank Hartley said to him: "You're not wearing your identity discs, Sir." The Colonel smiled and replied: "I shan't need them."

As the order 'fix bayonets' rang out among the waiting companies of the 18th Battalion, Corporal Norman Goldthorpe's Platoon Commander, Lieutenant Foizey, turned to him and said "I shan't come back." Corporal Goldthorpe told him to believe he would as "I certainly believe I shall. " However, his premonition was to prove correct. At 8.40am they began to leave their trenches. The first wave, 'A' and 'D' Companies from Dunmow trench', 'C' and 'B' Companies from Languard trench. These positions had been subjected to a heavy bombardment of high explosives and shrapnel since some fifteen minutes before zero. As Ernest Wilson clambered over the parapet he saw the Adjutant, Captain F. T. Williams, who had climbed out in front of him, thrown 20 feet into the air by a shell burst. He advanced a few paces and was himself struck down by a shrapnel ball. Captain C. H. C. Keen who commanded 'A' Company fell, seriously wounded, almost as soon as he left the parapet. Frank Burn described the scene as 'a hell on earth'.

Less than a hundred yards in front of Dunmow trench they came under a heavy cross fire from machine guns firing from their right, probably from the Quadrilateral Redoubt and south of the Serre Road. Almost everyone dropped flat on their stomachs to escape this murderous scythe, except their commanding Officer, Lieutenant-Colonel M. N. Kennard. Standing calm and erect amid the crack and whine of bullets and carrying only a walking stick he called out "come on boys, up you get", turned and began to walk at an easy gait towards the enemy. The Battalion rose to their feet and followed him. As they came out of the dead ground in which their assembly trenches were dug they were additionally engaged by a rapid rifle fire from the front. Casualties were heavy, particularly amongst the officers and including Lieutenant-Colonel Kennard, who was killed by a shell which burst close by him.

Lieutenant R. S. Cross who commanded No. 4, the lead platoon, of 'A' Company wrote:

> ". . . an intense bombardment was in progress on our front line and support trenches by the time I took my platoon out. Cannister bombs, high explosives and shrapnel catching all men as they reached the support line. This curtain of fire was extended to our support trenches. The heavy guns appeared to be working from Puisieux and the shrapnel from Serre. My platoon was in Dunmow and my line of advance about 20 yards south of SAP A.
>
> Our artillery seemed to me to have been concentrating mainly on the German trenches with good effect in smashing them up, but evidently, judging by the rifle fire, it did not smash up their dug-outs."

In his report Captain A. D. Stephenson, who commanded 'C' Company wrote:

> ". . . the enemy artillery was a great surprise to our troops who had expected to find most of the enemy guns put out of action. The enemy infantry, standing on the parapet firing at our advancing troops, seemed to consider themselves quite safe from our guns. Could our advancing troops not have laid down while our guns shelled the enemy down with shrapnel?"

Captain Stephenson went on to point out that, although the platoons moved off in four lines, the lack of bridges over the trenches to be crossed, and the width of these trenches due to the shelling, had caused the lines of men to 'bunch' at each crossing, a point that did not go unnoticed by the German machine gunners. He also suggested that, had the brigade machine gun teams been given a more flexible role, they could have been used to enfilade the enemy parapet, or to combat his machine guns. 'C' Company were the last to leave the assembly trenches and all four platoons reached the British front line. Few, however, were able to advance beyond it. Nevertheless, it was reported that Lieutenant Akam, of 'B' Company reached the German front line with his platoon as did Sergeant Bullock, the Battalion's Signals Sergeant, together with one man and a party of men from the 4th Division.

Corporal Goldthorpe had scrambled out behind Lieutenant Foizey with his section of 'Bombers', each wearing a canvas waistcoat with pockets for eight Mills grenades in addition to carrying a rifle and bayonet. Their task, on reaching the objective, was to proceed another 150 yards down a communication trench and build a barricade to forestall any counter attack. Having travelled not more than 30 yards or so the section was reduced to four men. Lieutenant Foizey ordered his small party to take cover behind a small hillock, whilst he went forward to see what was happening; but he was killed after covering only a couple of yards. Now there was not a living soul in sight. It was obvious that they could not go forward, but they had been warned that anyone who returned to the trenches unwounded would be shot.

After some considerable time, when things appeared to have quietened down a little, a Private Smith volunteered to go back for instructions. Although he was continually fired on he managed to do so, and returned to within hailing distance with instructions to go back. Corporal Goldthorpe ordered the remaining two to go back in short dashes at three minute intervals, following himself three minutes after the last man. Despite heavy fire all safely reached their own lines. Here they joined about twenty other men and the only surviving officer in "A" Company.

Private Frank Hartley had reached and crossed the front line trenches from which the 15th Battalion had started. He went on. The earth all around him was being thrown up in a spray by exploding shells, whilst the sky rained clods of earth. Suddenly, he felt a heavy blow and his right leg crumpled under him, pouring blood. Around him bursting shrapnel shells were turning wounded into dead so he crawled back half a mile, dragging Ralph Holmes with him, until he found ground offering some shelter from the barrage. Then he fell unconscious.

By 9.00 a.m. the front line trenches were crowded with men but with no officers or N.C.O.'s to organize them. Let us take up Sergeant Major Cussons' story again.

> '. . . I made my way to what I took to be Brigade Headquarters, as I saw a board to that effect, but it turned out to be the 94th Brigade. They telephoned my information to Division and also gave me orders to proceed to 93rd Brigade Headquarters. This took some time and on getting to

Sackville Street, I was ordered, with others, to line that trench in the need to quell a German counter attack which had just started (this report proved to be false). As soon as the necessity for this was over, I reported myself to the 93rd Brigade Headquarters who told me that what was left of the 16th Battalion were being collected in Sackville Street and that I was to return there and look after them.

In the day, somewhere between 3.00 and 4.00 p.m. in the afternoon, I was ordered to form up the remainder of the Battalion in Legend Street, near Brigade Headquarters. After two hours I was ordered to take the Battalion down to Dunmow trench, which I did.

During the wait at Brigade Headquarters, I took the names and numbers of the men of the Regiment who I had with me, about fifty in all. Just as I was going down to Dunmow trench, the first reinforcements, in the form of officers and N.C.O.'s arrived. Until the arrival of these reinforcements, I had no N.C.O. with me above the rank of Lance Corporal."

In point of fact Lieutenant Ransome was sent to Monk trench at 9.00 a.m. to try to reorganise the Battalion. He was killed very shortly afterwards.

At 9.50 a.m. the Brigadier General left his Headquarters for the front line to make a personal assessment of the situation. By 11.45 a.m. he had returned and decided that any further attempt to advance would be fruitless due to the heavy casualties that had been suffered and also that there were scarcely any officers or N.C.O.'s available.

In front of the British trenches, the dead and wounded lay in clumps whilst the German parapet was manned by confident troops who sniped at anything which moved. Here and there a wounded man, still able to lift a rifle, sniped back.

The front line was now held by Lieutenant Peace, who was wounded and looking very ill, Lieutenant Whitaker and Lieutenant Cross, all of the 18th Battalion, and about 200 men of all regiments. The Durhams had two companies in Monk trench and one company in Maitland trench. Fearing a counter attack, Brigade now ordered the Durhams to hold the front line where possible, although much of it was now untenable, with a company in support in Monk trench. What was left of the 16th Battalion was withdrawn to Dunmow trench which they were ordered to hold. Major H. H. Kennedy was given command of the Battalion.

At 4.00 p.m. on instructions from Divisional Headquarters, Major H. F. G. Carter reported to Brigade Headquarters and assumed command of the 18th Battalion whose survivors were then being collected by Lieutenant-Colonel Bowes of the 18th Durhams. At that time there were some sixty members of the Battalion in Dunmow trench. Major Carter searched Grey, Bradford, Monk and Bleneau trenches and 'SAP A' for survivors but, apart from a few wounded, found these trenches deserted. At 8.45 p.m. he received orders to occupy and hold Monk

Lt. Colonel H. F. G. Carter

trench. By then he had with him Lieutenants Cross and Howarth, 2nd Lieutenants Whitaker, Stephenson and Thornton and 120 other ranks. Later, he received orders to retire to Languard trench after being relieved by the 92nd Brigade who were to attack Serre on the following day. The plan for this attack was subsequently abandoned.

On the right, during the afternoon, another Bradford battalion, the 6th (Territorial) Battalion of the Regiment, had fallen in heaps in their attack on Thiepval.

During the night of July 1st/2nd stretcher bearers of the 11th Battalion East Yorkshire Regiment together with rations and reinforcements of 75 men per battalion arrived in the line. The Brigade War Diary for the 2nd and 3rd read respectively "quiet day in front - wounded and dead brought in" and "nothing to report, wounded and dead brought in all day". As soon as night fell parties were formed as stretcher bearers to bring in wounded still lying out in the open, and to identify the dead who were too numerous to bring in. Those who performed this task were never to forget it. As they turned over bodies so as to retrieve pay books from breast pockets and red identification discs from around the neck (green discs to be left to enable a later identification of the bodies), the violent manner of their deaths was revealed. Here were men with only half a face, with an empty brain cavity, or chest or stomach cavity. Here men with no limbs, even heads. The ground they walked on was carpeted with intestines, bits of men and offal.

Here and there wounded men called out for help, some babbled in delirium whilst others breathed with that horrible gurgling, snorting snore of those who are seriously hurt. Great numbers lay still, breathing shallowly. Many of these were left for dead.

There seems to have been an unwritten truce as this work went on long after daybreak, the Germans, presumably, were also carrying their wounded out of the trenches.

Later, men were brought in who had lain, badly wounded, in shell holes for up to two days. Amongst these was one of the few surviving officers from the 15th Battalion. There was Dick Collins, who had lain unconscious for two days with half his face torn away, having been left for dead. Fortunately, he had regained consciousness in time, and was able to attract attention. In contrast, Frank Hartley woke up to find himself in a field hospital with a red tag pinned to his blanket, indicating that his wounded leg was to be amputated. Fortunately for Frank, the arrival of another train-load of wounded diverted attention, and his wounded leg was left to heal of its own accord.

After dark the Germans left their trenches and searched in front of the wire for survivors.

Walking wounded 1: British and German wounded on their way to a dressing station. Imperial War Museum negative Q800.

In his book "A Victorian Son" (Collins, 1972) Stuart Cloete, whose battalion months later recovered British dead from the proximity of the then abandoned German front line, said that the wounded had been despatched by bayonetting them in the throat, whilst the skulls of the dead were smashed as if by sledge hammer. He said of these dead: "They hung like washing on the barbs [of the wire], like scarecrows who scared no crows since they were edible." In his 1972 letter to the author Stuart Cloete wrote: "We cleaned up the bodies at Somme, I do not know what regiment they were (West Yorks?). I think the troops I refer to in Vic/ Son must be the ones you are trying to trace. The German wire had not been cut."

At noon on the 4th of July a severe thunderstorm caused heavy flooding of the trenches, in some cases up to four feet deep, which created great difficulties in evacuating the wounded who were now laying in heaps around the Casualty Clearing Station in Basin Wood. Here Major MacTavish and Captains Roche and Horner worked in shirt sleeves, non-stop, at trestle tables with the dead piled around them. Captain E. V. Tempest of the Regiment's 6th Battalion, describing a Casualty Clearing Station further to the South, Paisley Dump, wrote:

> ". . . as one approached, one became aware of a noise a noise inhuman. A wail as of enormous fingers on an enormous wet glass, a wail that rose and fell, interminable, unbearable. Then suddenly one became aware whence the wail came. All along the muddy roadway they lay -the wounded, hundreds of them, brown blanket shapes, some muttering, some moaning, some singing in delirium, some quite still."

Major MacTavish, a Canadian serving with the 18th Battalion, was to write to a friend: "I'll never forget July 1st as long as I live. It was an awful day."On July 1st., at 10.00 a.m., Fred Rawnsley wrote in his diary: "Rumours that advance has been

> Box 164
> Normanvos [?]
> 12/6/72
>
> Dear Mr Hudson,
>
> We cleared up the bodies at Serre. I do not know what regiment they were (West Yorks?) I think the troops I refer to on V[ic]/[tory] must be the ones you are trying to trace. The ground was very much cut.
>
> Sorry I can't be of more help
>
> Yours sincerely
>
> Stewart C[?] 65/3

successful". At 12.00 a.m. he added: "Wounded commenced to struggle through. Heartrending sight. Pals badly smashed up. Thank God I didn't take part."

On the evening of July 1st, before going to dinner, Field-Marshal Haig wrote in his diary "I am inclined to believe from further reports that few of VIII Corps left their trenches". Perhaps the Field Marshall had been misinformed?

George Morgan spent the 2nd and 3rd of July helping to carry stretcher cases from Basin Wood to Euston Dump, the collecting point for ambulances. Here he found Billy Booth laying on a stretcher. He had lain in the open for three days waiting to be collected as had Corporal Metcalf. Billy Booth died of his wounds. Corporal Metcalf survived but was to walk with a limp for the rest of his life. He helped to carry out Abe Waddington, the Yorkshire Cricketer, who grumbled loudly at every bump or jolt. When finally they arrived at Euston Dump a Medical Officer read Private Waddington's wound tag and ordered him to "get off the stretcher and walk to the ambulance". After some remonstrations, Private Waddington did as he was

Advanced Dressing Station, Somme, 1916. Imperial War Museum, Negative Q2023.

ordered! Later George Morgan was called down to Bus-les-Artois where he found his friend, Bill Kenny, laying on a table, paralysed from the neck down. He said "Will you write to my fiancee, George, and tell her I shall soon be with her?" The medical orderly slowly shook his head. Bill Kenny died shortly afterwards. George kept his promise.

On the evening of July 4th, the Brigade was relieved by the 144th Infantry Brigade. The journey out of the trenches occupied a great deal of time, hampered by the flooded condition of the trenches caused by torrential rain, and by the numerous stretcher cases which still clogged many of the bays. Further difficulties arose when the 94th Brigade accidentally used Railway Avenue instead of Northern Avenue. As they struggled along Northern Avenue a voice from the dark called out: "Come on, boys, only another dozen yards." A rather short soldier, who hailed from Halifax, replied in a loud, clear voice: "It's awreet for thee thi big bugger, arz almust drowning down 'ere!" This brought a titter back from the darkness. Apparently his remark was addressed to the Divisional Commander.

The remnants of the 16th Battalion were led out by a Lieutenant of the Royal Engineers in whose charge they had been placed. This gentleman was newly commissioned from the ranks and wore a private soldier's uniform with cloth pips sewn on his shoulder straps. His small stature earned him the nickname 'four-by-two' after the piece of cloth used to clean the bore of rifles. While his simple attire caused George and his friends some amusement he was, unlike many of his brother officers, at least dressed in accordance with orders (see page 27). He later accused George Morgan of losing his 'British Warm' which, he said, he had placed in his charge. From subsequent enquiries it was learnt that the missing coat had been

Walking wounded 2 : a British soldier who probably died of shock on his way to a dressing station. Imperial War Museum nagative Q42261

placed on the back of a limber by another private. The limber had then been driven off at full gallop before the unfortunate private could retrieve it.

Both battalions then moved to Louvencourt on the same day. The 16th went via Colincamps where they ate a meal and were greeted by the villagers with a glass of wine. The 18th moved via Bertrancourt where there was a welcome issue of tea and rum. They were told that there would be no reveille - they could sleep as long as they wished.

However, on the 5th of July after only four hours sleep, both battalions were paraded and addressed by the Corps Commander, Lieutenant-General Hunter-Weston, mounted on his charger and flanked by two Lancers. His address is reproduced here:

> FROM: Lieut-Gen. Sir Aylmer Hunter-Weston, K.C.B., D.S.O.
> TO: All officers, N.C.O.'s and men of the VIII Army Corps
>
> "In so big a command as an Army Corps of four Divisions (about 80,000 men) it is impossible for me to come round all front line trenches and all billets to see every man as I wish to do. You must take the will for the deed, and accept this printed message in place of the spoken word.
>
> It is difficult for me to express my admiration for the splendid courage, determination and discipline displayed by every Officer, N.C.O. and man of the battalions that took part in the great attack on the Beaumont Hamel- Serre position on the 1st July. All observers agree in

stating that the various waves of men issued from their trenches and moved forward at the appointed time in perfect order, undismayed by the heavy artillery fire and deadly machine gun fire. There were no cowards nor waverers, and not a man fell out. It was a magnificent display of disciplined courage worthy of the best traditions of the British race. Very few are left of my old comrades, the original 'Contemptibles' but their successors in the 4th Division have shown that they are worthy to bear the honours gained by the 4th Division at their first great fight at Fontaine-au-Pire and Ligny, during the great Retreat and greater Advance across the Marne and Aisne, and in all the hard fighting at Ploegsteert and at Ypres.

Though but few of my old comrades, the heroes of the historic landing at Cape Helles, are still with us, the 29th Division of today has shown itself capable of maintaining its high traditions, and has proved itself worthy of its hard earned title of 'The Incomparable 29th'.

The 31st New Army Division and the 48th Territorial Division, by the heroism and discipline of the units, engaged in this, their first big battle, have proved themselves worthy to fight by the side of such magnificent regular Divisions as the 4th and 29th. There can be no higher praise.

We had the most difficult part of the line to attack. The Germans had fortified it with skill and immense labour for many months, they had kept their best troops here, and had assembled north, east and south-east of it a formidable collection of artillery and many machine guns.

By your splendid attack you held these enemy forces here in the north and so enabled our friends in the south, both British and French, to achieve the brilliant success that they have. Therefore, though we did not do all we hoped to do, you have more than pulled your weight, and you and our even more glorious comrades who have preceded us across the Great Divide have nobly done your duty.

We have got to stick it out and go on hammering. Next time we attack, if it please God, we will not only pull our weight but will pull off a big thing. With such troops as you, who are determined to stick it out and do your duty, we are certain of winning through to a glorious victory.

I salute each Officer, N.C.O. and Man of the 4th, 29th, 31st and 48th Divisions as a comrade-in-arms and I rejoice to have the privilege of commanding such a band of heroes as the VIII Corps have proved themselves to be."

H. Q., VIII Corps	AYLMER HUNTER-WESTON
4th July, 1916	Lieutenant-General

THE SOMME

Lieutenant-Colonel Carter said that the three battalions of the West Yorkshire Regiment, and the Company of the Durhams, advanced into the enemy fire, rifles held at the port "as if on parade."

The 16th Battalion went into the line with a strength of 24 officers, including med-ical officers, and 750 other ranks. During the period June 30th to July 3rd, they lost 11 officers killed, one missing and ten wounded. 69 other ranks killed or died of wounds, 111 missing and 313 wounded, a total of 515, or nearly 67% of the strength. The 18th Battalion's casualties were 16 officers and 400 other ranks, only seven officers and 170 other ranks surviving, a loss of 70%.

Lieutenant-Colonel Maurice Nicholl Kennard was born in 1883, the second son of Mr and Mrs Robert William Kennard. In 1903 he joined the 6th Dragoon Guards from the Militia, and, after holding the adjutancy of the Regiment for a period from April 1910 he became Captain in 1913. Whilst serving with the Dragoon Guards in the early days of the war he was wounded and was mentioned in dispatches as early as October 1914. In 1915 he was promoted to Major and took command of the 13th Battalion of the York and Lancaster Regiment, later to be transferred to the command of the 18th Battalion of the West Yorkshire Regiment. His body was never found; his name appears on the Thiepval Memorial as 'Missing with no known grave.'

Captain Pringle, the commander of 'C' Company of whom Lieutenant Laxton had spoken, was killed. His body was found 20 years later and interred in Sucrerie Cemetery, near Colincamps.

The body of 2nd Lieutenant Frank James Symonds was never found, nor was that of his Company Commander, Captain Donald C. Smith, despite the efforts of his father Mr. E. J. Smith, a Bradford councillor. Before the war, Donald Smith had played rugby for Yorkshire and, despite his spartan ways, which were the cause of some amusement amongst those he led, he was regarded by all as a very brave officer.

Lieutenant Robert Sutcliffe, a distinguished looking managed thirty six, died of wounds whilst travelling back to England on a hospital ship. An old boy of Bradford Grammar School, he joined the public school's battalion of the Middlesex Regiment at the outbreak of war and later obtained a commission in his County Regiment. He is buried in the Chapel ceme-tery extension in the village of Slack, Yorkshire, near his family home

Percy Bateman

Another to be buried near his home was Percy Bateman of the 18th Battalion.

Private Harry Redman

Suffering from a leg wound which had become heavily infected with gangrene he was shipped from France to a London hospital where, unfortunately, and amputation failed to save him. The 31year-old corporal told his wife, who had travelled to London to be with him: "I know I won't go to Hell when I die, I've already been there!" Some of his last words to her were "I'm lucky to have had such a long life, most of those who are dying up there [at the Front] are only boys." His grave is in Bowling Cemetery, Bradford..

The body of Private Dawson Horne, who "couldn't wait to get at 'em", was recovered from the German wire on August 8th, 1916. Unfortunately the location of his grave was lost and his name is to be found on the Memorial for the Missing on Thiepval Ridge. The body of Lieutenant Harold Egbert Foizey, is buried in Euston Road Cemetery, on the site then known as Euston Dump.

Among the missing was Private Harry Redman, of just twenty years. In an age when those bereaved, especially by dramatic tragedy, receive help and counselling, it is difficult to imagine the feelings of Harry Redman's parents who received only a telegram bearing the bald statement that their son was missing in action. Until the day of her death Mrs Redman never accepted that her son was dead, insisting that he was alive in some hospital having lost his memory.

Also listed amongst the dead was Private William Whitaker, aged 17 years and 10 months.

Sir Douglas Haig's Staff Officer was to write 'It would seem as if the only differences that numbers in an attack make to a properly located machine gun defence, when there is light and time to see, is to provide a better target'. With regard to this piece of wisdom Sir Winston Churchill was to comment: "No one can quarrel with such a conclusion.'

Lieutenant Robert Sutcliffe

THE SOMME

Major George S. Guyon
o/c 16th. Battn. West Yorks

Major Guyon's body was never identified. However, in Serre 3 cemetery there is a headstone engraved with the West Yorkshire Regiment badge and inscribed
An unknown British Officer Known unto God.
In 2003, whilst seeking his grandfather's grave, David Guyon located the site of 'SAP A' where the Major died. In the ploughing season, approximately half way between the Serre Road and Serre 3 cemeteries, a strip of paler earth can be seen indicating the previous presence of a trench.

Frank Burn (centre) with Fred Hall and Frank Booth standing in the remains of the British Front Line facing Serre, July 1st, 1966. Bradford Telegraph and Argus.

Shrapnel balls picked up by the author from the fields of the Somme with a pound coin for comparison.

CHAPTER 4: NEUVE CHAPELLE, FESTUBERT, GIVENCHY

> *Through darkness curves a spume of falling flares*
> *That flood the field with shallow, blanching light*
> *The huddled sentry stares . . . .*
>
> Siegfried Sassoon

On July 6th, both battalions left the Somme area. The 16th Battalion marched to Lestram, where they spent almost three weeks before moving to Les Lobes. The 18th Battalion marched to L'Ecleme. Here they were addressed by the Divisional Commander who congratulated them on the fighting of July 1st to the 4th and spoke of the necessity to inspire all reinforcements with the same efficient spirit as that shown by all ranks. He expressed his extreme regret that the Battalion had lost so many officers, N.C.O.'s and men, especially their Commanding Officer, Lieutenant-Colonel Kennard.

On July 27th, the 18th Battalion plus a composite company from the 16th, known as 'X' Company, took over the front line trenches from the 13th York and Lancaster Regiment in the Neuve Chapelle Right Sub Sector. Here, unlike the valley of the Somme, the landscape was flat and enclosed. Owing to the wet nature of the ground the defences consisted, in the main, of breast works. The front line had, before the Battle of Neuve Chapelle, been the German third and fourth support lines. Most men who fought in this sector were never to forget the dead, most of them British, who lay in putrescent rows in No Man's Land. It was said that parapets were built up with them and that corpses served as landmarks for patrols and direction aids to dug-outs and communication trenches. In his history of the 6th (Territorial) Battalion of the Regiment. Captain E. V. Tempest described the area as "a vast cemetery where no one had been buried" and said that "the heavy stench which lay like a cloud over the trenches, could be felt miles away."

On completion of the relief, Headquarters Company had established themselves in the ruined farm in Square S3d. 'X' Company held the right section. 'A' Company, commanded by Lieutenant R S. Cross, held the centre section and 'B' Company, led by Lieutenant L. C. Watson, held the left section of the sub-sector. 'D' Company, commanded by Lieutenant A. Howarth, were in support at Port Arthur and Edgware Road, Captain B. Tooke, together with 2nd Lieutenant J. L. Wood and 'C' Company, were in reserve at Lansdown Post, Hen Post and Edward Post. These positions are shown in Map 3.

In the meantime the 16th Battalion, less the composite company, marched to Croix Barbes and took over from the 11th East Lancashire Regiment the front line posts, 'Rags,' 'Bones,' 'Grotto,' 'Angle' and Saint Vaast, Loretto and Euston. The verdict of the Field General Courts Martial (dated 14th July, 1916) who had considered Private Patchet's crime of 'writing by candlelight' was now received and he departed to base to begin his sentence - after his experience on July 1st, perhaps thankfully. Nevertheless, by today's standards this would seem a strange reward for a gallant soldier.

At 9.30 p.m. on the night of the 27th, the 18th Battalion left company section, came under heavy H.E., shrapnel and minen werfer bombardment, whilst the entire front line was swept continuously by machine gun fire. At 10.27 p.m., a runner from 'D' Company arrived at Battalion Headquarters saying that German troops had broken into the front line trenches 10 minutes previously, and Lieutenant Howarth had sent a message to Port Arthur for bombers, as he had none with him. Brigade ordered 'D' Company to launch an immediate counter-attack.

At 11.30 p.m. Private H. L. Riley of 'B' Company arrived at Battalion Headquarters supporting Corporal Lee who was wounded. He said that a minen werfer had struck a sentry post and immediately afterwards a party of Germans, dressed in black, 25 to 30 strong, had broken into the trench. The Germans, in two parties of about 16, armed with pistols and bombs and under one officer, broke into the British front line at two points: working inwards. On uniting they left with several prisoners, including Dickie Bond. Their arrival was unexpected and rapid, they advanced under cover of their own bombardment and broke into the line immediately after the barrage lifted. Many of the Pals were surprised in their dug-outs, the first inkling of the raid being when electric torches carried by the raiders flashed in their faces. Corporal Lee and Private Riley were in such a dug-out when a German, armed with a pistol and a Knob Kerry or, perhaps, a hand grenade, threw a light on them and told them to put up their hands. Lee and Riley made a dash for it and got away; Lee being hit in the leg whilst making his escape.

When they left, the trench was held by Germans. Those who were not taken prisoner defended themselves with rifles but were reluctant to use bombs for fear of injuring their comrades. Witnesses reported that several of the enemy inflicted slight wounds on their prisoners, presumably to prevent them escaping, although it is noteworthy that one man was bandaged up by a German who had wounded him first with a bomb and then a pistol. Lance Corporal Denton of 'B' Company was

Captain Harry H. Dalley

taken prisoner in this trench and led about 300 yards towards the German line. There he knocked over his man and escaped, reaching his own lines at about 10.00 a.m. the following morning. He was slightly wounded. Lieutenants Howarth and Watson and 2nd Lieutenant Walton were all taken prisoner. According to a soldier who was left behind because of his wounds, the raiders were in the front line for about twenty minutes. In addition to their prisoners they took away with them a Vickers gun and a box of ammunition. A dead German left in the trench was identified as a member of the 3rd Ersatz Company of the 248th Ersatz Battalion Reserve Infantry Regiment. This identification was made from the only document found on his body, his leave pass from April, 1916.

When news of the raid was received at Battalion Headquarters, 'B' and 'D' Companies were ordered to report their situation. In the meantime a message was received from Brigade that 150 men of the 15th Battalion were proceeding down Lansdown. 'C' Company was ordered to move to reinforce 'D' Company by way of 'Covered way' as soon as the 15th Battalion men arrived. Runners brought in news that 'B' Company was uncertain of the situation but that they had a bombing party proceeding to clear the line from the left. At 12.50 a.m. a message, timed 11.35 p.m. was received from the officer then commanding 'D' Company, probably the Adjutant, Captain Harry L. Dalley, which read: "Am in front line of 'B' Company. Have found Williams but practically only ten 'B' Company men. Am manning front line with 25 men. Several wounded but cannot spare men to bring them out. No bosche. Lieutenants Burton and Fletcher with me".

By 4.00 a.m. the front line had been reinforced and a party of sappers despatched to repair the heavy damage in the trenches caused by the shell fire. In the preceding affairs the Battalion had lost six killed, including Lieutenant Cross, 2nd Lieutenant W. R. Humphries and Company Sergeant Major G. H. Lipton, 42 wounded, of whom four died later, and 36 missing, believed prisoners.

From this time, until the Battalion was relieved on August 4th, little of significance beyond patrol activity, enemy sniping and shelling, is recorded in the War Diary. On that day the 16th Battalion was relieved by the 13th Battalion the York and Lancaster Regiment and marched to billets in Les Lobes whilst the 18th Battalion were relieved by a composite battalion of the 16th East Yorkshire Regiment and the 11th and 12th York and Lancaster Regiment, and moved to billets in Lestram. The composite company, X Company, rejoined their own battalion after their spell of duty with the 18th but less Sergeant W. Culling of 'D' Company and Lance Corporal McConnel and Privates J. Moore, Cussons and W. Ackroyd, all of 'C' Company who had lost their lives in the preceding actions.

After a few days rest in billets, both battalions received orders to take over the Festubert left sub-sector. Both had completed the relief by midnight on August 10th, the 16th Battalion occupying positions on the right, the 18th Battalion on the left. The terrain was similar to the Neuve Chapelle sector, the defences consisting, in the main, of breast works. This was a sector in which enemy snipers were constantly active and in which the parapet was swept at regular intervals by machine gun fire. Enemy artillery was very active, making Cover, Richmond, Shetland and Pioneer trenches particularly unhealthy locations. On the evening of the 15th, the 18th Battalion suffered four casualties, one other rank killed and three wounded by snipers. One sniper was reported to be in Canadian Orchard, not 60 yards from their positions.

A patrol which attempted to move into No Man's Land from three successive bays was met by sniper fire on each occasion. On the following evening snipers again prevented a patrol from going out from Islands 31 and 32 and also drove back a wiring party.

On the night of the 17th, the 18th Battalion were relieved by the 11th East Yorkshire Regiment and moved to billets in Rue de L'Epinette as mobile reserve. 'B' Company and 30 men from 'A' Company however, remained in the trenches moving to the right sub-sector in the old British front line and coming under the orders of the 15th West Yorkshire Regiment. The following day the 16th Battalion was relieved by the 11th East Yorkshire Regiment. Four officers and 75 other ranks were attached to the 15th Battalion of the Regiment whilst the remainder of the Battalion took over the defence of the Village Line which consisted of five posts named Le Plantin North, Festubert (Central), Festubert (East), Cailloux South, Cailloux East and various other small posts. Shortly after occupying these positions Lieutenant A. S. Gibson suffered a serious wound to the left hand and was evacuated to a casualty clearing station and, subsequently, struck off the strength.

The Givenchy sector had been very active, the engineers on both sides competing to blow up large mines beneath opposing trenches. The sector became a line of very large craters with both sides building saps on their sides of the craters. Being only yards from each other there was considerable hand and rifle grenade activity from both sides. At 8 pm. on the 20th, a mine was blown by the enemy in the Givenchy Sector which destroyed 'I SAP'. This was followed by a heavy bombardment which switched on to the right of the Festubert section, being particularly intense between Islands 9 and 13. At 8.45 p.m. the barrage lifted on to the old British lines and then dropped again on to the front line. At this time a strong party of the enemy attempted to force an entry into the British lines between Islands 10a, 11 and 12, but were driven off without achieving their objective. A barrage was put down in

31st Division Men in a SAP-Head, Givenchy. Imperial War Museum, Q7265.

No-Man's Land in an attempt to cut off their retreat. Later a patrol went out to try to obtain identification, but failed to find any dead or wounded.

The 16th Battalion received news in August that Major H. H. Kennedy was promoted to the rank of Acting Lieutenant-Colonel. Sergeant A. W. Ashforth was granted a field commission, becoming a 2nd Lieutenant with the Battalion. Also, Company Sergeant Major G. Cussons and Private T. Pearson were both awarded the Distinguished Conduct Medal for bravery in action and for their devotion to duty on July 1st, 1916.

The first part of September found the 16th Battalion in the right sub-section in the Neuve Chapelle section of trenches. The 18th Battalion were located in the Festubert left sub-section occupying positions in Hun Street and Port Arthur.

The 18th Battalion then spent a few days resting at Croix Barbes, but mid-September found both battalions employed in the right sub-sector of the Givenchy sector. As the month closed, the 16th Battalion were holding the Village Line', a series of posts known as 'Givenchy Keep', 'Orchard Redoubt', 'Moat Farm', 'Hilders Redoubt', 'Herts Redoubt', and 'Pont Fixe South'. The 18th Battalion were occupying positions at 'Windy Corner' and in 'Poppy Redoubt'.

On October 3rd, the 31st Division was taken out of the line and moved to the Bethune area. After a brief respite in billets in the town the 18th Battalion moved to billets in L'Ecleme whilst the 16th marched to La Miquellerie. Here they occupied billets which had been organized by 2nd Lieutenant E. Wilson, the billeting officer, and Sergeant Harry Drake, the Battalion interpreter. A sample of the latter's work can be seen further on in this book, as Sergeant Drake was to be the secretary of "The Tyke", the Battalion magazine. In later years he was to teach in several Bradford schools and was to be revered by generations of young Bradfordians.

On the 7th October, the 93rd Infantry Brigade, left the 1st Army area, marching to Lillers where they entrained for Doullens, arriving in the late afternoon. Here they detrained and marched to the village of Thievres where the 18th Battalion took billets. The 16th marched on to billets in Famechon.

In October news was received that Captain Harry L. Dalley, Adjutant of the 18th Battalion, had been awarded the Military Cross for his conspicuous gallantry during the recent fighting and that Major H. F. G. Carter was promoted to the rank of Lieutenant Colonel.

Captain Alan Clough

Captain Harry Dalley with his wife after receiving the Military Cross at Buckingham Palace from George V on June 20th, 1917

.303" Short Magazine Lee Enfield (SMLE) Mk3 rifle with Bayonet. MOD Pattern Room,

CHAPTER 5: HEBUTERNE

*I see them in foul dug-outs, gnawed by rats,
And in the ruined trenches, lashed with rain,
Dreaming of things they did with balls and bats,
And mocked by hopeless longing to regain
Bank holidays, and picture shows, and spats,
And going to the office in the train.*
                                            Siegfried Sassoon.

On October 21st, the 93rd Brigade took over the Hebuterne Sector, the 16th Battalion occupying the right sub-section with the 18th Battalion on the left (see map 5). This sector had originally been held by the French, who had made several novel innovations. In the centre of the village they had sunk a deep well into which drained several others. It was equipped with a pump, driven by a petrol engine, so that there was always a plentiful supply of water. Under a small waterfall they had installed a turbine-driven generator which supplied electricity to light the numerous deep dug-outs in the village. A number of communication trenches radiated from the village, three of the most important being Yellow Street, Yankee Street and Woman Street. The last named got its name from the decomposing body of a young woman which had been discovered near its entrance in a pool of putrid water, once the village pond.

Here undulating country, long grass and bushes, provided excellent opportunities for patrol activity, particularly 'Winkling', an activity first practised by the Canadians. This exercise involved a small party surprising an enemy sentry in an isolated post and then winkling prisoners out of the dug-outs behind him.

On the night of the 23rd and again on the night of the 26th, the 16th Battalion sent out raiding parties under 2nd Lieutenants C. P. Graham and D. T. King with 30 other ranks. Their intention was to find two gaps in the enemy wire, previously reconnoitred, and to penetrate the German line. On both these occasions they were unsuccessful, finding the gaps to have been filled.

On the night of the 24th, 2nd Lieutenant D. A. Gill, Sergeant G. Quigley and Private H. Sutcliffe of the 18th Battalion left their lines at 8.45 p.m. to investigate the German wire. They proceeded eastward to the enemy wire and then about 100 yards to the south, where they found a gap, about 30 yards wide. They proceeded through the gap to within 10 yards of the enemy parapet. Unfortunately at this point they were seen by a German sentry who fired three shots, mortally wounding 2nd Lieutenant Gill. The enemy immediately swept the area with machine gun fire. Sergeant Quigley and Private Sutcliffe succeeded in extricating themselves from their predicament and returned to their own lines, unwounded, and carrying their officer's body.

From 11.00pm until approximately 11.15pm, in response to British shelling, the enemy opened a rapid retaliatory barrage, apparently searching for a British battery east and south east of 18th Battalion headquarters. About 500 high explosive, tear gas and gas shells were fired, the gas shells causing several casualties. These casualties may well have been higher if it had not been for Private Victor Alred who, regardless of personal risk, made his way to the headquarters dugout to give warning.

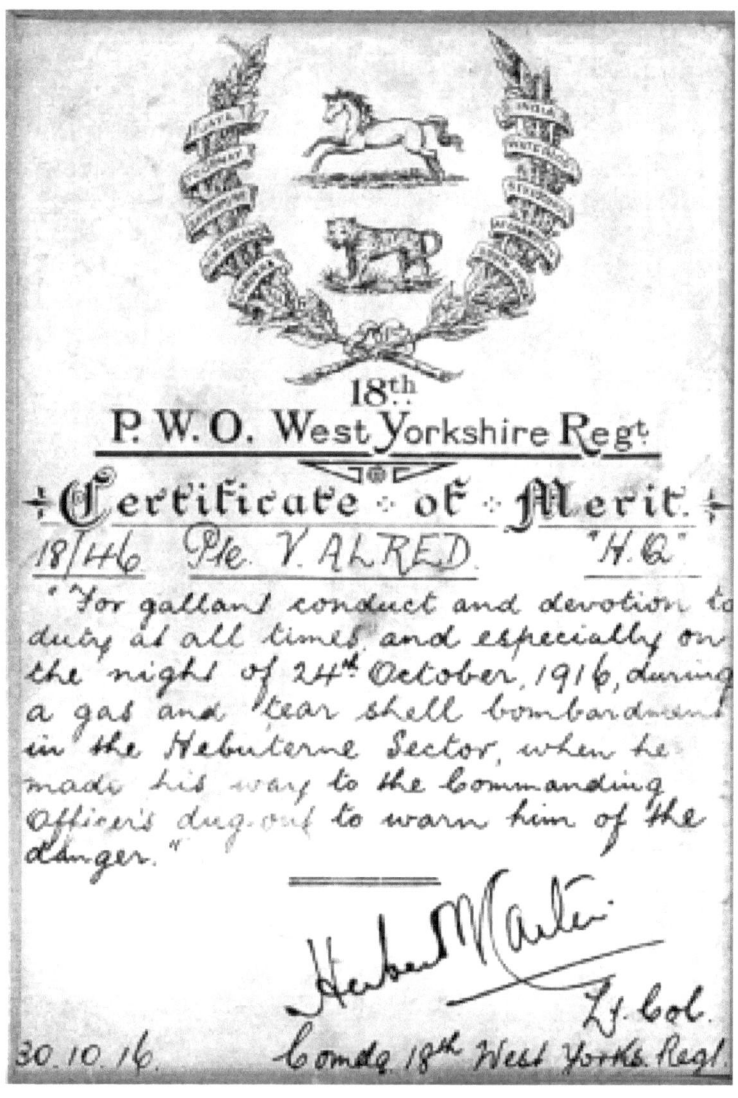

Both battalions were relieved from the front line on October 26th, and returned to support billets in Sailly aux Bois. From there they provided nightly working parties and fighting patrols.

Again on the night of the 27th a raiding party of 30 other ranks led by 2nd Lieutenants J. Luke and H. R. Mason, left the lines at 10.30 p.m., intent on penetrating the enemy trenches. Unfortunately whilst the advanced parties were engaged in getting through the wire nearest the enemy trenches they were spotted by a sentry and heavily fired on. They were compelled to withdraw, suffering one other rank killed. 2nd Lieutenant Luke and three other ranks were wounded.

On the 30th October the 16th proceeded to billets in Thievres whilst 'C' and 'D' Companies of the 18th went into bivouacs near Courcelles. The rest of the Battalion went into hutments at Coigneux. Both battalions now enjoyed a brief respite from front line duties but, on November 7th, they moved back into support billets in Sailly aux Bois. On the 11th November, between the hours of 10.00 p.m. and 3.00 a.m. and again at 6.00 a.m. the village was heavily shelled with high explosives and gas shells.

One of the last H. E. shells fired in this bombardment was a direct hit on one of the 16th Battalion's billets, killing eight other ranks and wounding 11 others, including 2nd Lieutenant G. Nicholls.

November 13th marked the beginning of the British offensive on both banks of the River Ancre. The 18th Battalion occupied the Hebuterne left sub-sector whilst 'A' and 'C' companies of the 16th Battalion occupied the left company section of the right sub-sector, coming under the command of the 18th. 'B' and 'D' Companies remained in bivouacs at Sailly aux Bois under the command of Major G. S. Blagbrough pending further orders. Lieutenant-Colonel Kennedy moved his headquarters into the dug-out which housed the 18th. Headquarters in Vercingetorix trench. The battalions were to hold the line during the attack on Serre and the German positions further south, while two battalions of the 92nd Brigade attacked on their front to cover the left flank of the assault. Zero hour was fixed at 5.45 a.m. when the British barrage opened promptly. Until 7.45 a.m. the enemy made no attempt to fire upon the front trenches. From then until 10.00 a.m. the enemy exhibited slightly more activity, shelling Brissoux and Knox trenches. This shelling became less as the morning advanced until about 11.45 a.m. when a heavy barrage was opened, chiefly directed at Jena Bart and Knox trenches and the junction of Jena and Vercingetorix trenches. During this time the 16th suffered ten casualties. The 18th Battalion suffered similarly. Just before noon 'C' Company Signals dug-out was blown in, killing two and wounding three. By 12.30 p.m. 'C' Company had lost nine dead and ten wounded. The bombardment slackened shortly after noon but increased to an intense barrage again around 2 p.m., costing the 16th a further ten casualties. The barrage had slackened by early evening, leaving the two battalions with a total of 55 casualties suffered.

The tour continued with spells in the trenches and brief respites in billets at Rossignol farm or Sailly aux Bois, although these 'respites' included the provision of working and carrying parties to, and into, the front line. On December 3rd, whilst occupying the right sub-sector the 16th Battalion were subjected to a heavy minenwerfer bombardment. The enemy scored one hit which killed five and wounded three other ranks.

Some relief from the monotony and hardships of trench life was provided to the 18th Battalion on December 9th when, around noon, an enemy deserter was seen approaching their lines along the Gommecourt-Hebuterne road. He was taken into custody and found to be very drunk. The inebriated German soldier was escorted to Brigade Headquarters by 2nd, Lieutenant Boweden and Corporal Broadhead of "C" Company. Corporal Broadhead recorded the incident in his diary with the comment "Got him to H.Q., after a bit of a struggle !"

On the same day the 16th received news that Corporal C. Higgins had been awarded the Distinguished Conduct Medal for gallantry and devotion to duty.

On December 23rd, Major G. S. Blagbrough was killed during a whizz-bang bombardment of the 16th Battalion's front. The Major, a former master at Bridlington Grammar School where he had been known affectionately by his pupils as Blags, had been with the Battalion since its formation and was second-in-command at the time of his death.

On December 31st, the 93rd Infantry Brigade were relieved by the 92nd Infantry Brigade. The 16th moved to Coigneux to rest but the 18th Battalion were required to remain in Hebuterne Keep and Sailly aux Bois until January 10th, 1917, when they were relieved in the front line by the 8th Battalion of the Gloucester Regiment.

The entire Brigade then spent over a month resting in the Doullens-Bernaville area. During this period both battalions commenced training in accordance with the newly introduced system of platoon organization under which platoon and company officers were entirely responsible for the training of their units including bombers, Lewis gunners and rifle grenadiers. Work was principally devoted to platoon drill, musketry, reorganization of platoons and route marching. Only half each working day was devoted to these tasks, the remainder on alternate afternoons and mornings by half battalions, being set aside for recreation. Football matches, running, tug-of-war, bayonet fighting, bomb throwing, and boxing matches were organized and all men, the diaries record, took part.

In January, Lieutenant-Colonel Kennedy left the Battalion to command the 6th Battalion of his own regiment, the Scottish Rifles. A tall genteel Scot, he always insisted on wearing the 'trews' and glengarry of his own regiment, and was well liked and respected by all. His place was taken by Lieutenant-Colonel A. C. Croydon, an officer who had risen from the ranks. Before receiving his commission he had been a Sergeant Major in the Lincolnshire Regiment. He was a strict disciplinarian of gruff manner. Coming events were to prove him a very proficient and professional officer.

Public concern at this time caused the War Office to forbid the employment of soldiers under the age of nineteen in the front line. Lance-Corporal Morgan and nineteen other young soldiers were, therefore, detached for instructional duties at the Infantry Training Depot at Etaples, known to British Tommies as "Eat Apples". The Depot included a large tract of land laid out with trenches, barbed wire, etc., known to soldiers as the Bull Ring. Here new drafts from Britain were taught the techniques of trench warfare by instructors who were known to their students as Canaries because of their yellow arm bands. George was to find, with some disgust, that many Canaries had never seen the front line. He described the shrieks, grunts and screams which these instuctors urged recruits to utter whilst thrusting bayonets into straw-filled sacks, as "rather silly." A detailed description of the regime at Eat Apples is to be found in Denis Winter's book "Death's Men".

Lance Corporal Morgan was to rejoin his battalion on achieving his 19th birthday.

George William Broadhead

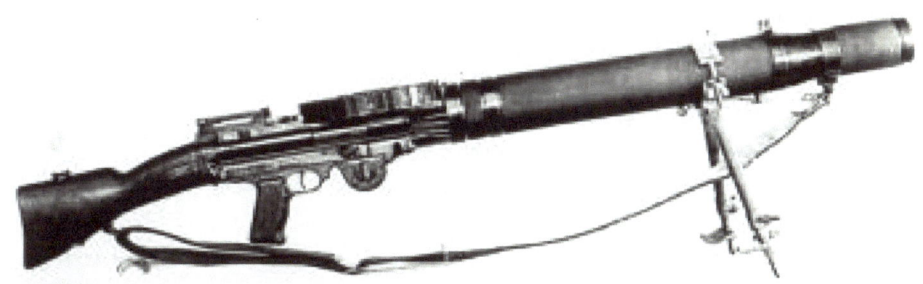

.303" Lewis Machine Gun. MOD Pattern Room, Nottingham

.303" Short Magazine Lee Enfield (SMLE) Mk3 rifle with Bayonet. MOD Pattern Room, Nottingham.

CHAPTER 6: GOMMECOURT PARK AND ROSSIGNOL WOOD

> *Men jostle and climb to meet the bristling fire*
> *Lines in grey, muttering faces, masked with fear,*
> *They leave their trenches, going over the top,*
> *While time ticks blank and busy on their wrists,*
> *And hope with furtive eyes and grappling fists*
> *Flounders in the mud. O Jesus make it stop!*
>
> Siegfried Sassoon

On February 21st, 1917, both battalions left Doullens and marched to Coigneux and hence into the trenches in the Hebuterne sector. The 16th Battalion occupied the L3 sub-sector with the 18th on their left flank in the L4 sub-sector. The 18th Battalion was now under the temporary command of Major C. W. Tilly of the 18th Durham Light Infantry, Lieutenant-Colonel H. F. G. Carter being hospitalised. Four days later Major Tilly became ill and Major A. W. Robinson assumed command.

On the 23rd February, the enemy began to evacuate his front line and fall back on to the Hindenburg line, a system of strong defences which straightened out his saliant between Arras and Vailly. The first indication that something unusual was taking place, on the opposite side of No-Man's Land, was when smoke was observed rising from the German trenches at two points. Artillery was informed and a barrage of 18 pounder fire directed at these points for several hours. At 11.00 p.m. on February 24th, Brigade Headquarters wired that the enemy was thought to have left his front line trenches opposite V Corps, and ordered patrols out to investigate, including two patrols from the 18th Battalion.

Company commanders were ordered to Battalion Headquarters and briefed for these operations. Two platoons from 'A' Company, on the left, were to reconnoitre the tongue of the Gommmecourt saliant; two platoons from 'C' Company, on the right, were to search the south-west corner of the Park, at 'Fir trench'. These were the first objectives. Two platoons each from 'D' and 'B' Companies were to support and proceed to points beyond the third line of German trenches and well inside the Park. These were the second objectives. Patrols were instructed that, if the enemy line was found to be unoccupied, they were to push forward to their objectives with vigour. The 18th Battalion the Durham Light Infantry were ordered to move up in support to enable the exploitation of any gains. Zero hour was fixed at 5.00 a.m. on February 25th (see map 5).

The patrols moved off at the appointed hour but at 6.40 a.m. 'B' Company were reporting bomb and rifle fire on each flank. Shortly after this the enemy artillery became very active. Ten minutes later, a report was received from Captain J. R. Thornton of 'A' Company, saying that his patrol had reached its first objective but that he was not in touch with 'C' Company. A little later 2nd Lieutenant Hartman, of the 19th Divisional Artillery, reported at Battalion Headquarters that Captain Thornton had gained the tongue of the salient and that Lieutenant Sleigh, leading the other platoon from 'A' Company, was moving through the woods of Gommecourt Park. A party of ten of the enemy had been seen on the left and had been dispersed by Lewis gun fire. 2nd Lieutenant Hartman was instructed to rejoin Captain Thornton and tell him to press on to the second objective. Captain Thornton wrote later:

> "I was in charge of No. 2 platoon and moved out from K3d 3.6 at 5.00 a.m. my objective being K2c2.9 to K3b 9.10. On moving into No-Man's Land a Very light was sent up from 'four tree SAP'. I moved northeast and entered a communication trench, at about K3b 9.5.10. Bombers were leading and we came into contact with an enemy post about K4c 9.0. The occupants of this post fled and we advanced to K4c 2.9.
>
> I stayed in this trench for about 45 minutes during which time I sent a patrol up 'Fin' towards 'Field' and another along 'Fish' [these were code names for three German trenches in Gommecourt Park] to about 100 yards past the communication trench at K4c 7.6 without coming into contact with any one. We were bombed from K4 2.2.05 and retaliated with bombs and claimed two hits. Shelling was heavy and as I could not get in touch with anyone I decided to return, leaving the enemy trench at about K4c 6.6, moving south of 'Yiddish'. I approached to a spot about K3d 9.8, from which smoke had been seen to issue for the last two days. This I found to be a burning dug-out, the wood around the entrance being charred."

At 7.20 a.m., a runner arrived at Battalion Headquarters with a message from 2nd Lieutenant Priday, who was in charge of the reserve platoon of the right patrol, saying that he had met a platoon of 'A' Company who had been ordered to retire. He had put them in support in Z Hedge and gone on with No. 6 platoon. By 7.30 a.m. 'C' Company had reported the return of the platoon that had formed the right patrol and led by 2nd Lieutenant O. H. Staff who reported:

"I left Z Hedge as ordered at 5.35 a.m. and proceeded to my objective through our own wire, which had been cut. I found the enemy wire strong and had some trouble cutting through it. I entered the enemy trench and bombed five dug-outs. I was met by a superior enemy force with a machine gun and, because my men's rifles were practically useless due to mud, I decided to withdraw."

The officer commanding 'C' Company was instructed to order the platoon forward again with support if necessary.

2nd Lieutenant O. H. Staff

At 7.42 a.m., 'A' Company reported that Lieutenant Sleigh's platoon had returned on his orders but that he was not with them. About this time a heavy enemy bombardment developed shelling 'A' Company out of 'The Mouse Trap' opposite Gommecourt Park. The enemy was, by then, laying a heavy barrage on his own front line. On the fate of Lieutenant Sleigh, Captain Thornton wrote:

"... Lieutenant Sleigh and No. 3 platoon followed behind me, I saw him enter at the same place (in the enemy line) as I had done. Apparently he continued north of 'Fin' and I heard bombing about 200 yards up. I did not see anything more of him. My casualties were nil."

Lieutenant Sleigh was subsequently posted missing, believed killed.

2nd Lieutenants Staff and Holt who had, by that time, submitted their reports to Battalion Headquarters were ordered out again with instructions to take the line and make every effort to hold it, but to return if this proved to be absolutely impossible. However, before this order could be executed, instructions were received from Brigade to withdraw all troops to their own lines. This decision was probably influenced by the fact that the 18th Battalion Durham Light Infantry was having difficulty in moving forward into support and, in fact, had not arrived by 7.47 a.m. The last patrol to return was No. 6 Platoon, led by 2nd Lieutenant N. H. Priday, who reported:

"No. 6 platoon left the line at 6.15 a.m. and on arrival at Z Hedge received a verbal message from the Officer commanding B' Company to the effect that I was to remain at Z Hedge in support. Here I met 2nd. Lieutenant Hartman of the 19th Division Royal Field Artillery who told me that he had just returned from the first German line. Soon after this I saw No. 2 platoon arriving at the junction of 'Yiddish Street' and 'C' line. I learned that this platoon had been bombed out. This decided me to move my own platoon forward and bring No.2 platoon into Z Hedge in support. This I effected and at 7.00 a.m.,I despatched a message to the officer commanding 'B' Company stating my intentions. I immediately moved forward in battle formation. A platoon of 'C' Company passed me here. They told me they had been bombed out and had lost direction. I explained what I was doing and continued my advance. I arrived at a point opposite K7c 5.7 and discovered two gaps in the wire. I immediately moved forward through these gaps into the Bosche line which I occupied at 7.30 a.m. I sent two runners to Z Hedge to bring forward No. 2 platoon under Sergeant Hustwick. On arrival of this party I pushed a point out about 50 yards inside Gommecourt Park and sent bombing parties along the trench on either flank, to try to get in touch with my flanks. These patrols returned, after half an hour's absence, stating that they had discovered no sign of anyone. I myself, with thrt men, pushed on into the Park to reconnoitre.

2nd Lieutenant N. H. Priday

The mist was by this time very thick so that I lost direction and with difficulty retraced my steps to my party. Whilst reconnoitring, three shots were fired in my direction from seemingly close at hand, but I could detect no sign of the enemy. On return I despatched a message to 'B' Company's commanding officer asking for reinforcements. Pending the arrival of these, I collected a quantity of enemy hand grenades, which I distributed amongst the men, at the same time explaining their use. At 9.00 a.m. my runners returned with a message stating that I was to retire as quickly as possible, which order I obeyed. During the hour and a half which I remained in the enemy's lines, no hostile movement was detected. All dug-outs in the vicinity were searched to no purpose and on retirement my party was not molested, but passed through a heavy hostile barrage, extending from the edge of our barbed wire entanglements to beyond Red line."

On the evening of the 26th, the 16th Battalion received orders to launch an attack on Rossignol Wood. The assault was to take place the following morning at 6.30 a.m., two companies forming the firing line with two companies in support. The two front companies were ordered to be clear of a line of posts on the Gommecourt-Puisieux Road at 6.30 a.m. Four, and later six, Lewis guns under the command of the battalion Lewis gun officer, were positioned on the 'Sunken Road' to cover the advance and to fire upon any favourable targets. Major H. B. Byles, second in command, together with the battalion signals, intelligence and medical officers took up a position at the Crucifix.

From there a line was laid to Battalion Headquarters in Woman Street. The extreme range ruled out a supporting barrage from the trench mortar battery.

The two companies, 'A' Company and 'C' Company, were clear of the enemy third line by 5.30 a.m. and deployed for the attack in No-Man's Land, moving forward at about 6.00 a.m. with scouts well in advance.

The first report received from the scouts was that the southern edge of the Wood was occupied. The officer commanding 'C' Company, on the left, sent one platoon to move towards Pioneer Graben and occupy the high ground there. On reaching the trench they were met by an enemy counter-attack which drove them back towards the Crucifix. A bombing party under 2nd Lieutenant E. Crowther was immediately sent against the enemy and succeeded in driving them back about 180 yards after killing one and wounding several others. The party were able to establish blocks in Moltke Graben and Pioneer Graben and a bombing post at the junction of these trenches. The remainder of the company pushed forward, some men getting into the Wood whilst the rest dug themselves in in Stump Alley, and Pioneer Graben, south-west of the Crucifix, after losing some seven men killed and nine wounded in trying to move forward.

At 11.00 a.m., two platoons from the reserve companies were ordered forward to assist 'C' Company, who were not making much headway. This Company, although under heavy fire from 6.00 a.m. consolidated all the positions taken and stayed in them until relieved that night.

On the right, 'A' Company pushed forward into the southern edge of the Wood, three platoons entering by way of the trenches. The enemy immediately opened heavy fire upon them, with machine guns, infilading these trenches and killing or wounding almost their entire strength. 2nd Lieutenant Ashworth, who commanded No. 2 platoon, said in his report:

> "We came under heavy machine gun fire on reaching the crest of the hill about 600 yards from Rossignol Wood. I entered a communication trench and got my Lewis gun working."

He went on to say that the machine gun fire was from three directions and that they were also subjected to a light field gun barrage. Private W. Higgins, who went into action with Sergeant Farrar, No. 4 platoon, recalled:

> "We took cover as soon as the German machine guns opened fire. The heavy fire was kept up and it was practically impossible to move. My platoon was on the right and I was fourth man from the right. All the N.C.O.'s of my platoon were killed or wounded. I lay in the same position from where I could see about seven or eight men lying on the ground either killed or wounded until about 4.00 p.m."

The Company's No. 3 platoon, commanded by 2nd Lieutenant Tucker, took cover in shell holes in the open and were able to rejoin the battalion that night. Corporal E. Keighley who went into action with this platoon was to recall:

> "After we had crossed the third German line we came under heavy machine gun fire. I found that we were too crowded in the shell hole in which we had taken cover, so I took four of my men to find a better position. As I got to the top of the communication trench, two of my men were killed. I hung on there for some time and, after about half an hour, 2nd Lieutenant Tucker came up and joined me."

Captain Armitage, the Company Commander, and Lieutenant Knight, were killed. Of the platoon commanders, Sergeant Farrar was killed and 2nd Lieutenants Ashworth and Tucker were wounded.

No messages were received from 'A' Company after 6.00 a.m. that morning until 2nd Lieutenant Tucker was able to report to Battalion Headquarters at 10.00 p.m. that night. Included in this Officer's Report, and referring to the wounded, are the following remarks:

> "I saw a number of men laying about, out in the open, wounded and unable to get back. It was impossible to get stretcher bearers near them as the enemy was constantly sniping from the Wood. Men who were laying wounded were sniped at on making any attempt to reach cover, as the ground where they were was practically without shell holes and absolutely exposed to enemy fire, and snipers were firing incessantly."

In point of fact both Stump Alley and Bulow Weg were too wet and muddy for the use of stretchers. In addition they were exposed to enfilade fire from the Wood, so that these trenches could not be used for the evacuation of the wounded.

When darkness came on the night of the 27th, Lieutenant-Colonel Croydon relieved the two companies in the front line at the Crucifix and the old German third line. Food and water together with ten boxes of ammunition and ten boxes of bombs were sent forward. At that time the Vickers and Lewis gun teams had been in their positions for 42 hours. During the attack the 16th Battalion had suffered 222 casualties, two officers and 64 other ranks had been killed, ten other ranks had died of their wounds, two officers and 83 other ranks had been wounded in actio and 65 persons were missing. 'A' Company had suffered particularly heavily. As we have seen both the officers killed and both the officers wounded were from this company. In addition, the company lost 38 N.C.O.'s and other ranks killed, 35 N.C.O.'s and other ranks wounded whilst six N.C.O.'s and other ranks died of their wounds and 61 persons were posted missing. Among the N.C.O.'s who lost their lives were Company Sergeant Major Wilkinson, Sergeant Barnes and Sergeant Cockroft who had already lost two brothers in the campaign. All these men had joined the Battalion on its formation in 1914. Sergeant Nelson was the only Sergeant in 'A' Company to survive the day.

On the 28th, the 18th Battalion received orders to relieve the two companies of the 16th Battalion, and the two companies of the 15th Battalion on the right, from their new positions. Major Robinson also received verbal instructions that his Battalion would be required to attack Rossignol Wood on the morning of March 1st. These instructions were subsequently amended to the morning of March 2nd.

The relief moved off at 7.00 p.m. Lieutenant Morgan with one platoon from 'D' Company relieved the 16th Battalion from their positions in the Crucifix. Here, he set up a report centre and telephone, and established a party of battalion bombers. Another platoon from 'D' Company relieved the 16th Battalion personnel in the old German line from K11d 3.7 to K11d 6.5. The remaining two platoons from this company relieved the 15th Battalion companies in their forward posts. 'A' and 'B' companies established themselves in the old German 3rd and 2nd line from K11d 3.8 to K11d 8.0 and from K11c 8.9 to K11d 3.0. 'C' Company moved into the old German front line from K11c 5.7 to K11d 1.0. Battalion Headquarters was set up in Woman Street. The relief was completed by 12.00 midnight, the Battalion suffering seven casualties, wounded by shell fire.

The 16th Battalion were now relieved from support by the 13th Battalion the York and Lancaster Regiment and proceeded to a camp near Coigneux on the Courcellers Road.

Throughout the afternoon of the 1st, heavy smoke continued to rise from burning dug-outs in the Wood. From the early hours and throughout the day of the 2nd, the 18th Battalion maintained strong patrol activity. At mid-day the officer commanding 'B' Company was informed by Battalion Headquarters that it was intended to occupy the Wood "that night". Shortly before 1.00 p.m. 'D' Company reported that they had a patrol, consisting of an N.C.O. and two other men, probing up Stump Alley. They had been unable to reach the enemy line at the west corner of the Wood owing to a sniper, who had killed one of their men. A second N.C.O. patrol from 'D' Company had penetrated up Bulow Weg trench as far as the Wood, experiencing no opposition except sniping. The Wood end of the trench was found to be blocked with trees and wire. Another patrol was immediately sent out by the same route. Shortly before 3.00 p.m. a message was received from Brigade Headquarters which read:

> "Every endeavour will be made to enter Rossignol Wood and 1st Garde Stellung with strong patrols tonight. All ground gained will be held by strong posts and consolidated . . ."

By 5.30 p.m. the Battalion had a patrol working into the Wood at K12b 0.6 whilst another patrol was working up the continuation of Bulow Weg trench towards the Wood. A stronger patrol was waiting at the top of Bulow Weg for information from the advanced patrols. At 7.00 p.m. a patrol from 'B' Company moved out from the Crucifix with instructions to meet up with 2nd Lieutenant Priday and his platoon at the north-west corner of the Wood. The company moved out by platoons while 'A' Company moved up behind them. At 8.30 p.m. 'B' Company reported from the Sunken Road, near Stump Alley, that 2nd Lieutenant Priday and his men were in the Wood and had met with no opposition. Their remaining platoons were following up at 15 minute intervals. By 10.00 p.m. both 'A' and 'B' Companies were in the Wood with their Company Headquarters established at its edge in the extension of Bulow Weg. At 10.25 p.m. instructions were received from Brigade Headquarters ordering the Battalion to press on, after the Wood had been cleared, and establish a series of six posts to defend its approaches from the east. The Wood was to be lightly held owing to the possibility of heavy retaliatory shelling. The objectives of the 'Durhams' on their left, was 1st Garde Stellung from the junction of Lehmann

Graben to the junction with Becker Graben thence working south-east along the trench to gain touch with the 18th Battalion at the point where the road intersected the trench. Posts were to be established at the junction of 1st Garde Stellung and the communication trench. At 11.50 p.m. advice was received from Brigade that patrols from the battalion on the right had been encountering serious opposition from K12d 7.8 and L7c 0.7 (some 200 and 500 yards to 'A' Company's right) since 7.30 p.m. The message from this battalion, the 6th Battalion the Wiltshire Regiment, continued: ". . . am endeavouring to obtain possession of the Berg Graben between these points to make a flank attack."

Major Robinson

By this time 'B' Company were consolidating a line a little to the north of the Wood, assisted by a platoon from 'A' Company. They had established the three strong points shown on map 5. 'A' Company had one and a half platoons at the north-east neck of the Wood and had established three strong points there, also shown on map 5. A further one and a half platoons were in the Wood's south-west corner and in the first 200 yards of Berg Graben. Six prisoners had been taken. By 12.40 a.m. the Wiltshires had occupied the rest of the Berg Graben.

Shortly after 5.00 a.m. the 18th Durham Light Infantry reported that one of their patrols, moving along 1st Garde Stellung, had met with heavy opposition and considered that the trench was strongly held. At 11.00 am. a message arrived from 2nd Lieutenant Bradford, of the Durhams, who reported:

> "I am quite near the barrier at the junction of Pioneer Graben and 1st Garde Stellung. Have patrols out myself. About 100 of the enemy have been seen in the vicinity, wiring and working on the parapet. His wire is very thick and deep and the barricade is the same also. He has evidently seen some of our men, also heard bombs thrown because he is now manning his line. The line is strongly held and, owing to the depth and thickness of the wire, chances of getting through are small."

When this information was passed to the Durhams, their Commanding Officer asked Major Robinson to render any assistance possible to help 2nd Lieutenant Bradford clear up the situation. He left it to the Major to decide upon and carry out what operations he considered necessary to help the lieutenant in achieving his objectives. Two patrols, one of Durhams and one from the 18th Battalion were immediately ordered out to ascertain the strength of the enemy. Both patrols reported the 1st Garde Stellung at point 70 andprobably the 2nd Garde Stellung at point 82 to be strongly held. After consultations with Brigade, Major Robinson decided to attack these strong points. His operational order read:

> "At 5 p.m. the Infantry of Keel (the 18th Battalion West Yorks) and the Infantry of Deck (the 18th Battalion the Durham Light Infantry) will get into battle formation extended order as close to the barrage as possible. At 5.10 p.m. the Infantry will rush the positions at K6c 82 and K6c 02, (these positions were, in fact, strong points). Before 5.00p.m. the Infantry of Keel and Deck must not be within 250 yards of the triangle formed by the neck of the north-west saliant of the wood and a line from K12b 2.4 to K12b 3.6."

The operation was carried out with dash and vigour and, by 6.10 p.m. 'B' Company had reported that 1st Garde Stellung had been entered, that 20 prisoners had been captured and that the position was being consolidated. Captain Thornton was reported wounded. At 7.27 p.m. Brigade signalled: "Wire directly you are in a satisfactory position for relief platoons and Company Headquarters must be forwarded before sanction is given for relief to take place".

The dispositions of the companies was then relayed to Brigade but, before requesting relief, Major Robinson visited all posts to check their positions stated (strong points K6c 9.1 and trench K6c 8.2). He led men to their correct positions and saw them consolidating their posts before moving on to inspect other posts. After visiting all the posts in the Garde Stellung and Rossignol Wood, and requesting the 13th Battalion York and Lancaster Regiment to relieve two platoons of 'C' Company in 2nd Garde Stellung, he returned to Battalion Headquarters and reported his situation to Brigade as being "quite satisfactory for relief."

By 12.30 a.m. on the 4th, relief had been completed by the 13th York and Lancaster Regiment, except for the two platoons of 'C' Company who were still busy consolidating their positions. These platoons were relieved at 2.30 a.m. The Battalion then moved to Hebuterne where they remained until the afternoon. Then they marched to billets in Bayencourt. The casualties suffered by the Battalion during these operations were described as light.

Captain J. R. Thornton was carried out of the trenches by his orderly and company runner, Private Frank Burn. The two had been inseparable since Festubert. When he attended a Company

Frank Burn on active service, September 1916

Commander's course at Condett, the Captain had taken Frank with him as his servant. Frank was at that time under the age of 19 and, therefore, not allowed to be employed in the trenches. Captain Thornton, happily, recovered from his wounds. The two were able to continue their comradeship in later years through the Bradford Pals Old Comrades' Association. Captain Thornton was, for many years, President of the Association, whilst Frank Burn held the office of Chairman until the Association was disbanded in 1979.

Lieutenant Norman Priday was awarded a Military Cross for his courage and initiative.

The courage displayed by Sergeant Albert E. Sands during operations in March/April earned him also a mention in the despatches of Field Marshall Douglas Haig.

The 16th Battalion had posted a screen of Lewis gun teams, out in No-Man's Land, to cover the approaches to their positions. Just before first light they realised that one of these teams, manned by men from "C" Company, had not received an order to retire. They were in danger of being isolated by an expected enemy artillery barrage.

Sergeant Sands of "C" Company answered a call for a volunteer to go out into No Man's Land to guide the team back to their own positions. Armed with a satchel full of grenades and his comrades' good wishes, he climbed over the parapet and began the long crawl on his belly across the wastes of the battlefield. When he reached the post, he found three men. One was dead, another badly

wounded, the third suffering from exhaustion and exposure. He had enlisted with all three. Sergeant Sands de-activated the Lewis gun, dumped all his gear (for which he was later castigated), took the wounded man on his back and, with the man who could still walk clinging on for support, began the long trek back. When he staggered back into "C" Company positions, the man on his back was found to be dead. Shaking Sands by the hand his Company Commander gave him a measure of rum.

In later life, when recounting the incident to his small son, Albert Sands would include the soldier's song:

> And then the officer will meet you,
> With a tot of rum he'll greet you
> And he'll say "Mate, retaliate,
> With a Mills' Number Five."

Gaverelle Trench, 1917. By Adrian Hill. Imperial War Museum picture No. 1648/314

No Man's Land in front of Serre, 1916. Imperial War Museum, Neg. Q1910.

CHAPTER 7: GAVRELLE AND OPPY WOOD

Lee, Arthur, b. Leicester, 40489, Pte., K. in a., F.&F., 3/5/17
Lee, Joseph, b. Leicester, 40488, Pte., K. in a., F.&F., 3/5/17
- *extract from the list of the men of the 18th Battalion who were killed {Appendix 4).*

Towards the end of March, 1917, the 93rd Brigade moved back to the Bethune area. The 18th Battalion was in billets in Feuillade Barracks in the town of Bethune whilst the 16th Battalion was accommodated in Neauvry. A brief period of cleaning up, training, route marching, etc. made a welcome break from life in the trenches.

On the 28th April, the 93rd Brigade was ordered back to the Arras front, where they relieved the 63rd Naval Division in the vicinity of Gavrelle. On arrival in this sector, the Brigade was immediately concentrated in the forward area. The 16th Battalion occupied the left sub-sector. On their right the 15th Battalion held Gavrelle. The 18th Battalion went into the support positions with 'B' Company on Hill 80, the remaining companies in the support trenches some 400 yards west of Gavrelle.

The beginning of the month had seen the opening of the Allied spring offensive. The British armies had driven the enemy from Vimy Ridge and broken his line east of Arras. The positions which both battalions now occupied had only recently been held by the Germans.

By the end of April the French offensive, in the south, was running into difficulties. On May 3rd, to take some of the pressure off their allies, the British First and Third armies struck towards Fresnoy. The 31st Division took part with the 2nd Division on their left and the 9th Division on their right. The 92nd Brigade attacked on the Division's left, the 93rd Brigade on the right. The objectives of the 31st Division were the German 1st and 2nd lines. These are shown, in so far as they affect the 93rd Brigade, on map no. 6.

2nd Lieutenant R. W. Clarkson of the 18th Battalion recalled:

"Before going up to the line a day before the attack, each officer was received by Colonel Carter, who wished luck to him and his men. Everyone was in good heart and determined not to let himself and others down."

For hours there had been almost continuous shelling by both sides and the first job was to advance an hour before zero in order to man the direction tapes at intervals extending over about 200 yards. This was done without interruption from the enemy.

2nd Lieutenant R.W. Clarkson

The Brigade lined up for the attack with the 16th Battalion on the left. Then the 18th Battalion, divided into two halves, one half on the right of the 16th and one half on the left of the 15th Battalion who formed the Brigade's right flank. The three battalions were each to attack on a double company front, and in four waves. The 18th were lined up in half companies in the order, left to right, '/\, 'D', 'C', 'B'. Thus '/\ and 'D' companies operated in conjunction with the 16th and 'C' and 'B' companies with the 15th Battalion.

The 16th Battalion was assembled with two platoons of 'D' Company on the right and two platoons of 'C' Company on the left in the first wave. The second wave was made up from the remaining platoons of these companies. 'B' Company, including George Morgan, now a Sergeant, formed the third wave and 'A Company the fourth.

The officers of the 16th Battalion who went forward with the attacking waves in 'A' Company were Captain Illingworth, 2nd Lieutenant Bantock, 2nd Lieutenant Cowell, 2nd Lieutenant L. Ashworth and 2nd Lieutenant Tucker, the Battalion Bombing Officer, who, with a party of Regimental bombers and rifle grenadiers, had been detailed to deal with the enemy strong points in, and around, the Link Maze. In 'B' Company the officers were Captain Ashworth, 2nd Lieutenant Platnauer, and 2nd Lieutenant Cook. In 'C' Company they were Lieutenant Crowther, 2nd Lieutenant Parker, and 2nd Lieutenant Greville. In 'D' Company they were Captain P. L. Parker, 2nd Lieutenant Barltrop, and 2nd Lieutenant Bantock, who was attached to this company for the operation.

With Lieutenant-Colonel Croydon in Battalion Headquarters were 2nd Lieutenant Stanley, acting as Adjutant, Lieutenant Barrow, the Battalion Intelligence Officer, 2nd Lieutenant Johnson, the Signals Officer, 2nd Lieutenant Bartlett, the Artillery Officer and 2nd Lieutenant Bentock, acting as Liaison Officer with the 18th Battalion, the East Yorkshire Regiment.

GAVRELLE AND OPPY WOOD

Artillery methods had improved since the Battle of the Somme. New techniques included the 'creeping barrage' where infantry advanced behind a moving wall of exploding shells; that is, if they were able to differentiate between their own barrage and that of the enemy. The technique was to be used on this occasion.

The Brigade attack itself was divided into two halves, the right, or southern attack, and the left or northern attack. The barrage on the left was only to move, or creep, at a rate of 100 yards in four minutes so as to conform with the brigade on the left who were to attack Oppy. The barrage on the right was to creep at the rate of 100 yards in two minutes. This was to conform with the brigade on the right. Zero hour was fixed for 3.45 a.m.

At 2 a.m. the enemy laid a heavy barrage on the British front line which lasted 20 minutes. It caught both battalions as they were preparing to leave the protection of their trenches to line up on the assembly guide tapes laid the night before. (Unfortunately, the Battalion's war diaries make no mention of the gallantry of, nor of the casualties suffered by, the officers and men who laid these direction tapes.) Many 18th Battalion men were killed or wounded. In his report on the attack, Lieutenant-Colonel Carter described how no one hung back but climbed out unhesitatingly and fearlessly into a bristling fire, in some cases treading over the bodies of their dead comrades to do so.

At 3.00 a.m. in response to an S.O.S. from Oppy Wood, the enemy laid a heavy barrage lasting 17 minutes on the British front line.

Promptly at 3.45 a.m. the British bombardment began and the three battalions rose to their feet and moved forward, close to the barrage, extended in good order. Unfortunately for them, No-Man's Land was bathed in bright moonlight.

At 3.49 a.m. an intense enemy barrage was directed at the entire British front, accompanied by heavy machine gun and rifle fire from the left flank and immediate front. The artillery barrage was to last until 12.00 noon.

By 4.00 a.m. the 16th Battalion's first waves had reached their first objectives, passing through the enemy wire, which was sparse, without difficulty. As the barrage lifted, they advanced into the enemy trench, which they found to be only lightly held and experienced a minimum of opposition. Prisoners were taken and the first wave set about consolidating the trench whilst the following waves pressed on, behind the barrage, to the second objective. The enemy was seen to leave this position in large numbers, retiring in disorder and suffering heavy casualties from fire brought to bear upon them from the advancing troops. This trench was occupied, but it was then that Captain Parker, leading 'D' Company, realized that the companies on his left had not come up. Steps were taken to consolidate the trench, which was very shallow. Digging proved to be difficult due to the chalky nature of the ground. Lewis gun posts were pushed well out.

In most cases the 18th's 'left half battalion' had reached their first and second objectives.

However, heavy machine gun fire had sadly depleted their ranks by the time they had reached the second objective. There was some considerable loss of direction, possibly because of the fact that two consecutive casualties in a line, left the men 24 yards apart. On the right, however, the 'right half battalion' did not get much further than their first objective. In one or two places they were held up by wire but in the main they were wiped out by machine gun fire before reaching the first line of German trenches. Many of these machine guns were firing from unmarked strong points, often consisting of shafts dug out from the bottom of large shell holes and leading to

Corporal W. Palframan

emplacements that opened out into the crest or the back of the hilly ground. Corporal Palframan of 'B' Company, who was second in command of No. 8 'Moppers-up' platoon, found such a post just past the Windmill and in front of the enemy line. He reported it as a very deep hole, about 20 feet deep, and funnel shaped. He got two prisoners out of it but elected not to investigate further. He therefore bombed it. Corporal Palframan was awarded a Distinguished Conduct Medal and, later, was to be commissioned in the field.

Here, let 2nd Lieutenant Clarkson take up his story:

> "'B' Company, including my platoon, formed part of the first wave on the right. Before zero hour advanced my platoon left the trenches to line up on the tapes which directed the attack, half left, towards the supposed enemy line, so far as the disjointed front was known. Guesswork, mostly.
> At 3.45 a.m. zero hour came in as a quiet, dark dawn. Our only orders were to advance behind the creeping barrage which, at that time moved slightly forward, at the same time the enemy barrage intensified, and would continue to do so until the German trenches were reached. We had no idea how far this would be. It was expected that our artillery would have made their front line uninhabitable so whatever trench we entered was to be made as defendable as possible. The expectation was that the second wave would pass through us to the second objective. All 'according to the book'! My platoon was depleted to about 20 including a Lewis gun section of four men carrying guns and ammunition. I remember that this seemed a bit weak for an advance attacking a line of about 200 yards.
> 'What', thought this young civilian Subaltern, 'is one supposed to do now?' Twenty men stretched over 150/200 yards in the gloom carrying bayonets at the ready, all trying to keep a straight line, not knowing what to expect, hoping for an abandoned front line but, in all probability, trenches full of quick-firing enemy. A Subaltern should be in front of his

Pals, first thought he to himself. Secondly, he should show a good example (God help me!) Perhaps talking in a loud voice, encouraging and directing. They may then know where you are. (But the noise was deafening - How could they hear what was being said?) The walking was anything but good, plenty of obstacles to step on, still dark before dawn, air thick with smoke and bursting shells and no view of one's troops except for the one or two on one's left and right , certainly no more. One remembers shouting at several figures: *Don't bunch! Spread out.*

Where are the N.C.O.'s? Doing what they can to keep things going but none to be seen in the gloom. One remembers calling to Batman Riley (a good chap): 'Riley, where are you?' 'Here, Sir,' someone replies. Then, after about ten minutes . . . . WHAM! Something hard hit on the right side somewhere and caused one to tumble to the ground. No real pain and finding walking was still possible, had to catch up with the platoon who must be somewhere in front by then. One was in the back now, instead of in the front. Finally, the light becoming a bit better, a German trench in front so jumped in hoping to find men of the platoon. What now! Wound bleeding a lot but not much pain. Found two dead Germans in the large Strong Point and about 12 of our men from different platoons all of whom were wounded pretty badly except one who kept a look out. No one strong e n o u g h to turn the trench the other way round [to prepare the trench against counter-attack]. Tried to keep the injured in good trim and hoped to find the second wave troops arriving to re-enforce. None, of-course, arrived and, at this point, now daylight and less firing, a friend, Lieutenant Daws, slipped into the trench having lost touch with his own lot. He'd managed to get this far without being wounded and realizing our situation decided to try and get back to Battalion Headquarters which I gather he did.

wrote a message and entrusted it to my only active soldier but I am certain he did not manage to make it.

To one's surprise a German F e l d w e b e l arrived in our trench.

'So,' one thought 'we have got a prisoner!' He was not carrying a gun but no doubt he had one whereas I was carrying one before being wounded but I now found that the shrapnel which I had stopped had severed my lanyard and dropped the revolver in No-Man's Land! We were of-course, at his mercy. He approached me being the only one showing any authority although didn't recognize me as an officer being, as usual, in private's uniform. He made it clear his reason for visiting us in daylight was to see what had happened to his own men. He was a civilized man and before leaving us he found my first aid kit and tied me up [dressed the wounds] and made me understand that we would be taken to a dressing station as soon as it became dusk. And so it happened.

I just managed a short walk and on the way I saw Norman Priday on a stretcher with leg wounds. We had only a minute or so to talk together . . . And so ended my association with the Bradford Pals."

Private Page of 'A' Company went forward with No. 3 platoon in the third wave. They got into the second line where they became mixed with 'B' Company. Lieutenant Robinson of that company was there, busily trying to service a German machine gun. However, there was no one on their left. They began to dig in but were sniped at from all sides and fired on by machine guns. They could see the Germans massing for a counter attack and extending around them. Then they saw the 16th Battalion retiring.

Sergeant Tidmarsh of 'C' Company and the 3rd wave got as far as the enemy wire, about 30 yards in front of the first objective. The wire was uncut and about four yards thick. They drove the enemy from his trench but, because of the uncut wire, they found themselves outflanked and had to retire.

Sergeant Calverley led a platoon from 'B' Company in the fourth wave. His objective was to make a strong point some 50 yards in front of the Windmill. The Sunken Road, just past the railway was manned by the enemy. There were some dug outs there and a machine gun post, although the latter appeared to have been knocked out. A big gap existed between the Sergeant's party and 'C' Company and it seemed to him that his own company had gone too far to the right and that they had become mixed up with 'C' Company. He got his platoon into the German first line where about seven of his men, together with the Company Sergeant Major, began to work their way along the trench. Then they saw on their left 'A' Company retiring with their arms slung. They were being followed, at a distance of about 180 yards, by a party of Germans who were firing on them. Since 'A' Company were retiring, Sergeant Calverley was forced to do the same. It was as they were going back that the Company Sergeant Major was killed.

At 6.13 a.m. runners brought a verbal message from Company Sergeant Major Nicholson, of Tarran's company, saying that all officers were missing, the majority of the men were casualties and that he himself was wounded. They had reached their first objective but, whilst making towards their second, machine guns firing on them from each flank had caused heavy losses.

Private Tarran of 'D' Company said that his company had followed the barrage to within 20 yards of the German trench. There they came under a cross fire from two machine guns, one firing from the main road and the other from a ditch. Although they reached the first objective, the first two waves had been practically wiped out. He crawled into a shell hole and, finding no other men there, returned to his own lines.

2nd Lieutenant Harris *of* 'A' Company said later that after the barrage commenced, the company had become somewhat disorganized and, after crossing the road, 16th and 18th Battalion men and those of different companies had become mixed together. A great number had congregated in a trench and he himself, together with a brother officer of the 16th Battalion, went over to their right and took ten prisoners. His companion then received information that they were being surrounded on both flanks. A party of the 16th Battalion appeared on their left. He took his party, and his prisoners, across to join them. The officer in charge of this party, presumably Captain Parker, told him he had better report at Battalion Headquarters. This he did, arriving with about 20 men and a Sergeant.

Captain Ashforth of 'B' Company, 16th Battalion, followed 'D' Company whilst his other two platoons led by 2nd Lieutenant Platnauer followed 'C' Company. After crossing the Sunken Road his men came under fire from several enemy posts, which they disposed of, but at this point found that they were out of touch with the battalion on the right. They reached the first objective at 4.00 a.m. and crossed over, advancing onto the second line which they took without difficulty. At this point, contact was established with both Captain Parker and Captain Illingworth.

An unknown N.C.O. and three other ranks, probably some of 2nd Lieutenant Platnauer's men, found themselves pinned down in a shell hole in front of an enemy post. From the post came a German who attempted to throw a grenade into their midst. He was immediately cut down by four simultaneous shots from the shell hole. This man was almost immediately replaced by a second grenadier who was also cut down. This procedure continued until some eight men had fallen before the party's rifles. When no others appeared the N.C.O., covered by his comrades, crawled out to investigate. He found that the entire garrison of the post laid shot dead in front of his shell hole. Had these gallant men launched a simultaneous bomb attack, the result for the N.C.O.'s party would have been less fortunate.

At about 5.00 a.m. a party of about 100 of the enemy was seen approaching Captain Parker's positions from half right and in three waves. At first it was thought that the party was coming to surrender and they were waved on. The enemy, however, immediately opened fire. This fire was returned with Lewis guns and rifles causing many casualties and forcing the enemy to fall back in disorder. Shortly afterwards Captain Duckitt, of the 18th Battalion, came up into 'C' Company positions with four men. At 5.30 a.m. the enemy opened up with heavy machine gun and rifle fire from the rear, killing Sergeant Manley, wounding 2nd Lieutenant Ashworth, and making digging and consolidation of the newly won positions difficult. By 7.30 a.m., however, the trench was in good condition for defense in the centre but still very shallow on the flanks. At this time Captain Parker estimated that he had 100 men with him. Very shortly after this the enemy began to advance in strength from the front, with waves in extended order leading and massed in the rear. The intensity of machine gun fire and sniping from the flank and the rear was considerably increased. It was about this time that Captain Illingworth was reported killed.

As the enemy waves came down the ridge and on to the front, heavy Lewis gun and rifle fire was directed against them, causing heavy casualties. Sergeant Agar, in charge of 'A' Company Lewis gun, estimated that he entirely wiped out a party of roughly 50 men, advancing in file and at a range of 50 to 60 yards. At this stage the enemy showed an inclination to surrender freely but, as the situation on the flanks became apparent, their morale recovered and the attack developed. Captains Parker, Ashworth and Duckitt held a short conference and, taking into consideration the fact that both flanks were open, and that, therefore, they would very soon be surrounded, they decided to retire to their own lines, and this from the left. The order "Lead on from the left" was given, but there was no exit from the left. So the order was given to withdraw from the trench by the rear. Practically all 'A' Company's casualties were suffered during the withdrawal, owing to heavy machine gun fire from all sides, and included 2nd Lieutenant Cowell who was hit between the shoulders.

Shortly after the barrage had started Lieutenant-Colonel Croydon had discovered that the battalion on his left had been held up, causing the gap referred to previously. He immediately ordered his adjutant, 2nd Lieutenant Stanley, to organize two bombing parties, composed of Headquarters, Signalers, Runners, and an artillery liaison officer, to block the trench. Some few minutes later a party of the enemy was seen coming down Wood Trench from Oppy. 2nd Lieutenant Stanley immediately jumped over the parapet with a party of bombers and bombed the enemy party from behind, thereby cutting off their line of retreat and compelling some fourteen of them to surrender. At that moment some men from the 10th East York's came doubling down the trench saying that they had been driven out of their positions by the enemy. Lieutenant-Colonel Croydon halted them and put them out in shell holes to the left and to the right, thus making a strong line of defence. In the meantime 2nd Lieutenant Stanley had taken out another party of bombers and worked around the back of the enemy, some of them surrendered immediately. It was then that 2nd Lieutenant Stanley was wounded. During this period, stragglers from various units who were coming back, were organized and directed into a defensive line by the Colonel. A bombing party with a Lewis gun had been established up the trench under the command of the Intelligence Officer together with the Signal's Officer, stragglers and battalion observers.

Lieutenant-Colonel Croydon was now able to get his wounded to the rear and to request reinforcements. The time was now 5.05 a.m. Lieutenant Colonel Carter, hearing of the request for assistance, visited Lieutenant-Colonel Croyden's Headquarters to confer. He reported the situation to Brigade as follows:

> "16th West York's holding B2 4d 6. 5. Apparently some of our men retiring from trench leading from railway towards Oppy Wood in first objective, about C 13c or C 19a. Enemy look as if he will counter-attack from Oppy Wood, and is putting a pretty heavy barrage on the eastern flank of our trenches between Sunken Road near old 16th West York's Headquarters and the railway (i.e. B30a and railway

B24d). Hill 80 should be held at once so as to prevent enemy turning our flanks, and if possible a machine gun or two placed between Hill 80 and our trenches along the railway. Situation on our right not known regarding holding of original trenches, because matters are so disorganized and the trenches so badly damaged that it is quite possible that the enemy will counter-attack and try to regain the whole of Gavrelle. Our original line should be held at all costs, and unless more troops are available, a further attack cannot be made. Machine guns and Lewis guns will be wanted but above all, Hill 80 should be held."

The enemy did not show any inclination to attack Lieutenant Colonel Carter's defence line in force but began to retire slowly towards Oppy. Heavy casualties were inflicted on them by Lewis gun and rifle fire. However the enemy artillery then brought a barrage of 5.9's and 8.0's to bear, making the position untenable. The Colonel, therefore, decided to withdraw his small force to a better position, in rear of the railway, which had been selected by Lieutenant-Colonel Carter. The force went back to their new positions two men at a time, where they dug themselves in on a 70 yard front. On arrival in his new positions Lieutenant-Colonel Croydon was struck on the helmet and knocked down by a shell burst, leaving him concussed. He was taken to the dug-out of Lieutenant-Colonel Carter who assumed temporary command of the situation. However, after a period of about four hours rest, Lieutenant Colonel Croydon was able to resume his command. By then, reinforcements from the Durham Light Infantry were beginning to arrive in his positions.

Lieut.- Col. A. C. Croydon

Many men were killed and a great number wounded during the retirement, owing to the trenches being blown in, thus providing excellent targets for the enemy machine gunners who constantly fired from the right and from the front. Later in the day an attempt was made to regain the original positions but it was found to be impossible to get beyond the railway until after dark, due to the continuous hostile bombardment, snipers and machine gun fire. At 3.15 p.m. Brigade ordered that a composite battalion be formed from the survivors of the 16th and 18th Battalions and placed under the command of Lieutenant-Colonel Croydon. All available 18th Battalion troops (less Battalion Headquarters) were put in the charge of 2nd Lieutenants Dams and Harris and placed at the disposal of Lieutenant-Colonel Croydon.

Later in the day Lieutenant-Colonel Croydon's small force began to work their way back to their original positions. They finally achieved these objectives on the following day. In addition to the men from the 18th Battalion, the force now comprised men from the East Yorkshire Regiment, 18th Battalion the Durham Light Infantry, The King's Own Yorkshire Light Infantry, the Royal Engineers, the Machine Gun Corps, the Light Trench Mortar Batteries and, of course, the 16th Battalion. About 50 prisoners were taken during the operation but many of these were killed by their own artillery fire as they made their way to the rear areas.

There seems little doubt that the Colonel's action thwarted the enemy's attempt to cut off all the troops who had gone forward during the attack. Had he not remained at the position taken up, the War Diary argues, many men would have been taken prisoner as they came back that way.

The casualties suffered among the 16th Battalion's officers on the 3rd were:

Captain O. Illingworth, 'A' Comp	Reported killed in action
2nd Lieut A. H. Barltrop,'A'Comp	Wounded in action
2nd Lieut F. T. Cowell, 'A'Comp	Wounded in action
2nd Lieut J. L. Stanley, 'C' Comp	Wounded in action
2nd Lieut E. Crowther, 'C" Comp	Missing, believed wounded
2nd Lieut L.M.Platnauer,'B' Comp	Wounded, and missing
2nd Lieut G. L. Tucker,	Missing
2nd Lieut L. Ashworth, 'A' Comp	Missing
2nd Lieut E. G. Bantock,'A'	Missing
2nd Lieut N. Parker, 'C' Comp	Missing
2nd Lieut D. O. Greville,'C' Comp	Missing

The casualties for other ranks for this day were:

	'A'	'B'	'C'	'D'
Killed in action	5	1	4	8
Missing	24	33	90	29
Missing believed killed			1	
Missing believed wounded			3	
Wounded and missing	1			
Wounded but still at post		5		
Wounded in action	25	23	19	32
Total	55	62	117	69

Total casualties for the day were, therefore, 11 officers and 303 other ranks.

GAVRELLE AND OPPY WOOD

The War Diaries do not contain a list of casualties suffered by the 18th Battalion on this day but, from the foregoing account the reader will, no doubt, conclude that they were equally heavy.

Lieutenant-Colonel Croydon's report on the operation ends with the following statement:

"I consider that the following lessons are learnt from these operations.

(1) The chief thing I noticed in the recent operations was first the preliminary bombardments in my opinion are unnecessary.

(2) Atmospheric conditions should be studied. Owing to bright moonlight the enemy saw our men forming up in No-Man's Land, which caused an S.O.S. signal from Oppy Wood followed by a barrage.

(3) Length of front was, in my opinion, too great, and caused the line to be very weak and extension great.

(4) Reserves should be brought up into the line which the attacking party vacates, and kept there for any emergency. They could also be used for filling up the attacking line where seen to be thin, or to deliver a counter attack.

(5) A Staff Officer should be detailed to view the ground previous to operations as battalions vary in strength and maps are not always accurate.

(6) A Battalion Commander should always have a small reserve at his disposal to enable him to meet any emergency.

(7) Owing to the weakness of the force that reached the final objective it was impossible to consolidate. Strength and depth should be considered.

(8) The concentration of Artillery fire on known strong points and their immediate vicinity."

The early hours of the 4th were marked by the enemy acting in a very nervous manner, Very lights and occasional S.O.S.'s appearing along the whole front. At 3.10 a.m. he put down a barrage along the British front line trench and around Gavrelle, the duration of which was about 20 minutes. His registration in the vicinity of the railway, and the point where it crossed the trench at B24b, was described as being "very accurate." Hostile machineguns maintained a constant bickering from around B 18d 7. 8. British artillery retaliated along the whole front during the night, systematically shelling the enemy front and support trenches, Hollow Copse and Freshness. Between 9.00 a.m. and noon, artillery activity decreased. Little enemy movement was seen with the exception of some activity south of Oppy and near Linkburn. At 9.00 a.m. the 'block' at B18d 45.50 was found to be occupied by a party of extremely alert German troops who challenged any approach with a shower of hand grenades.

The positions occupied by the 16th and 18th Battalions now ran from near the Windmill to B24d, then to B24d 3.7, B24 6.3.0. and then northwards to B18d 4.5. The Battalions also occupied a newly constructed trench from B24c 9.5 to B24c 7.3.

THE BRADFORD PALS

On the night of the 4th/5th both battalions were relieved by the 14th York and Lancaster Regiment and proceeded to a camp at St. Catherine, near Arras.

During the 5th, 6th and 7th May, both battalions rested. With the exception of cleaning up clothing and kit, there were no parades. Each battalion was reorganized into two companies, designated No. 1 Company and No. 2 Company, which gives some indication of battalion strengths at that time.

The following is an extract from a letter which Private Albert Hanson wrote to his wife Mabel during this period.

> "May 5th, 1917
> Dear Mab,
>
> Well, thank God I came out of it alive once more. Never was I in such a tight place as the last affair. Not that we were beaten, far from it. Our Battalion swept all before it. It was a glorious fight as far as fights are concerned but I never faced death as much in all the war as I did the last time in the trenches. I got one or two of your letters whilst in the trenches. In fact I got one about an hour before we went over the top. I have had enough experiences to last all my life in the last fighting. You can imagine what I went through when I was buried four times in one day. The sensation was awful but I am none the worse for it. I prayed to God to spare me and He did. I seemed to bear a charmed life, in fact, two seconds hesitation on my part saved me from being blown to pieces on one occasion. So you can guess what I have been through this time. I have never told you much about it before but this is the worst I have been in. However, the sun is still shinning once again, so thank God for that. I got the paper as soon as I got out of the trenches so that cheered me up to a certain extent. You will quite under- stand why it is that you have not heard from me for such a long time. I sent you a Field Card the other day so I think you will have received it by now. I am rather sorry about the fellows you mention in your last letter. One exciting job I had was going for the lads' rations one day. Just fancy, my pal and I went 10 miles under shell fire for them. The young fellow who brought my ring home is amongst the missing. Anyhow, enough about the war, let's hope it will soon be over. The sooner the better . . . "

Unfortunately the sun was not to shine for Albert Hanson for much longer.

On the 8th, the 93rd Brigade received orders to relieve the Gavrelle sector, the 16th being detailed as 'Brigade Reserve' and relieving the 13th York and Lancaster Regiment in a system of trenches west of Railway Cutting whilst the 18th Battalion occupied the support trenches. On the night of the 16th both battalions moved forward and took over the trenches occupied by the 18th Durham Light Infantry who were to make an attack on Gavrelle trench. Much work was done by the 16th Battalion in strengthening and deepening the trench north and south of the Gavrelle-Fresnes Road with a view to making a good taking-off trench for the Durhams. This activity did not go unnoticed by the enemy who directed a continuous barrage of 4.2 inch and 5.9 inch shells on to the front line. The work was not therefore completed without casualties. The Battalion lost three killed and eight wounded on the 12th and two killed and thirteen wounded on the 13th. Among these was Private Hanson who died on the 12th in a casualty clearing station from gun shot wounds to the head.

May 17th found the 16th Battalion in the support trenches Jewel and Joyous as Brigade reserve. The 18th Battalion had a half battalion in the support trenches and a half battalion in 'Willie', the front line trench, from a point adjacent to Gavrelle Cemetery to where it crossed the road at 11b 2.7. The latter half were to be 'in support' to the 18th Battalion, the Durham Light Infantry, who were to attack Gavrelle trench during the hours of darkness.

At 12.30 a.m. on May 18th, the barrage began and the 'Durhams' went forward. Three parties of that Battalion actually reached their objectives, the two smaller groups were driven out immediately although the third party, numbering about 40 men, stayed in the German trench for about 30 minutes before they too were driven out. The company attacking on the south side were met by a bomb barrage and failed to reach their objective. By noon the attack had been declared a failure.

Both battalions were now relieved by units of the 63rd Naval Division on the evening of the 19th, the 16th moving into a camp near Roclincourt and the 18th to a camp near Ecurie.

From this date until the 27th, both battalions were mainly employed in the provision of working and carrying parties. On that day the 16th Battalion moved to billets at Maroeuil whilst the 18th Battalion marched to hutments in Bray. The 16th's departure for Maroeuil was marked by a grenade, accidentally thrown into an incinerator during 'last minute clearing up', exploding

Albert and Mabel Hanson

and wounding 11 men. Both battalions now enjoyed a brief respite of a few days which were employed in battalion training, musketry, etc. Sufficient replacements were received to enable both battalions to be reorganized into four companies. News was received on June 5th that the courage of 16th Battalion personnel had been recognised by the following awards: Captain Parker - Military Cross, 2nd Lieutenant L.Stanley - Distinguished Service Order, Private Hallam Distinguished Conduct Medal.

On June 9th, both battalions began another spell in the trenches of the Gavrelle Sector. The weather was wet and rain storms on the 11th badly flooded the trenches making them, in many places, impassable. Considerable labour was needed in clearing them, digging sump holes and laying duck boards to render movement possible.

The period was marked by a great deal of patrol activity by both battalions. On the night of the 18th one such patrol included Frank Burn. After spending some time studying the antics of an enemy seen signalling from his parapet with a red lamp, they returned with a Lewis gun which they had found in front of the wire. Even in recent years this gun has proved to be the source of much inter-battalion banter. Frank Burn always maintained that the gun was the property of the 16th Battalion who had left it there during the attack on the 3rd May. Needless to say, this has always been hotly denied.

On the night of the 23rd June, while the 18th Battalion was resting in bivouacs behind Railway Cutting, a long range gun shelled the vicinity of the encampment. One shell fell on the orderly room tent, killing Privates C. Burgoyne, W. Kellet and S. Tweedale and wounding Lieutenant-Colonel Carter.

During June, news was received that Captain Illingworth, reported killed in action, Lieutenant Crowther and 2nd Lieutenants Ashworth, Bentock, Barker and Tucker, reported missing since the attack on May 3rd, all of the 16th Battalion, were prisoners-of-war in Germany.

July opened with the Brigade still in the Gavrelle Sector and maintaining strong patrol activity. On the night of the 2nd, at 10.30 p.m. 2nd Lieutenant O. H. Staff, of the 18th Battalion, took out a patrol of eight men, leaving the trench at H1b 4.9 and moving down each side of the road. After completing his task 2nd Lieutenant Staff returned with his patrol but stated that he had seen Very lights go up on the left of the road. He declared his intention to go out again, in the hope of capturing some of the men who were sending up the lights. He departed again with Sergeant Steele and Private Morris. As they approached the point in question a machine gun opened fire on them and they were bombarded by a shower of hand grenades, one of them wounding Sergeant Steele. They were then pounced upon from behind by a party of Germans. In the following fight the trio became separated but Sergeant

GAVRELLE AND OPPY WOOD

Steele was able to escape to the British lines. Some time later, he was followed by Private Morris, unwounded, who said that when he last saw 2nd Lieutenant Staff he was unwounded and fighting a party of about 12 Germans single-handed.

In the morning and afternoon of the 3rd, enemy artillery was very active, shelling the support trenches heavily. This, coupled with the experiences of the previous night, produced a tendency to 'over react'. As a result Private Gaunt was accidentally shot as he returned from an advanced post.

Corporal D Hunter of the 16th Battalion, attached to the 93rd Brigade trench mortar battery was awarded the Distinguished Conduct Medal for conspicuous gallantry during the attack on May 3rd.

Charles A. Bottomley
16th Battalion 1918

Harold P. Whitehead
with his mother 1918

Lieutenant-Colonel H.F.G. Carter photographed in 1917 with sergeants under his command. They include Sergeant Major H. Scott (back row 3rd from left) who appears in Chapter 1 of this narrative, and Sergeant W. H. Revill (front row 1st on the left), formerly of the Lincolnshire Regiment, who was awarded the Belgium Croix-de-Guerre for distinguished service during 1917. After the war Billie Revill returned to his small-holding in Sturton, near Lincoln, where he lived to the grand old age of 96.

The Interior of a Dug-out, Gavrelle, 1917. By Adrian Hill. Imperial War Museum, picture no. 888/342

No-Man's Land in front of Serre, 1916. Imperial War Museum, Neg. Q1910.

CHAPTER 8: ARLEUX AND MERICOURT

Next week the bloody Roll of Honour said
"Wounded and missing" - - - (That's the thing to do
When lads are left in shell holes dying slow,
With nothing but blank sky and wounds that ache,
Moaning for water till they know
It's night, and then it's not worth while to wake!)

Siegfried Sassoon

On July 20th, the Brigade received orders to move to Neuville St. Vaast and thence to the line. The 16th Battalion reached their destination at 8.30 a.m. and rested until sundown in temporary billets before moving up to the trenches in front of Acheville. While the companies were moving off by platoons a few shells fell in the vicinity. One H.E. shell fell directly in front of 'D' Company who were just about to march off. 2nd Lieutenants Buchanan and Robb and four other ranks were killed, 41 others were wounded, one of whom later died.

The 16th Battalion occupied the front line with Battalion Headquarters in New Brunswick trench. The 15th Battalion were on the 16th's right, with the 11th East Yorks of the 92nd Brigade on their left. Their front line, with advanced posts which in fact were fortified shell holes, about 200 yards out, covered a frontage of about 1100 yards. The 18th Battalion moved into the trenches as battalion in support and worked as two 'double companies', 'A' and 'B' Company under Captain Key-Jones.

On the morning of the 22nd at 'stand down,' Corporal W. Ingram of 'A' Company, 16th Battalion, was found to be missing from one of the advanced posts. The circumstances pointed to him having been 'snatched' by an enemy patrol while making his way to a latrine. After this incident 'A' Company sent out patrols each night determined to catch an enemy straggler in order to even the score. One patrol, on the night of the 26th waited for 30 minutes outside the enemy wire, but without success. On the night of the 28th, which was exceedingly dark, Sergeant

Nelson led out a patrol of six other ranks. Fifty yards out from their own wire, they were surprised by an enemy patrol who opened fire on them at point blank range, from a shell hole concealed in long grass. The Sergeant fell, mortally wounded, whilst one other member of his party received lesser wounds.

The patrol was taken so unawares by the suddenness of the attack that with the exception of one bomb being thrown at the enemy, no retaliation was made. Two members of the patrol brought in the Sergeant's body, but Privates Claydon and Martin did not return and were posted missing.

Another misfortune befell the 16th Battalion that night when, at 1.00 a.m., the enemy shelled Quebec trench heavily. One shell fell outside 'C' Company Headquarters, killing a stretcher bearer of the 18th Battalion, mortally wounding 2nd Lieutenant O. L. Paus and wounding 2nd Lieutenant W. F. Caniey and three other ranks.

On the 29th, the 16th Battalion were relieved by the llth East Lancashire Regiment, of the 94th Brigade and proceeded to the rear of the left Brigade L3 (Mericourt) Sector in Canada and 'Gertie Miller' trenches. The 18th Battalion occupied the front line on the right with the 18th Durhams on their left.

For the 16th, this dreary month closed with one bright spot. Each day, while in Brigade support, a party of 60 other ranks, together with a group of officers, proceeded after sundown to a point near Neuville St. Vaast to take hot baths, returning the following evening after sundown. George Morgan remembered this occasion well since it was his first opportunity to take a hot bath since he arrived in France. He had the dubious honour of sharing the same tub, in point of fact, a wine vat, with Company Sergeant Major Cussons.

On the night of August 1st, the 18th Battalion sent out patrols to examine the enemy wire. Patrol No. 1, under 2nd Lieutenant Burton with two N.C.O.'s and 19 other ranks with a Lewis gun, found the German wire to be three to four feet high and about seven yards deep with lots of loose wire, but no gaps. They returned to their own positions at 1.25 a.m. without incident. Patrol No. 2, under 2nd Lieutenant Kiddle with two N.C.O.'s and 20 other ranks with a Lewis gun, left their own lines at 9.40 a.m. at T17a 95 and moved north-east to the enemy entanglements and then moved south-east along the wire for about 280 yards. At this point they were challenged by a German sentry. Very lights were sent up and machine gun and rifle fire directed against them together with about 30 grenades thrown towards them. They withdrew without casualties after throwing grenades into the enemy trenches which were believed to cause casualties.

Both battalions were relieved on the night of August 6th and rested for ten days, the 16th at Ottowa Camp and the 18th at Fraser Camp near Mont St. Eloy. On August 16th they returned to the line, transported by train to Neuville St. Vaast and from there moving into the trenches. The 16th occupied the right sub-section in Totnes, Nova Scotia and Montreal trenches. 'A', 'B' and 'C' Companies were now commanded by Lieutenant E. Wilson, Captain G. W. Ashforth and Captain J. D. Ballantyne respectively.

The 18th had two companies in the railway embankment, known as Brown Line (see map 7) and two companies with Battalion Headquarters about A6c. The 16th spent their first day in the line generally cleaning up their trenches, and strengthening and deepening them. Patrols examined the wire, finding it deep and continuous. On the following day the Germans registered strong disapproval of their activities by bombarding the line with trench mortars and blowing in 15 yards of trench. The Battalion suffered four casualties from this fire, one of whom later died of his wounds.

On the night of August 19th, 540 gas projectors were discharged over Acheville. The attack was considered a success, the wind being favourable. Information obtained from a prisoner, captured later, indicated that his Regiment had suffered over 80 casualties from the gas with at least 20 dead. As dawn broke, the enemy retaliated with a minen werfer bombardment, 14 bombs bursting in and near the front line. One round burst in a bay, blowing to pieces a soldier who had just walked around the traverse and was actually saying "Good morning" to Sergeant Morgan who, with another soldier, was wounded by fragments. Suffering one large and two small wounds George Morgan, together with his comrade, was carried out amid calls of "What a lovely blighty". 2nd Lieutenant Metcalf was also wounded that day, hit by machine gun fire whilst visiting a forward post.

On the night of the 23rd patrols, each of one N.C.O. and ten other ranks, went out to examine the enemy wire on the Battalion's front. They found it to be deep and continuous.

On the following night, the 16th Battalion was relieved by the 13th Battalion the York and Lancaster Regiment and moved into the reserve line with 'A' and 'B' Companies in the Brickstacks. Battalion Headquarters was located in La Folie Wood. The troops were accommodated in dug outs in the old German line and although those in Vimy were continually shelled, everyone was said to be comfortable. Bath houses had now been erected for the use of the troops, in the Brickfields and in Vimy East, no doubt making a considerable contribution to the comfort of the accommodation. They were to remain in the reserve line engaged in fatigues, deepening and widening Teddie Gerade trench and carrying mining cases and gun pit frames to Hudson trench until the night of the 4th September when they were relieved by the 4th Canadian Mounted Rifles and moved to Kitchener Camp, north of Roclincourt.

From 2.00 a.m. to 3.00 a.m. on the 30th August, the enemy heavily shelled the 18th Battalion's Headquarters in the Quarry, their front line in Totnes trench and their close support and support positions in Quebec and New Brunswick trenches, more especially on the front line where this trench cut the Quarries Road. From 9.00 a.m. to 12 noon and from 2.00 p.m. until nearly 7.00 p.m., with very isolated intervals, the Battalion Headquarters was shelled severely, about 1,000 shells of all calibres falling in and around the Quarry. So indiscriminate and careless was the nature of this shelling against the various lines of trenches that it hardly gave the idea of registration or barrage firing. Lieutenant-Colonel Carter reached the conclusion that the enemy was trying to hide his registration and practise barrage firing by excessive shelling in the guise of a destructive shoot against the Colonel's Headquarters, and that the enemy's intention was to raid his positions.

The front line, Totnes trench, was manned by 100 men. Another 80 men were in close support in Quebec trench whilst the strength of the Company of the 15th Battalion in New Brunswick was roughly 70 men. On studying the map, Lieutenant-Colonel Carter realised that if the enemy were to make an accurate entry into some definite point in the front line, he would need some obvious mark to guide him, in the dark, across a No-Man's Land of some 600 to 800 yards width. As most of the shelling had been on the left and the fact that the Quarries Road would make the only definite guide for the enemy to a specific point, he concluded that the most probable point of attack would be the junction of Totnes trench and Quarries Road and its vicinity. Lieutenant-Colonel Carter therefore issued the following instructions:

> (1) The following orders were sent to companies at 1 p.m., the letter being addressed to 'C' Company (left flank) and copies sent to other companies: "The shelling today looks as if the Bosche may be thinking of a raid on your front. With this in view do no wiring tonight, nor will the other companies. f you think it advisable you can put a small listening patrol just in front of your wire and possibly a post to your left rear in that old disused trench, south of the Quarries Road and behind your front line, in case he tries to get in behind you.
> Warn your men, and 'D' Company Commander will lend you half his strength, whom you can put on your left in Quebec, and these with any of 'A' or 'B' Companies left in the line can be used for counter attacking. The working party of 20 in 12th Avenue belonging to Hilt [15th Battalion the West Yorkshire Regiment] will in case of trouble, come automatically under your orders and I will write to them to this effect.
> Directly you counter attack, send a runner over the top to Hilt's Company in New Brunswick and tell them to come up and reinforce you in Quebec. Send a wire to me when you have counter attacked too. I will send the remainder of Hilt to you in case they have not received your message. This is only in case a raid takes place. If of course the raid is on 'A' or 'B' Company's front, 'A' or 'B' Company will take charge of the counter attack with the oddments of 'A', 'B', 'C' Companies and half 'D' Company.
> No stores will be drawn tonight and half 'D' Company will do all the ration carrying for tonight. Be careful of water today in case the well is blown in."

(2) The following orders have been given to Hilt Company attached to me. "The shelling today rather points to the possibility of a raid on our left front.

In this case we have to counter attack, you will, if you receive orders from either me or one of the Company Commanders in Quebec move across over the lid and take up the defence of Quebec. Explain this to your men, and that they are only on the defensive, and that my Battalion will be in front of them. Also, do not move your bombing post just north of junction of Quarries Road and New Brunswick trench.

Your working party in 12th Avenue will, in case of trouble, report to officer commanding 'C' Company in Quebec."

Lieutenant-Colonel
Commanding Officer Haze

A standing patrol was positioned between the Battalion's left (point A on map 8) and the 18th Durham Light Infantry to cover the gap which existed there.

The night of the 31st was quiet until 2.45 a.m. when the enemy put down a heavy barrage of 5.9's, 4.2's, 4.1's and 77mm shells on the front line, close support and support trenches. Lieutenant-Colonel Carter went to the top of the Quarry and watched the barrage develop.

Between 2.45 a.m. and 3.00 a.m. the Lewis gun post on the left flank spotted a party of about 30 Germans approaching the wire in single file. At the same time No. 3 post of the left company observed a similar party, carrying a machine gun, approaching. Immediately both posts opened rapid fire. In answer to the sentries shouts of "Stand to! They're comin' ower" men leapt to the parapet and, with rifles and Lewis guns, poured a fire into the enemy parties, the companies on the right firing half left. Many enemy were seen to drop. During all this time the enemy artillery barrage continued to rain down on the pararet, killing 2nd Lieutenant R. G. Dalton and one other rank and wounding eight other ranks.

Shortly after the fight began, a wounded man came back into the support trench and told Captain Whittaker, who commanded 'A' Company, that he thought the enemy had entered the line on the left. Captain Whittaker immediately signalled by telephone 'S.O.S.L3' and ordered the officer-in-charge of the light trench mortar battery to "Open fire."

Following the orders previously received, Captain Peace, Commanding 'C' Company, together with the half of 'D' Company attached to him, counter attacked 'Over the lid' to Totnes trench. The leading party jumped into an empty bay and began working up the trench whilst the men following worked from outside the trench. At the same time as the counter attack moved off, the 15th West Yorks Company moved forward to take up the defence of Quebec trench (marked E on the map).

Captain W. Peace

As soon as this was done Lieutenant - Colonel Carter sent a message to the front line companies instructing them that as soon as the front line was clear they were to push out strong patrols to search for German dead and wounded and that, if possible, all men were to be back in their original positions by dawn. In point of fact the enemy had not entered the front line and had not penetrated beyond the wire. There was some delay in sending out patrols due to difficulties in stopping the trench mortar barrage, which had been deadly accurate and caused a great deal of damage. Many of the enemy killed or wounded by Lewis gun and rifle fire were blown to bits where they lay. Decimated remains of many German corpses were found in front of the wire. Only one wounded German, with both his legs broken, was found and brought in, together with the body of an officer wearing the ribbon of the Iron Cross and other orders. Both men belonged to the 54th Infantry Regiment. Although the remains of some six to ten dead Germans were found, these were in such a decimated state that identification was impossible and collection for burial considered "not worthwhile." The booty recovered by the search parties included a light machine gun, in good condition and clean, a wooden encased bangalore torpedo, a Very pistol and three rifles.

Four snipers, in camouflage suits, crawled out into No-Man's Land and searched the ground for any wounded or dead. Each carried a card, written in German, explaining to anyone they found that they were in good hands and if they remained quiet they would be brought in after dark. These men returned at 3.30 p.m. without finding anyone.

The following memorandums, congratulating the Battalion in their repulse of the raid, were later received from Brigadier-General J. D. Ingles and Brigadier-General Ian Stewart:

> C. C. HAZE
> I congratulate you on the thoroughness and excellence of your arrangements in repelling the raid attempted by the enemy against your lines on the morning of the 31st and on your success which you thoroughly deserved.
>
> I also wish to express my great appreciation of the splendid behaviour and prompt action of the Officers, N.C.O.'s and men of your Battalion and the determined manner in which they carried out your orders.
>
> 31st August 1917   J. D. Ingles, Brigadier-General
> Commanding 93rd Infantry Brigade, 31st Division

ARLEUX AND MERICOURT

The Corps Commander has read with interest the report on the attempted raid of the 31st August, and requests that you will convey his congratulations to the C.O. 18th West Yorks Regiment, and the troops under his command on the accurate appreciation of the enemy's intentions, and adequate steps taken to frustrate them and the confidence and promptitude displayed in meeting the attack.

4th September 1917

Signed: Ian Stewart
Brigadier-General, General Staff, XIII Corps

On the 4th September, the 18th Battalion mounted two daylight patrols. Here are their official reports:

18th West Yorks Regiment
DAYLIGHT PATROL REPORT
4th September, 1917

Two observers in camouflaged suits left our left company front at 4.35 a.m., crossed the Quarries Road and the Miericourt Road and proceeded to about T11a 25.

At 5.45 a.m., they saw a party of 12 men leave the sandbag structure at T11a 55 (approx.) previously reported and proceeded to their front line. 100 yards to left of sandbag structure is an S-shaped SAP, the head of which is apparently a shell hole. At 6.30 a.m. six enemy with a M.G. left this SAP for their front line. In the SAP head is a T.M. [trench mortar] about 12 inches long pointing in the direction of the battalion on our left.

The White House is about 100 yards behind enemy line, in a direct line with the sandbag structure. Behind and to the right of White House there is a house built at right angles, and in the end of this, about 15 feet from the ground is a square sandbagged hole, probably a M.G. emplacement or an O.P. In front of White House, quite close, is a dump of barbed wire, trench elements and iron stakes.

At 1.00 p.m., about 14 stretchers were taken to the cemetery. Could not be seen whether they contained dead or wounded.

At 1.30 p.m., observers saw what was apparently a long round periscope in enemy front line to the right of communication trench leading to the White House. They thought they might be seen, so fired simultaneously and smashed it.

3.00 p.m. Four Germans were seen to move along front line and climb over portion of trench which had been blown in. On their backs were strapped metal objects 2 feet by 1 foot 6 inches, with a tube on the top. Probably Vermosel sprayers.

At 5.30 pm observers saw working party of 100 men carrying shovels and rifles going past the White House, to the rear of enemy lines.

At 6.00 p.m, on the left edge of the Quarries Road, about T11a 55.15, there are three dead Germans, recently killed, probably some of the raiding party of 31.8.17. They could not get close enough to examine them because the road at this point is in full view of the enemy.

The enemy has put out a lot of wire since the last patrol, on 30.8.17. The fork roads at T11a 61 are heavily wired.

11.30 a.m. Our artillery were firing on the enemy line in rear of the sandbag structure. Observers think enemy had a number of casualties, for whistles were constantly being blown. They think this was a signal for stretcher bearers. They report that artillery which was firing on the enemy front line to the right of Quarries Road was making accurate shooting, shells were falling in the trench and on the parapet.

When the enemy fired at our aircraft, they noticed there were quite a number of machine guns between SAP referred to before, and the Quarries Road. Eight machine guns were plainly seen. Observers returned to our lines at 8.30 p.m.

DAYLIGHT PATROL 3rd September, 1917

Patrol of two other ranks left our lines at 4.30 a.m. At 5.30 a.m. patrol saw enemy moving back from front line to support line independently. About 90 O. R. were seen. This confirms previous report and would seem to indicate that the enemy vacates his front line during the day. If our artillery shelled between 5.00 a.m. and 6.00 a.m. each morning they would be certain of causing casualties. Communication trench running into MericourtAcheville Road, seems to be a popular route. M.G.'s fired on our planes from front and support lines. Enemy guns, 4.2's, were observed to be firing from behind hedges at T18d 57. There seem to be several batteries firing from this part of Acheville.

The 18th Battalion were relieved from the line on the night of the 5th September, and moved back to Neuville St. Vaast where they later entrained for Bray. Both battalions now enjoyed a brief respite from the front line in their respective camps. Their time was spent in resting or training, although the 16th Battalion detached one company, first 'C' and later 'A', on a working detail in Long Wood.

On September 19th, both battalions returned to trench duty, the 16th relieving the 11th East Yorkshire Regiment in the L2 sub-section of the Arleux Sector, the 15th West Yorkshire Regiment being on their right and the 14th York and Lancaster Regiment, 94th Brigade, being the battalion on their left. The relief was completed in daylight via Tired Alley. The 18th Battalion moved into the support positions known as Red Line (see map 7) relieving the 10th East Yorkshire Regiment.

On the 25th the 18th Battalion moved into the front line, relieving the 15th West

Yorkshire Regiment, in the right battalion position, whilst the 16th were relieved by the 18th Durham Light Infantry and took over that Battalion's position in the left support sector, with 'A' Company in the Arleux Loop and 'B', 'C' and 'D' Companies in Red Line. The War Diary records that during the preceding tour in the front line, the Battalion suffered only two casualties, both wounded although one seriously, and one case of suspected shell shock. On October 1st, the 16th was relieved by the 12th East Yorkshire Regiment and moved to Bray. The 18th was relieved by the 10th East Yorkshire Regiment and occupied the support line for five-days. Then they too moved to Bray, having been relieved from support by the 13th East Yorkshire Regiment. There followed for both battalions a spell of eight days of rest, specialist training with Lewis guns, bangolore torpedoes and practice firing on the Bray range. On the 13th, both battalions were moved back into the line, the 18th occupying the support trenches.

On the 16th October at 5.10 a.m., the enemy brought down an extra heavy bombardment on the positions occupied by the 16th Battalion, wounding Lieutenant J. L. Stanley, D.S.O., and three other ranks, one from 'C' Company the others from 'D' Company. The bombardment also extended to the battalions on their left and right flanks, the 14th York and Lancaster Regiment and the 15th West Yorks respectively. Lieutenant-Colonel A. C. Croydon, M.C., seeing this to be no ordinary affair called for artillery retaliation, soon after which the York and Lancaster Battalion sent up S.O.S. rockets. The artillery retaliation which resulted probably stopped the enemy mounting a raid. He did mount a raid against the York and Lancaster Regiment, but his efforts proved unsuccessful. Half the enemy troops never reached the British wire, having been caught in the S.O.S. barrage. One prisoner was taken by the York and Lancaster's who subsequently counted 27 dead in their wire. At 10.00 a.m. a Red Cross flag was waved from the German second line, the enemy presumably wishing to search for and bring in wounded, but as no one appeared and enemy shelling continued, no action was taken in response to this gesture.

After the raid, as it was thought that a number of the enemy might be laying out in No-Man's Land awaiting an opportunity to 'crawl in' after dark, Sergeant G. Meadows of 'C' Company, 16th Battalion, asked permission to go out, dressed in a camouflaged suit, and see if he could spot any of the enemy and if so, "account for them." Permission was granted and he crawled out, with one other rank following in the rear to give support and assistance. After they had crawled about 150 yards, they saw two enemy soldiers laying a telephone wire. Sergeant Meadows fired at and killed the leading man. The other man immediately took cover but presently reappeared, whereupon the Sergeant fired again killing this man also. A third man then appeared but, although the Sergeant fired at him, he was successful in getting away. After this Sergeant Meadows and his companion remained in No-Man's Land for some considerable time but, observing no other enemy, they then returned to their own lines. Sergeant Meadows was later awarded a Military Medal.

On the night of 19th October, the 18th Battalion relieved the 15th West Yorks in the front line, whilst the 16th Battalion were relieved by the 18th Durhams and moved into left support with three companies in Red Line and one company in Arleux Loop South.

Both battalions remained in these positions until the 25th October when they were relieved from the line, the 16th Battalion moving to Durham and Lancaster camps whilst the 18th Battalion moved to Bray. This was followed by almost two weeks rest and training before both battalions returned to trench duty. This pattern of movement was to continue for the next three months.

The winter of 1917-1918 was one of the hardest on record. Extremely cold weather froze the ground to the hardness of iron. The battle front was covered by a carpet of snow. Operations were impeded on both sides and although the front was officially described as 'quiet', life in the trenches was exceedingly difficult. Nevertheless, both battalions maintained a policy of aggressive patrolling in No-Man's Land.

Examples of these activities recorded in the 18th Battalion's diary are:

> 23rd October-Daylight patrol from 'C' Company commenced detailed reconnaissance of enemy wire.
>
> 25th October - Daylight patrol located three enemy machine guns in a shell hole at B12b 80.05.
>
> 10th November - Daylight patrol went out at 6.30 a.m. returning at 11.00 a.m. after reconnoitring enemy defences. Three hostile machine guns located. Second daylight patrol examined enemy wire. Third daylight patrol worked south-east along Oppy-Arleux Road as far as Willows. Reported light trench mortar firing from SAP in front of enemy line behind Willows.
>
> 14th November - Patrol of five men led by Corporal Barker took up a position in No-Man's Land under cover of mist. At about 7.15 a.m., a sentry was seen with his head and shoulders above parapet of enemy SAP. Corporal Barker fired at this man who threw up his hands and disappeared groaning.

An interesting example of ground / air liaison occurred on November 15th, when three patrols, each of two other ranks crawled out into No-Man's Land and marked the position of enemy machine guns firing at British aeroplanes which, by arrangement, flew low overhead to draw fire from the enemy's guns.

On January 4th, news was received that Temporary Major (Acting Lieutenant-Colonel) A. C. Croydon was promoted to the rank of Temporary Lieutenant-Colonel. Also an extract from the London Gazette, War Office, dated 18thDecember, 1917 was published in Battalion Orders:

> Mentioned in Despatches 7th November, 1917:
>
> Lieutenant-Colonel A. C. Croydon, M.C.
> Lieutenant J. L. Stanley, D.S.O.
> Lieutenant J. M. Barrow
> Lieutenant D. T. King
> Lance Corporal W. Francis

The hard winter weather was followed by heavy rain and a rapid thaw. Conditions became very bad, subsidences taking place and the bottom of the trenches becoming, in places, two or three feet deep in thick adhesive mud. Communication trenches became impassable and movement was only possible 'over the top'. Consequently during the hours of daylight the advanced posts were completely isolated. However, Mother Nature was not selective, the conditions in the German line being equally abhorrent. The 18th Battalion War Diaries record that "visibility was very bad and there was exceedingly little around the Tunnel Headquarters and some artillery fire directed at the Sucrerie and Willerval".

On the night of the 19th the 18th Battalion were relieved from the front line by the 18th Durham Light Infantry and moved to Ecurie Wood. This completed their last tour in the front line. The 16th, on the night of the 23rd, moved into close support in Red Line, with 'D' Company in Arleux Loop North. Until their relief from these positions on the 27th, when they moved to billets in Ecoivres every available man was employed in making the trenches passable, particularly Arleux Loop and Tired Alley. At Ecoivres, after the usual cleaning up and kit inspections, the companies were reorganized into three platoons per company.

On January 31st, orders were received by the 18th to "disband the battalion." The 16th, however, were to complete one more tour of trench duty. On February 5th they relieved the 11th East Yorkshire Regiment in the Arleux Sub-Sector. The companies were distributed as follows:

> 'A' and 'B' Companies under Captain Battishill, M.C., in Arleux Post;
> 'C' Company under Captain L. L. de Souza in Oak Post;
> 'D' Company under Captain A. H. Evans in Tommy Post.

Arleux Loop had been heavily bombarded by howitzers during the morning prior to the relief and about 50 yards of trench had been blown in. Baron trench was also subjected to heavy machine gun fire during the day. The 6th was marked by the heavy artillery bombardment of the German lines owing to the expected relief of the 240th Division by the 5th Bavarian Regiment. The Battalion participated with machine gun, Lewis gun and trench mortar fire.

During the next few days, a great deal of work was done in clearing the mud from Arleux Loop and repairing the damage to Baron trench. These activities were interrupted on the night of the 8th when the enemy put down a heavy barrage on the right divisional sector, occupied by the 62nd Division. This was followed by a raid, which was repulsed, two of the enemy and two British soldiers being killed.

On the 11th February 1918 the Battalion was relieved from the front line for the last time, by the 18th Durham Light Infantry, and moved to Fraser Camp. On the following day they marched to Maroeuil where they were billeted in the town. On the 13th, Company Sergeant Major G. Cussons ceased to perform the duties of acting Regimental Sergeant Major, being posted to the 15th Battalion West Yorkshire Regiment. Captain L. H. Croxford and Lieutenant D. T. King of 'A' Company, together with 2nd Lieutenant J. Luke of 'D' Company were also 'cross posted' to the 15th Battalion, as were 192 other ranks.

2nd Lieut. Frank James Symonds killed in action 1/7/16 aged 20 years

CHAPTER 9: AND IN THE END

On February 15th, 1918, the 16th Battalion marched to Mont St. Eloi Station and entrained for Pernes. From there they marched to Sachin, about two miles to the east, where they were billeted under XIII Corps instructions. The last entry in the battalion's War Diary reads:

"February 28th - The total strength of the Battalion (583 other ranks) and the undermentioned officers are posted to the 3rd Entrenching Battalion and proceed to join."

Officers on the Battalion strength at that time were:

Headquarters

Lieutenant-Colonel A. C. Croydon, M.C., D.C.M., Commanding
Acting Major W. D. Coles
Captain and Adjutant J. J. G. Greenwood
Captain A. J. Brightwell
Captain G. A. McK Morant, M.C.
Lieutenant J. M. Barrow
2nd Lieutenant T. S. Campbell

'A' Company
Captain P. H. Battishill, M.C.
Captain L. H. Croxford
Lieut E. Wilson
2nd Lieut J. R. Brown
2nd Lieut F. de B. Price
2nd Lieut L. Crabtree
2nd Lieut S. S. L. Jackson
2nd Lieut K. T. Makin

'C' Company
Captain J. D. Ballantyne
Captain L. L. de Souza
Lieutenant A. Dickes
2nd Lieut G. A. Brown
2nd Lieut A. J. Comerford
2nd Lieut J. J. Walton
2nd Lieut A. B. P. Wood

'B' Company
Captain H. S. Nesbitt
2nd Lieut W. Barrie
2nd Lieut J. F. Farrar
2nd Lieut J. P. Lawson
2nd Lieut L. Parsey, D.C.M.
2nd Lt. A .L. Pearson, D.C.M.

'D' Company
Captain H. Evans
Captain E. Murgatroyd, D.C.M.
Lieut O. V. L. Hough
Lieut J. L. Richard
2nd Lieutt H. J. Clements
2nd Lieut J. P. Feather
2nd Lieut D. G. Garbutt
2nd Lt. R. W. Jackson, D.C.M.
2nd Lieut E. Jowett
2nd Lieut G.L. Lyall
2nd Lieut J. W. Marsden

Attached to Battalion
Captain C. Roche, M.C., R.A.M.C. (Medical Officer)
Captain J. Calderbank (Church of England Chaplain)

The 18th Battalion, having spent four days as Brigade support in the Arleux Sector, moved to Bray camp. On February 1st, all officers and other ranks assembled in the camp Church Army hut where Lieutenant-Colonel Carter explained the reasons for disbanding the Battalion and expressed his appreciation of the manner in which all ranks had worked under him.

On the days which followed, drafts began to leave the Battalion, although it was a great consolation to all that the drafts were to other battalions in the Regiment. Officers on the strength at that time were:

> Lieutenant - Colonel H. F. G. Carter, M.C., Commanding
> Captain H. L. Dalley, M.C., Adjutant
> Captain M. Clough
> Captain F. W. Whittacker
> Captain L. H. Bakes
> Major A. W. Robinson
> Lieutenant J. L. Wood
> Lieutenant F. R. Kennington
> Lieutenant and Q/ M B. Hammond
> Lieutenant J. R. King

AND IN THE END

Lieutenant F. D. Dams
Lieutenant E. Williams
Lieutenant A. Cockenham
Lieutenant E. A. Ramsden

2nd Lieut A. Atkinson	2nd Lieut G. R. Lorel
2nd Lieut F. G. Baker	2nd Lieut A. S. Penn
2nd Lieut T. E. Dickenson	2nd Lieut H. Salmons
2nd Lieut C. H. Duckworth	2nd Lieut P. H. Scott
2nd Lieut H. Gill	2nd Lieut E. Smith
2nd Lieut J. Gray	2nd Lieut G. W. Smith
2nd Lieutenant J. D. Hollis	2nd Lieut C. A. F. Thornton
2nd Lieutenant W. R. Horner	2nd Lieut J. Whithead
2nd Lieutenant F. H. Hoyle	2nd Lieut J. Whithead
2nd Lieut C. F. Kiddle	2nd Lieut R. B. Wright

On February 11th, a farewell message from the Brigadier, was received:

> "The Brigade Commander feels sure that Brigadier-General J. D. Ingles, D.S.O., who is now on leave would wish to express to Lieutenant Colonel H. F. G. Carter, M.C., and Lieutenant Colonel A. C. Croydon, M.C., and all ranks of the 16th and 18th Battalions, West Yorkshire Regiment his deep sense of regret at parting from them as units of the 93rd Brigade. Both these battalions have served in the 93rd Brigade since its formation in May 1915, and have loyally and devotedly upheld the splendid traditions of their Regiment, and have by their good work and efficiency, largely contributed to the high reputation of the Brigade.
>
> The severance of these battalions from the Brigade is necessary in the interests of the whole army, but that does not lessen the deep regret felt throughout all the remaining ranks of the Brigade.
>
> In times of hardship and danger, the 16th and 18th Battalions of the West Yorkshire Regiment have proved themselves brave, cheerful soldiers and good comrades.
>
> To all ranks of these battalions, the best wishes of the Brigade are tendered for their success and welfare in the future, and they will never be forgotten."

On February 15th, Lieutenant-Colonel Carter, Major A. W. Robinson, Captain L. H. Bakes, Lieutenant J. L. Wood, Lieutenant B. Hammond, Lieutenant F. R. Kennington, 2nd Lieutenant G. W. Smith and 2nd Lieutenant F. H. Hoyle together with 42 other ranks proceeded by rail to the XIII Corps reinforcement camp at Pernes. The last entry in the Diary, referring to this posting, reads:

"This reduced the strength of the battalion in the field to NIL".

THE BRADFORD PALS

So ends the story of the Bradford Pals. No longer the keen boisterous battalions of volunteers who had marched from Bradford three and a half years previously and been thrice decimated in battle, but men who never lost faith for all that.

After the war the survivors formed the "Bradford Pals Old Comrades' Association" with its headquarters at: 'Claremont', Morley Street, Bradford. This Association was active until March 1979.

The King's Colours of both battalions now hang in Bradford Cathedral, near the side door. However, one cannot fail to comment on the fact that, when peace came, the City which had raised them did not put up a memorial or a plaque to those Pals who did not return until July 1979.

It is fashionable now to write of these men as 'brainwashed by the system'; 'carried away by misguided enthusiasm'; 'men who did not know what they were fighting for.' Anyone who has had the fortune, indeed the honour, to meet these men, knows this not to be so. In 1976 after spending an evening in the Blighty Club with a group of Old Pals, which included George Morgan, Frank Burn and Frank Hartley, listening to their experiences on the Somme and the other battlefields of the First World War, the author expressed the view that what seemed so incredible was the impression that, if asked to do the same again, they would. Almost as one voice these old comrades replied: "Yes, we would!"

Perhaps the words of Winston Churchill in his book "World Crisis" would make a fitting farewell to these battalions:

If only Generals had not been content to fight machine gun bullets with the breasts of gallant men, and to think that that was waging war.

Field Marshal Haig: "I consider the machine gun to be a greatly over-rated weapon."
The photograph is of George Taylor at Serre Cemetery in 1974, taken by Stan Barraclough.

Aftermath

Have you forgotten yet? . . .
For the world's events have rumbled on since those gagged days,
Like traffic checked while at the crossing of city-ways:
And the haunted gap in your mind has filled with thoughts that flow
Like clouds in the lit heaven of life; and you're a man reprieved to go,
Taking your peaceful share of time, with joy to spare.
But the past is just the same - and War's a bloody game . . .
Have you forgotten yet? . . .
Look down, and swear by the slain of the War that you'll never forget.

Do you remember the dark months you held the sector at Mametz -
The nights you watched and wired and dug and piled sandbags on parapets?
Do you remember the rats; and the stench
Of corpses rotting in front of the front line trench -
And dawn coming, dirty-white, and chill with a hopeless rain?
Do you ever stop and ask, "Is it all going to happen again?"

Do you remember that hour of din before the attack -
And the anger, the blind compassion that seized and shook you then
As you peered at the doomed and haggard faces of your men?
Do you remember the stretcher cases lurching back
With dying eyes and lolling heads - those ashen-grey
Masks of the lads who once were keen and kind and gay?

Have you forgotten yet? . . .
Look up, and swear by the green of the spring that you'll never forget.

Siegfried Sassoon. March, 1919.

The Prince of Wales inspects Old Comrades in Bradford in the Twenties.

Survivors of the Pals battalions at Bradford Cenotaph, July 1st, 1977.
Bradford Telegraph & Argus

APPENDICES

Regimental Sergeant Major G. Cussons
16th. Battalion

APPENDIX 1 : The Tyke, No. 2,

a surviving example of the Battalion Journal which, it is worth remembering, was written by young soldiers on active service, not by veterans writing some sixty years later. This facsimile is taken from an original copy which belonged to the daughter of George Arthur Fishwick who was killed whilst serving with the 10th Battalion of the West Yorkshire Regiment. In Bradford he had been a dyer's labourer. His daughter gave "The Tyke, No.2" to Alan Petcher who has done much research into the history of the Bradford Pals.

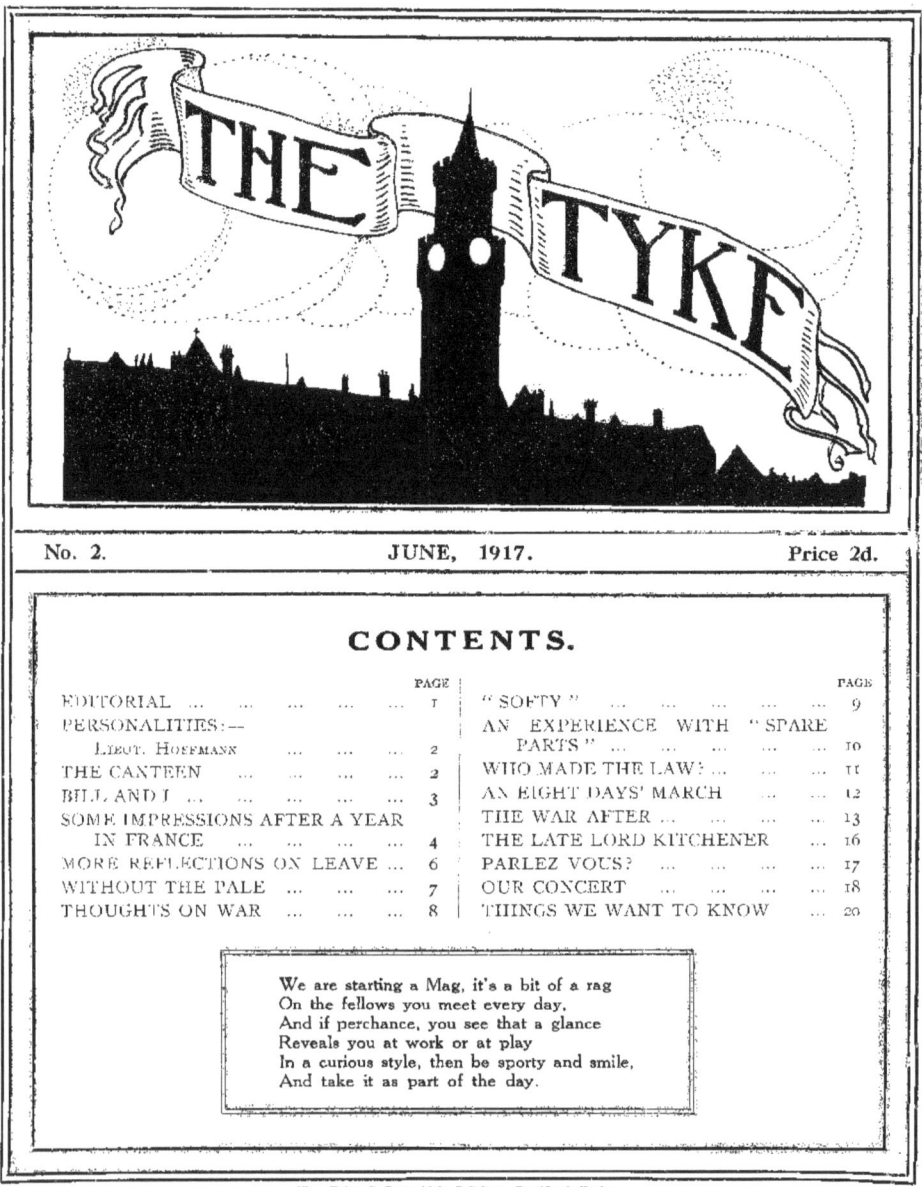

APPENDIX 1

The Tyke

No. 2. JUNE, 1917 Price 2p

We have made for you a song,
And it may be right or wrong,
But only you can tell us if it's true;
We have tried for to explain,
Both your pleasure and your pain,
And Tommy, here's our best respects to you.

Oh there'll surely come a day,
When they'll give you all your pay,
And they'll treat you as a Christian ought to do.
So until that day comes round,
Heaven keep you safe and sound,
And Tommy, here's our best respects to you.
-RUDYARD KIPLING.

• EDITORIAL •

In bringing this second venture to the notice of our readers we must first of all render our hearty thanks to everybody for the very cordial reception accorded to our first number. We have been overwhelmed with the good wishes of friends both here and in the homeland. To all such we give our hearty thanks, and promise, so far as we can, to endeavour to be worthy of all the kind things which have been said of us. We hope that in the days that are in front - days probably of great stress and strain - that we may in these pages form a close connecting link between our lads here and friends at home. We believe that we are on the eve of great and vital events - events which will go to mould the future of our race for generations yet unborn, and if in our humble way we can ease the burden and lighten the task of the men who are bravely bearing the heat and burden of the day in this time of
national crisis, we shall feel amply repaid for all the efforts we have made. Perhaps in the days to come some of us may be - will be - called upon to make the supreme sacrifice in the cause we all have at heart. If so be, may we do our duty, and at the supreme moment leave the arena with our faces to the Sun. The days to come are days of glorious promise, rich with opportunities for service, golden with the hope of freedom, and full of assurance of the freedom of the civilised world and a great step forward in humanity's march onward.

So to all, good luck and good wishes.

TO OUR READERS

The Editor and Staff most cordially invite any members of the Battalion to write to us on matters of interest. It is not our intention to confine the contributions to this magazine to a limited few. As a Battalion Magazine we want everybody to feel they have a real living personal interest in it, and anything which they can do to make it a success we ask them for. Poetry, jokes, trench incidents, anything in which all of us are interested, is always welcome, and we are sure that many things of general interest of which we never hear occur daily, and we invite our readers, when they find any such incidents, to drop us a line.

Take as a motto "Don't be shy," and let us hear from you.

THE STAFF.

★ ★ ★

ON THIS ROCK.
Landlady: "Dinah, are you a good cook?"
New Girl: "Lawdy, yaas, ma'am. Ah goes to church twice every Sunday - yaas' m."

PERSONALITIES

CHARACTER SKETCH.-No. 2.

The oldest officer in the Battalion in length of service, the subject of our sketch is also one of the most popular with all ranks. Those of us who have been in daily contact with him can bear evidence to his kindness and consideration to all who in any way had dealings with him. The elder of two brothers the subject of our sketch was educated at Bradford Grammar School, and joined the Battalion on its formation. A keen lover of all outdoor sports, with a strong preference for Rugby football, Lieutenant Hoffmann soon made his mark in the field as a thorough sportsman. Was for a long time in charge of the Transport Section, which under his management became a very efficient force in the Brigade, and acted as President of the Band, for a long period. Carries with him the good wishes for a safe return from all who have had the privilege of being associated with him, both in duty and in pleasure, and having found thereby a thorough sportsman and gentleman.

-H. L.

CAPTAIN ROCHE, M.C.,
the subject of last month's Character Sketch

THE CANTEEN.

There is one institution in the Regiment which is continually ascending and descending the ladder of popularity. I speak of the Regimental Canteen. Now let me explain that a Canteen at the Front is far different from those in the camps at home. Mine, for instance, is situated in an old leaky, draughty barn which simply swarms with rats, so much so that every night I have to pack all my goods up in their cases, nail them down, and then sleep on them to keep the rodents from sampling Tommy's dainties. Again, we do not sell beer. This is a great grievance. I should describe the Canteen as a Tuck-shop on a large scale, but no Tuck-shop ever sold as much chocolate or biscuits as a Regimental Canteen. When we have beaucoup choc. and biscuits we are on the topmost rung of the ladder mentioned above, and when we have none we come down with a bump to the bottom one of all. We are right there just now, which is the reason why I have found time to write these few notes.

The following dialogue will show Tommy's disgust when the dainties are "Napoo":-
Tommy: " Any choc., mate?"
I: " No, Jim."
Tommy "Any biscuits?"
I: "No; nothing to eat."
Tommy: "' What a blankety-blank canteen!

This sort of thing goes on all day long. Then, when the stuff actually does arrive, the news flies round like wildfire, and for as long as the stuff lasts I am besieged. They simply swarm round the old shop, and my assistant and myself cannot take money fast enough, and are heartily glad when closing time comes and we can pack up for the night. We stock almost every kind of cigarette, and I shudder to think, what would happen if we ever ran short of Woodbines.

When the Battalion goes in the trenches "the old shop." goes with them, and has already had several narrow escapes. The last time we were in I established myself in a draughty archway (no other place being available) in a village which is frequently shelled by the enemy and had quite a lively time, but the old shop came through all right. Sold out as usual.

The rate of exchange causes considerable bother to the lads, especially when I am obliged to give change in both English and French currency. They turn it over, stare at it in a bewildered manner, and go away shaking their heads over it and wondering if they have been done or not.

I shall have to finish now. The goods have arrived and the biscuit-wallahs are gathering in their thousands.
Now for two solid hours' hard work.

-E. S.

APPENDIX 1

THE TYKE

"BILL and I"

No. 1.

"WE JOIN THE ARMY."

Bill and I are soldiers now. We state this fact for the benefit of our readers who might take our disguise to mean something less complimentary. Bill is just 21, and I (Ebenezer) am nearly 20. Bill is fat and podgy, with an appetite like a horse and a thirst that is the envy of the neighbourhood. In private life Bill's business career is that of an errand boy to a coal hawker, and the illustrious profession of your humble servant is that of being head manager to the proprietor of a coffee-stall on Saturday nights - at other times living the life of an independent gentleman. In the course of our professional wanderings one day Bill and I saw a placard which stated "Your King and Country Need You!" and having nothing else to do, and lacking the necessary financial stability wherewith to purchase the essential liquid refreshment which we require in the course of our arduous labours - and the recruiting station being near at hand - we decided to oblige His Most Gracious Majesty to the best of our ability. Our reception was most cordial on arrival. In fact, the whole staff greeted us with smiling faces, and the fellow with the twiddly-iddly things on his cap asked us if we had not made a mistake, as the baths were next door. After having corrected this mistaken impression on the part of this gentleman, we informed him that we had come to place the flower of our blooming manhood at the disposal of the nation. This, alas, did not produce the impression we desired. In fact, it only produced ribald laughter on the part of all concerned. However, the recruiting sergeant took Bill into another room, where he was examined by the doctor, who pronounced him fit, and soon after the same fate befell myself. Then we were taken before a fat old buffer - he was a magistrate - whom we had frequently met in other walks of life, chiefly about 11 a.m. on Monday mornings, who gave us 5s. and costs - we mean words of fatherly advice - and wished us well in our new career, though the sergeant muttered under his breath " Thank God we have a navy." Then we were sworn in - how often since then we have been sworn at - and handed the sum of one shilling and ninepence by the representative of the grateful nation. This performance being over, we adjourned to the nearest house of refreshment to discuss the probable effect of this increase in His Majesty's Forces on the German nation when their secret service reported in Berlin. After disposing of various liquid rations not specified on Army Forms, the recruiting sergeant-who, under the influence of our magnetic personalities and other things, had become quite friendly told us to report to him next morning at the head-quarters of the 999th Blankshires. We left for home. On our arrival we found that the news had rapidly travelled before us, and on turning into the old familiar haunts we were greeted with a most flattering reception - " England's last hope!" "Are we winning?" "What are we coming to?" "The King wants Men!" and so on. We were deeply moved by this warm greeting- in fact, if we had not moved quickly the police would have performed this operation for us. From here we adjourned to the "Pig and Whistle" to receive the congratulations - and beer - of our many friends. Here time passed quickly on, and at a late hour of the night two gallant warriors wended their way homeward with faltering but martial tread ready for the bloodthirsty deeds of the following day.   -H. L.

NEXT MONTH:

"BILL AND I GO TO CAMP."

A YOUNG WIFE'S AUTUMN THOUGHTS.

(Found in No Man's Land.)

When you come back from that stricken land,
  My heart says-" Only a little while,"
I think that the flowers will take your hand,
The solemn old church clock see and smile.

The village is wrapt in a dim low light
And the seashore white with the autumn foam,
But the stars will shine for us blue and bright,
When you return, when you come home.

Ah, we who wait in the autumn here,
  Quiet and still 'neath the sky's wide dome,
Pray God to cherish and watch you, dear,
  To guard you and bring you home.

SOME IMPRESSIONS AFTER A YEAR IN FRANCE.

Looking back over the experiences of the last twelve months one recalls to mind a certain expression used by one of the Battalion as our boat steamed into the French port at which we disembarked. " Well," he said, " we're here at last, and I'm glad to leave Egypt behind. Now perhaps we shall see what War really is." Those of us who are left will agree with me that in grim reality we have seen what War really is. France is, at present, perhaps the most wonderful country in the world. Wonderful in resource, wonderful in her power of recovery, and most wonderful for the Spirit of Victory which animates her people. Villages and farms behind the line are not all entirely ruined. If the inhabitants had all fled from the range of the German big guns, to the region devastated by war would have been added a region devastated by fear, a band thirty or forty kilometres deep of uncultivated fields and factories shut down. Instead, the vast clayey, chalky plains of France in the war zone-swept by cannon, covered with the burnt skeletons of farmhouses and villages, where the few trees that have been spared by the Allied troops have been gnawed white by transport horses and mules, and even the agricultural implements have been burned in the camp fires - these places will soon be green with wheat. It will again stretch fair and tall to the very edge of the firing line as if nothing had happened in France but sun and wind and rain. As I have said, France is wonderful in her resources, and not the least wonderful is the marvellous way in which the women have taken up the burden laid down by the menfolk who are at the war. In agriculture, in industry, and in all the intricate problems which perplex the mind of man in modern commerce, she has taken up the burdens laid down by the menfolk-increased by the stress and strain of war-and worthily upheld the best traditions of her race. Wonderful in resource, equally wonderful in her power of recovery, the French people have also shown an example to the world. You take hold of a ruined village: if successful you press forward, and on your return the place is rebuilding. They are re-creating a New France out of the ashes of the old, and the process is going on under our own eyes, in our own day and generation. And the spirit of ultimate success never wavers. To them the victory is as secure as the eternity of the hills.

And about ourselves. We settled down in what was then a pretty typical French country village on our arrival. Here, on Good Friday of last year, we entered the Line for the first time. Good Friday was ever a Devil's day in the history of mankind, and on the Monday following the Company to which the writer belongs lost its first man as a casualty of war. Since then one has almost become indifferent to the issues of life and death, and one passes such sights in a far different spirit nowadays, but the death of this man - a close friend - is one of those recollections one carries away in one's thoughts. We buried him two days later in a quiet little cemetery, amid the bombardment of English and German artillery in, to use the Padre's words, the sure and certain hope of a better resurrection. Five of us paid our last tribute at his resting place, and of those five, to-day the writer is the only one left in France. Three of that little company have crossed the Great River, and the other one is still in England recovering from wounds received in action. We stayed here for four months until the beginning of the advance on the Somme on July 1st. In this we took part. It is neither the time nor the place in this magazine for the writer to enter into detail his impression and opinion as to the happenings of that day. Sufficient to say that the best of Bradford's sons at the time worthily upheld the honour of the City to which they belonged, and gave to its history fresh honour and glory. They went to their death as steady as if on parade, and Bradford will do well to hold their memory sacred, and if she is poorer today by the loss of these her best, she - if she has learnt the lesson rightly - ought to he infinitely richer by the sacrifice made. To the writer, July 1st will ever be a black day in the calendar, one of those perpetual yesterdays which will haunt the memory for ever. One did not wish to mention names, but no reference to this event would be complete without reference to the work done bythe Battalion Medical Officer, Captain C. H. Roche,M.C., for the magnificent work untiringly and ungrudgingly performed, under great difficulty and heavy fire, at considerable personal risk. Many Bradford lads are under a deep debt of gratitude to him for the splendid work he did on their behalf that day. After this black - for us - week-end we left the Line, for a short time and proceeded to a lovely little spot, far away front the noise and tumult of the battlefield, here to rest awhile and take stock, as it were. Then into the Line again, but away from the old spot, and here for three months we held the trenches among a different class of people, and in lovely country at the best of the year. After this we again took up our journey back to the Somme. Here again amid the storm of shot and shell and scenes indescribable almost, but besides which Dante's Inferno was a picnic, we took our place once more. Nothing I think, will ever bring home to the English people the real true horror and tragedy of it all but actual bitter experience. Of the present one cannot here speak.Sufficient that we are still keeping our end up and doing our best. Of the days to be, what? Some of us can see, stretching down the days to come, a greater realisation of the value of humanity than hitherto. To gain this the road may be hard, but we hold the faith that it will not now be long. By the memory of our comrades gone before we press on, their efforts have been for the best, and at least our happy dead have escaped the worst fate of all, the fate of our elders grown old and cold and weary, all their ideals shattered, their illusions swept away. They have been taken in the very hey-day of their youth, caught up by the Gods to play in the Elysian Fields, where falls not hail or rain or snow, nor any wind blows loudly. Schoolboys but yesterday, their laughter still re-echoes through the familiar places that knew them so well; their spirits hover over the ground where they won their laurels. Nothing is lost. The God of War may have taken and smashed their bodies, but their souls are beyond any power of man to hurt, and we press on towards the crowning good - the Brotherhood of Man - and, as one writer ably puts it -" Then not in vain shall the Motherhood in her need call unto us that remain to face our duty on the battlefield of life, ever faithful soldiers of God." For the ancient saying stands fast that the chief end of man is to magnify the glory of God and through suffering to enjoy Him for ever.

"LOOKER ON."

* * * * *

PACKAGE FOR HENRY.

"Yes, Henry and I certainly possess similar tastes," exclaimed the adoring bride. "We are surely interested in the same things."

"Yes," agreed Henry's mother-in-law grimly, "you certainly are. You care more for dear Henry than anyone else in the world, and so does he."

LIEUT.-COLONEL A. C. CROYDON. M.C., D.C.M.

MORE REFLECTIONS ON LEAVE.

(BY A LADY CORRESPONDENT.)

My sympathy (or perhaps I had better substitute fellow feeling in case Tommy chooses to mischievously misinterpret the word) is entirely with the Boys regarding the question of leave. Yet, unselfish as he is during those ten glorious days of liberty, I would venture to estimate that only the barest percentage of Tommies dream of viewing the question of " leave " from any point of view but their own. During his brief excursion to "Blighty" he is so very much engrossed in studying the turnings and twistings of his own mind that "to see himself as others see him" will perhaps prove a refreshing draught.

There is something magical about the word "leave," something enchanting. Suggest the possibility of it to the most anxious soul and her eye will brighten at once, whilst the old vigour of bygone days will spring into life again. To us, it speaks of fairies at work - witchcraft once more on this solid old earth of ours. To Tommy it whispers " home," and delights such as have nearly faded from his memory.

The first glimpse of Tommy - who can describe that? We have the advantage of him here, for he has only just returned from a long and tedious journey. He wants sleep, rest and food before he can begin to take pleasure in the things around him; we are ready to welcome him, keen of eye and quick to note all the changes which a year of campaign has wrought for him. His appearance and manner of speech have altered, but what of that? He is still ours, and proves it before he has been in the house a few minutes. However, we know that one fleeting hour is just about as much torture as he can stand the first night. and then it's "Girls, stand aside and let mother put him to bed".He escapes with a sigh of rapture, thinking, no doubt, what heaps more value there is to be found in a bed than these chattering civilians. As a rule, on saying " good night," he will enquire what time he needs to rise the following morning, and on being given a decent hour. such as eight or nine o'clock, he will chuckle, saying that he is not going to waste so much time in bed; he can do that when he gets back again, and let the breakfast be ready for him at 7.30 a.m. prompt. But where is he to be found at 7.30 in the morning? Either the bed has refused to yield up her weary burden, or Tommy has suddenly, on the first morning, become a victim to meditation. He yells for his " Petit dejeuner " to be taken up to his bedroom, not forgetting to inform his waitress, whilst she is almost feeding him. that this is what the Army manages for him once a week (waitress included, I expect).

Oh, yes! By the end of the first day everybody in the house, including the dog, has to confess that Tommy " has a way with him." Mark the word "confess," and secretly the feminine members of the household are putting their heads together to decide what is going to be done with him after the war. They find this too big a question for an immediate decision, so put it aside for the time being.

Next comes the important question of how Tommy is going to dispose of his time. Now if he has been in France for the last twelve months he desires the time of his life but oh! the number of poor mis-guided people who believe in giving him a taste of their own particular "good time" Whether his parents have come to the painful conclusion that he cannot be depended on to choose the nature of own enjoyment or whether they think that France has robbed him of all power of judgement and discrimination is a question. At any rate, the outcome is the usual "follow me" system, and, as a result Tommy is bored. For Tommy to be bored , whilst on leave is tragic. It is imperative that this danger should be averted. but how? Simply let the younger members of the family take control of the entertaining part of the programme. Give the sisters a free hand, and they'll make the thing go. They have the spirit which is essential to making. things a success: they have been deprived of such a pleasure for a long time, and when such a chance as this crops up, they are only too willing to make the most of it. Besides, most of them see further into their brother's mind (and are therefore capable of anticipating his every wish) than a host of widely-spread relations.

On these auspicious occasions the food question always gives rise to many both amusing and painful scenes. If Tommy is setting much store on the good things he is to eat, he will do well to send his mother a wire from London. Then, with the rapidity of a house on fire, she will in half an hour have suffcient eatables in the house to feed about three times the usual number, for twice the usual length of time. You can therefore calculate for yourself the answer to this mathematical problem, and at the same time think of poor Tommy. He, knowing that many of the dishes have been specially concocted for his benefit. bravely tries to do his part, whilst the rest of the family watch him, most likely to make sure that the food disappears in the right quarter. When Tommy quietly drops off to sleep after such a banquet as this a murmur of "poor lad, poor lad," goes round the company again; they are a little wide of the mark. Tommy awakes at the rattling of the tea cups (a natural instinct by the way) and braces himself up for another attack, after which he succumbs on to the piano stool to play a series of doleful hymns. Let me add that s without a trace of self-consciousness. His mother, taking advantage of this opportunity, borrows his top note to clean the knives with (Bairnsfather) and retires gleefully to the kitchen.

Tommy has adopted many of the French customs. He aggravates the family by interspersing his remarks with a word or two of French. This gives relish to the conversation, but they, who are hanging on his every word, think it absolute gibberish. Most likely they demand a translation, whereat Tommy

THE TYKE

begins to look foolish. He is not used to translating French idioms to a wondering open-mouthed family -" C'est impossible! " he mutters.

His manners, considering that he has only mixed in masculine society for the last twelve months, are not bad. He very quickly adapts himself to the use of such marvellous things as white serviettes and to drinking water at dinner. Cheese he abhors, and is polite enough to tell you so.

He has developed many new habits, such as smoking in bed, disappearing for hours together, and paying extravagant prices for everything he buys. He must have the best. " Never mind the cost," he says loftily. In these days of rigid economy (where sugar is not found in every woman's cupboard) such practice calls up the remembrance of days of yore, when we all had extravagant tastes. Tommy has not experienced the sensation of visiting a grocer's shop and being refused a pound of sugar, however much he offered to pay for it!

In order to let his family witness what a strong animal he has become, also to keep his muscles up to scratch, he likes to engage each member of the family in a "turn" every morning. (This generally happens when the water is plentiful.) If the plaster overhead should give way, and you hear a series of thuds on the ceiling above you, which threaten to send it on your head at any moment, there is no necessity for you to become alarmed - it is only Tommy taking his daily exercise with a small brother as victim. Hurry to the room where such an engagement is taking place and you will find it deserted- Tommy has quietly disappeared, taking his victim along with him. The room, in an absolutely chaotic state, has got to be made fit for habitation again, and it is your honour and pleasure to do it. So much for that wonderful and heroic boy, Tommy.

Tommy returns to France with the firm conviction that the dear old people are just the same as ever. He is mistaken. Some eminent philosopher, speaking or writing lately about the war, said that it had already produced an almost refreshing sense of seriousness. Certainly it is serious enough, but I cannot yet admit the sense of refreshment. On his leave Tommy sees us pretty lively, but although a change is taking place slowly in " Blighty," yet there is one taking place. His experience in France has quickly changed his outlook on life; ours is taking the form of a slower, more refined torture. As Sir Walter Scott says in his diary, it is not always the heavy blow which hurts most; sometimes the dreading and expectancy of it are equally as hard to bear. However, Tommy thinks we don't understand the seriousness of war, and he obtains the impression by the utter senselessness of the questions put to him when on leave. As Yorkshire people say, "There be fowk and fowk", and I honestly believe it is just an effort at geniality - a very poor one indeed. Tommy should judge by actions, not words, and in heart of hearts I think he does.

Therefore, take no offence for any words of mine, Tommy. You are all just our dear boys away from home and we want you. all back again to prove our gratitude in a more pleasing way. -E. G. P

WITHOUT THE PALE.

(BY " H. C.")

As most readers of this magazine know, the active or fighting portion of the British Army in France spend most of their time in small villages just behind the Line. These villages usually consist of a couple of estaminets (densely overcrowded during the hours they are open), a few dilapidated cottages, occupied by more dilapidated women, and some derelict barns.

These latter are the soldiers' temporary homes. Weeks come and go, and the life of the soldier is one monotonous medley, alternating between going into the trenches and resting in these so-called villages. But one day, very occasionally, comes the news that No. — Battalion of the So and So Regiment will change fronts, or perhaps go back to some big railhead for heavy fatigues. Rumour is soon busy, and the ultimate destination is soon known, and always are we going to a large French town. Visions of life, cinemas, theatres and big dinners open out before the vista. And preparations are made for a good time in the near future. Then comes the long five or six days' march, or the tedious uncomfortable railway journey. These are made easy by the hopes and aspirations of coming days. Very soon, only a few days, and the soldier reaches the Mecca of his dreams. The large town he has pictured is now in the distance, and the morrow will see the realisation of all his desires fulfilled. But,- lo and behold! the town is reached and the march is no way finished. On through the town and once again into the open country. Many are the guesses, and more the growls of the disappointed Tommy, now that his hopes are dashed to despair. But soon, some five kilometres or so, the Battalion is called to a halt, and they are once more housed in the usual small village, in the usual derelict barns. And just without the pale. Imagine, dear reader, the murmurings and ill wishes of the disappointed soldier as lie sits and contemplates what might have been, but never is. In the distance can be seen the chimneys and towers of P—, but it is out of bounds. Consolation must be found in the adjacent estaminets or, to the man of higher ideals, the Y.M.C.A. or Church Army may be employed. And the time goes on; a percentage of passes are granted to any place of interest in the vicinity, but we do not forget that we are here on very serious business. The C.O. and other Officers are as indulgent as they can possibly be under the circumstances. Some time, perhaps, we shall have the good fortune to be billeted in a large town, when all our wishes may be gratified. Meanwhile, let us remember we are not on a picnic. Our whole object is to smash the Teuton, and, to use a favourite maxim of our lads, " We can do it! Aye, and we will do it, and then, well - wait and see. Our object now is, England and home, but before we can realise this hope we must wind up the watch on the Rhine. This done and our work finished, we can gladly, gloriously and honourably, bid a long farewell to La Belle France

-H.C.

THOUGHTS ON WAR.

To write upon war in the midst of a world conflagration is perhaps somewhat of an anomaly, but, nevertheless, even at this time it is not too late to learn some lessons as to its causes, consquences and results. And the causes of war are threefold, but practically one in principle - jealousy, ambtion and greed - but the real name of them all is money. All the wars in history are in the ultimate issue capitalist wars.

The present conflict, which is such a reflection on our Christian civilisation of the last 2,000 years, and which has dragged half humanity into the mire, is solely the result of the greed and ambition of the German people to extend their Empire, and to rule the world with Prussian militarism. General Sherman, in the American Civil War, asked for a definition of a state of war, tersely replied "War is Hell." Those three words perhaps sum up better the state of things that prevail on a modern battlefield, perhaps better than any other descrition could. There is the loss of life, the economic waste to all concerned, the depopulation of the best of the nations' manhood, and the burden of debt which is piled up for future generations. Nothing that will ever be written will ever really bring home to those that have not seen it the abominable waste and destructiveness of modern warfare.

Everything that in any way has had natural form or beauty is entirely swept away, or defaced, ruined, mutilated and lying about in an unsightly confusion of revolting ugliness and filth. Trees and flowers and grass, and roads and buildings and furniture, and clothes and men's equipment, are burnt and torn, and broken and shattered, rendered useless and defiled. The earth around is broken up into deep shell holes with the hellish artillery fire, and the ground is cumbered and the air poisoned with the dead bodies of men and horses putrefying and offensive. The war zone is simply a foul rubbish heap, and the face of nature little more than a repellant nightmare. There is neither beauty nor dignity left in any of the works of either God or man. A canker has to all intents and purposes devoured the land, and day after day, and night after night it cankers and corrupts. Day after day, night after night, the same terrible waste goes on - the waste of valuable human life, the life of healthy flesh and vigorous blood, the waste of human skill and human work, the work of farmer and husbandman, of builder and manufacturer, the waste of intellectual greatness and intellectual gain. The waste of material, the material of shells and chemical products which waste not only the breath of life, but every stick of property that they can reach, but themselves as well. And this continues week after week and month after month, and all the time the energy of these millions of fighting men, instead of being usefully productive, is devoted solely and simply to the destruction of their fellow men and, as a necessary consequence, of the lifelong happiness of those other millions of human beings, especially women and children, to whom they are dear. Truly, as the American General has said, "War is hell," and to-day, when the nations of the earth are called on to exercise all the hellish ingenuity which science has worked into modern warfare in order to preserve the civil liberties, of Europe from the corruption and demoralising influence of modern Germanism, it is the duty of every man to put all his heart and soul into the winning of this - one hopes and trusts - the last great war, and so to place the nations of the world for ever beyond the reach of this microbe of militarism, and thus make the world a sweeter and cleaner place to live in.

It has ever been the pride of this nation of ours to be the champions of the weak and the oppressed, and when the German people trampled on the rights of Belgium, we were ready to take up the gage of battle on her behalf, and to-day, in battle array, we stand with the other champions of civil and religious liberty defending the rights and privileges which have been handed down to us from generation to generation by our forefathers.

Russia, through this war, is a new nation. America is beginning to see farther than the almighty dollar, and recognise that men are more valuable than gold. France is giving of her best for freedom. The smaller states of Europe are slowly but surely recognising that right is the great standby for nations as well as men. And Germany - what of her?

Is all her proud record of the ancient past to be trampled in the dust and mire through the greed and ambition and the folly of an Emperor whose Kultur is a blood lust, and whose ambition is a terrorised world with himself as "Over-Lord?"

And so to-day, as never before in the history of mankind, humanity stands at the parting of the ways. One road leads to death and the destruction of all those things which we have been taught to hold as precious and of value - home, liberty and freedom - the divinest gifts of God, and the other, clear and shining, points humanity onward and upward to the things that are better than our best thoughts, and higher than our highest ideal, to all that we can conceive of best but have not yet reached.

For these the best and bravest of the sons of men have laid down their lives to protect; and it is up to us, the living - every one of us - to see that the sacrifices of our dead are not made in vain, but that from their example and sacrifice may be built a new England and a better world.
-H.L

★ ★ ★ ★ ★

NO TIME FOR A LOAF.

Some time ago when a local corps was reviewed by Sir Ian Hamilton, one officer was mounted on a horse that had previously distinguished itself in a bakery business. Somebody recognised the horse and shouted "Baker!" The horse promptly stopped dead, and nothing could urge it on. The situation was getting painful when the officer was struck with a brilliant idea, and remarked- "Not to-day, thank you." The procession then moved on.

APPENDIX 1

THE TYKE

A STORY WITHOUT WORDS

"SOFTY."

He was only a Simple Soul in his Battalion. He was known as "Softy" to his companions. Slow of action and timid of speech, his was a quiet and reserved nature, and he was the butt of his Platoon's jokes and the despair of his Platoon Commander. But he was always on parade in time, spotlessly clean, and ready in his own peculiar way for anything he had to do.

Although continually plagued and tormented by his comrades, his language was as clean as his person, and his character beyond reproach. But he was slow of understanding and dull of comprehension. On working parties he invariably did the wrong thing, and when corrected invariably did it worse at the second attempt. But tell him to do a thing, and once he grasped it you could rely on it being done, in his own peculiar way, and when the time came for his Battalion to participate in a "Push," and men were excitedly discussing the chances of life and death according to their mood - some in laughter, some in bravado, some in fear, and some with oaths upon their lips. "Softy" said nothing, but went his was quietly. Men called him "Windy," but he only smiled in his quiet way, and the night came when the Battalion went up to the Line to go "over the lid" in the morning, and "Softy" went as his Platoon Commander's runner, and when the hour arrived "Softy" went with the rest, and faced a hellish and murderous machine gun and shell fire from the enemy.

The order was given to "retire," and in the confusion "Softy's " Commander and "Softy" got parted. "Softy," with the remnants of his Company got back, but when they "called the roll" his Commander was missing. Volunteers were asked for to go and try to find him, but the men were worn out with the strain of the morning's work, and only "Softy" came out, nervous, hesitating and shy. He took his orders in his own dull way, and ambled off on his perilous journey. About two hours later a solitary figure with a burden on his back came staggering and bleeding into the trenches.

It was "Softy," wounded unto death, with his unconscious Platoon Commander on his back. He placed his burden down gently, and then, utterly done, fell to the ground with the cry "Is he right?" Willing hands did all they could for "Softy," but it was too late. The Angel of Death laid his finger on those poor stammering lips, and claimed him for his last rest.

"Softy" lies in a beautiful little cemetery, and above the White Wooden Cross which is the soldier's heritage are these words- "Greater love hath no man than this, that a man lay down his life for his friend," and it seems to me that "Softy" is only a type of many.

Men of the shy nature and the hesitant speech, but the brave heart and the resolute spirit, just the common clay like you and I, but oh, so wonderfully moulded in the Potter's hand as to do great things, and these men are daily dying for us.

Let us see to it, then, that we live for their sakes'.

RANKER.

AN EXPERIENCE WITH "SPARE PARTS."

They had just come up from G.H.Q. and were feeling quite the real thing as their mess mates gathered round them in the smoky atmosphere of their quarters on the evening of their arrival.

They were questioned, cross-examined, pumped for stories, and by 9.30 p.m. were at last able to ask a few questions themselves. "Where can we complete our kit?" "The nearest town is twelve miles away, but if you can get there you will be able to purchase all you require". "But how are we to get there?" "Oh, horses." "Of course, of course," said one, the other looked as if the word horse had given him a short arm jab; he exclaimed, " Why, I can't ride". "Oh, don't worry," said his chum, a strange light coming into his eyes. "It is just as easy as sitting on that box, and a jolly sight more comfortable, and by the time we have rubbed the two first kilos off, which, by the way, we shall do at a walk, you will be an enthusiastic horseman, filled with an ambition to become a Company Commander, when you may have one of those noble animals entirely at your own disposal." And so, with many nods, handshakes, and expressions of confidence, the two Turpinites sought the shelter of their respective sleeping bags.

The one sleeping peacefully, the other wakeful, and thinking of the ordeal which tomorrow's dawnwould oblige hint to undertake. " Oh, I do hope it will be wet," he murmured as he dozed off into a troubled sleep.

The following. morning, while breakfasting, an orderly announced that the horses were awaiting their jockeys in the yard outside. This news was the cause of another outburst from the amateur, who had been asking all and sundry tips as to how to hold on, and if it had not been for the confidence he had in his companion, this experience would have not been chronicled. The horses up to this point were both unknown quantities.

We see the two exponents come into the yard together. Bespurred and bewhipped they approached the awaiting steeds, and we see that it is only by a powerful effort that the experienced one is able to hide his true feelings. Turning to the other, he explained that one cannot always judge a horse by its looks, and, putting his hand on the other's shoulder, led him blindly to the groom, to whom he whispered, " Get him on its back before he sees it." At last the rider was up, and it was some job, but he got up at last, and never do I hope to see a sight to equal them - it was a great combination. The horse was as calm and serene as a late September afternoon, and sat upon his back was something which resembled the hottest part of July, both in appearance and temper.

After the third smack on its noble rump, and a click of the heels, he got the noble beast to move forward at a slow walk. In the first hundred yards of the ride the experienced one was leading by fifty yards, and when the kilometre post had been reached, it was necessary for the leader to return, and see what had become of his friend. He found him fuming in the road, and even threatened to return if he couldn't exercise more control over his mount and make it walk slower! So the arrangement was made that mutually they would try and urge the slower mount to quicker movement, and, much to the surprise of both, the mount broke into a trot and careered in a zigzag manner down the road. Nothing seemed to matter to the animal now; he had entered into the spirit of the thing properly, he whinnied and snorted, and, much as its rider desired him to walk, it was of no avail. By this time their way lay through a village. The soldiers billeted there had a rare view, they turned out en masse to watch the spectacle go by, and, it is said, telephoned through to the next village, because here again a great reception awaited them.

The horse was enjoying himself thoroughly. And what about its rider, poor devil. First he clung, to the saddle, and then he tried to grip with his knees, but in the end he had to allow himself to be tossed about at the will of his charger.

How he kept aboard is a mystery to himself and to all who were witness. When three villages had been passed, a hill loomed in sight, and this proved too much for the animal's enthusiasm, and with a final whinny he started to walk again, and when his rider had somewhat recovered himself he managed to stop him and dismount, and it might have proved a sorry day for his friend had he not had the good sense to keep out of the way for a little time. When he did come on the scene the horse was peacefully grazing in an adjoining field, his rider stamping up and down the road, and swearing that henceforth they should be as big enemies as they had been friends in the past. He absolutely declined to have anything further to do with the horse, and intended waiting until the first lorry came along in which he could complete his journey. However, the tactical one offered him a cigarette, and they sat down together under a haystack, and after some little discussion it was decided to resume the journey together.

At the slowest of slow paces they went along. After a kilometre of this, and a positive refusal on the part of the novice to indulge in a trot, the two chums parted company, hoping that they might not meet each other again. However, fate decided otherwise, and some hours later they ran into each other in the main street of the town they had been making for, and, seeing that half the battle was over, they set out to make the best of the two hours that remained before dusk.

Regardless of the journey back, they enjoyed those two hours. We see them next both smiling at each other and mounted. The novice suggests that they should try a trot, which was quite a success for two kilos; here they met some opposition in the shape of a traction engine. After several delays they reached a spot where it seemed they would have to remain for the night. They got separated, each losing the other in a maze of motor lorries. Half an hour later they met

APPENDIX 1

again, still threading their way through the traffic. But the animal on which the novice sat was in no mood for turning, and had reached the stage when even walking was too much for him. Nothing could impress the animal to go forward. Its only desire seemed to be to take part in the game of obstructing the highway. However, a solution was arrived at by the jockey unconsciously backing him on to the hot radiator of a motor lorry in rear. This had the desired effect, he got his head in the air and made another start for his stable, but its rider being a most conscientious fellow, and possessing a large heart, he somehow thought his weight was to blame for the horse's condition, and therefore dismounted to make things easier (for himself). After this he had no choice in the matter. Although he was eight kilos from home, he led his horse bravely the whole hog, at least to the foot of the last hill. Here the horse required the assistance of both the novice and the expert.

Next we see them emerging through the door of the stables, and we hear them say one to the other, "No, never again!" and the novice swears there isn't an atom of pleasure to be had riding a horse The horse has since become famous, and is on the Establishment as "S.P." -E.M.

IN MEMORIAM.
(Dedicated to the Bradford Pals.)

Unto you our homage we pay, brave lads of our own town,
Your memory will never die but will be of world renown.
When duty called you nobly went, just like an Englishman would,
Ready to obey a Country's command, and do just what you could.
What a grand body of noble men you were as you marched along,
Husbands and brothers, fathers and sons, marched on with a cheering song;
How proud we were as you marched away, clad in your suit of blue,
And many a humble yearning prayer went up to God for you.
Oh, Bradford Pals, you gallantly fought, we only know too well,
Our hearts thrill with pride when we think of the day you charged into that gaping hell.
Many poor hearts have ached and bled for dear ones we lost in the fray,
But nobly you taught your enemies all that prepared you for "The Day."
The tiny crosses that mark your graves are surmounted by God's own love,
Your lives laid down for us at home, our loss - your gain above;
We pray your sacrifice may not be in vain, but through the coming years,
A purer England we shall have, built up on our prayers and tears.

Listerhills, Bradford. **HYLDA BRADLEY.**

WHO MADE THE LAW?

(Reprinted from the Sunday Chronicle.)

On the body of Sergeant Leslie Coulson, killed in the Somme fighting, on October 8th last, was found, with his pipe and the last letter from his father, the following tragic poem, evidently written a day or so before, for it bore after his signature the date October, 1916. The mementoes only reached England a few days ago. The verses will be read with great interest, especially by those who knew the great accomplishment and the greater promise of the young author:

Who made the Law that men should die in meadows,
Who spake the Word that blood should splash in lanes,
Who gave it forth that gardens should be boneyards,
Who, spread the hills with flesh and blood and brains
  WHO made the Law?

Who made the Law that Death should stalk the valleys,
Who spake the Word to kill among the sheaves.
Who gave it forth that death should lurk in hedgerows,
Who flung the dead among the fallen leaves?
  WHO made the Law?

Those who return shall find that Peace endures,
Find old things old, and know the things they knew,
Walk in the garden, slumber by the fireside,
Share the peace of dawn, and dream amid the dew-
  THOSE WHO RETURN.

Those who return shall till the ancient pastures,
Clean-hearted men shall guide the plough horse reins,
Some shall grow apples and flowers in the village,
Some shall go courting in summer - down the lanes-
  Those who return.

But Who made the Law? The trees shall whisper to him,
"See, See, the blood - the splashes on our bark,"
Walking the meadows he shall hear bones crackle,
And fleshless mouths shall gibber in silent lanes at dark.
  WHO made the Law?

Who made the Law? At noon upon the hillside,
His ears shall hear a moan, his cheek shall feel a breath,
And all along the valleys, past garden crofts and homesteads,
He who made the Law,
He who made the Law,
HE who made the Law shall walk alone with Death -
  WHO made the Law?

AN EIGHT DAYS' MARCH.

After our somewhat strenuous time in the Somme Valley, it was with a certain amount of relief that we set sail - or should it be set foot - upon an eight days' march to - at that time - a destination unknown. We left our billets in a somewhat jubilant frame of mind, glad to turn our backs - our hopes for ever - on a neighbourhood which has no pleasant recollections for Bradfordians, a neighbourhood in which we have left many of our best and bravest friends and comrades to sleep their last long sleep. Our destination was a matter of ten miles, through roads which were at the beginning little better than a mud bath. This was reached about 2 p.m., a small but rather pretty French village with a long straggling main street, and old-fashioned country houses typical of the French kind. After a meal we at once proceeded to wash all our carts and limbers, and also to grease them, and by the time this was done darkness was coming on, and one wended one's way to the billet ready for a night's sleep.

Next morning, after breakfast, and the mail had been distributed, in which men seemed liberally supplied with parcels, we resumed our journey over a distance of about 11 miles to the village where recently we were "resting." Once here, again about 2 p.m. the boys soon got into the old familiar haunts, and although the night turned out nasty, nevertheless an enjoyable evening was spent. Once again we thoroughly cleaned and washed and greased our limbers and carts to improve their appearance.

Next morning broke chill and cold, but fortunately the weather kept fine and dry, and we resumed our pilgrimage. This time the distance was but a short one, and we arrived at our resting-place - a big but uninteresting place - about twelve o'clock, having covered a matter of about eight miles. Here, after having washed the carts and limbers, there was nothing much to either see or do, and for the most part the evening was spent in billets. At 8.30 p.m. the men were served with hot rum and tea, which was greatly appreciated, for the night was very cold indeed. Teetotal cranks please note.

Next morning we were off in good time, for twelve miles lay between us and our billets for the night. The roads were very heavy, and the country bleak and hilly, but to the cheery music of the band we made good progress, and after passing through one of the big centres of France, we arrived safe and sound about 3.30 p.m. In this pleasant village the Battalion were widely scattered, and the different companies were some distance apart. It was pleasant to view the surrounding country here, and after the carts and limbers had had their daily bath we thoroughly enjoyed a walk in old-fashioned country lanes, which reminded one of the Homeland.

Next day our journey was one of eleven miles, and if in the last place our men were scattered about, in this one we were even more so, one company being at least five kilometres away from the others. Our own particular billet here was an estaminet, and a fairly good one too. After the carts and limbers had been duly attended to we paid a visit to the church, which had some very pretty carvings in old oak, apparently of very great age.

Next day was quietly spent resting, and one afterwards enjoyed a quiet stroll mid pretty scenery - of course after the usual treatment of carts, etc.

Next day found us on the move early, with a matter of 13 miles to go. The day was fine and dry, the roads in good condition, and the whole march went with a swing. On the road we received the congratulations of the Brigadier-General on the general excellence of our marching, which all the way reached a very high standard indeed. Arriving at the village where we were to spend the night, we immediately set to work to clean the afore-mentioned carts and limbers, and then, after a good meal, set out to enjoy the delights of one of the prettiest little villages we have been in during our wanderings through France. After rum and tea at eight o'clock we settled down to sleep with the prospect of a long hard day before us. The distance on this the last day was a matter of 16 1/2 miles. We set off in good spirits on a somewhat trying passage. After going about half the distance we halted for a hot mid-day meal; on this particular occasion we did not wash the limbers and carts; then on again. Our Brigadier, who saw the whole of his Brigade at a given point near the end of our journey, again gave us the credit of being - in his opinion - the fittest Battalion to finish.

We arrived at our final destination at about 4 p.m. after having covered a matter of 81 1/2 miles in eight days of hard marching, without the loss of a single man. When we add that this was done with each man carrying a full pack: - Greatcoat, shirt, socks, towel, etc. and all the accessories a wise and thoughtful Government think it necessary to hang on to a soldier, together with a rifle and 150 rounds of ammunition, we think our readers in the Homeland will agree that it was, on the whole, a very creditable performance, and that the "boys" are not lacking in physical fitness, at all events.

We could enlarge much more upon this subject, but as the aforementioned never-to-be-forgotten carts and limbers are to be washed, we regretfully come to a close.

P.S. - We have just heard the carts and limbers have to be painted.

- H.L.

SERGEANT-MAJOR WILKINSON.

We are pleased to be able to record in this number that C. S. M. Wilkinson, who in our previous issue was reported as "Missing - believed killed," is now a prisoner of war in Germany.

Although we all regret his position as a prisoner, we rejoice to know that he is still alive, and hope and trust that his stay in such unpleasant conditions will not be of very long duration. May the time soon come when once more we shall have the pleasure of his cheerful and entertaining personality with us.

APPENDIX 1

THE TYKE

THE WAR AFTER.

It is perhaps a little early and out of place to think about the state of things in England after the war is over, but nevertheless it is a thing that must not be lost sight of, and I think that steps should be taken now to meet the problem that is bound to arise between Capital and Labour and between employer and employee if England is to maintain her supremacy in the commercial world.

It is very true to say that a nation cannot stand still or "mark time," either she must go forward or backward, and as to which of these two England is going to do depends almost entirely upon the plan or scheme that will be adopted to further and better co-operation between employer and employee.

There is no doubt that if, after this war is over, we are still going to be troubled and harassed with strikes and the working at cross purposes between employers of labour, unions of employers and the various Trade Unions, England will lose her place as leader of the commercial world. The problem should be faced now, and the thing looked at by both sides in a straightforward way. Capital is dependent upon capital labour, and labour is equally dependent upon capital, and there are bound to be employers and also employees.

One scheme would be the nationalisation of the chief industries, etc. in the country; this certainly has many points in its favour, but I am convinced that this scheme would be a wrong one. For a nation to progress the element of competition in all industries, etc. must be fostered, and anything in the form of monopoly or trusts must always be avoided. The nationalisation of any industry would tend to lessen the element of competition in that industry. Take for example the railways. It is the competition between the various railway companies that has made our railway system the best in the world. In the Woollen District of Yorkshire there is in many cases the choice of four companies for the transport of the material, both raw and finished; it is because of this independence that makes the service so good as it is. Imagine in peace time, and normal conditions, the railways under the Government, total monopoly, and the satisfaction that small manufacturers, etc. would be likely to get. It would be much the same in all industries carried on by the Government.

One scheme I suggest, if adopted in a systematic way throughout the country, that would further the co-operation between employer and employee, and that is the Profit Sharing System. I do not suggest that it would do away altogether with labour troubles, because that, I believe, is practically impossible, but I do say that it would, if adopted by both sides in the proper spirit, solve the labour disputes to a large extent

There are at Present in the country some large concerns that have adopted this scheme, and although their systems are not in detail the same, the main principle, that is, the work people are given a personal interest in the concern, and that they share in the profits of the concern, is the same in all these systems.

It has been found where these systems are adopted that the work people have more interest in their work, more work is done, and better work is turned out. The life in the Army has certainly taught our millions of soldiers (peace time employees) many things, and the chief one, I consider, is that they are taught to take interest in everything that is going on around them. Before any military operations the greatest care is taken by the higher authorities that all ranks should know all the details of the operations, the organisation, the why and wherefore of everything that is done: this is done to gain the confidence of and to further the incentive in all ranks.

This teaching, will most certainly have its effect in civilian life, and prove of the greatest value in the commercial war to come. I think that the reason why the Profit Sharing System has not been more universally adopted is - because of the ignorance of the subject by the large employers of labour in the country. Now is the time for the Government to organise propaganda throughout the country on the subject, with the object of educating and enlightening people on this subject, which certainly has great possibilities, and is as yet in its infancy.

There is a saying "Never trouble trouble till trouble troubles you," but when you know and can see the trouble coming this is most certainly a fallacy; this country has in the past been too prone to believe this saying, but this present war and its duration is certainly an example of the fallacy of this old saying.

For this war to come let us prepare for it now, and deal with the problem in a straightforward way and gain the confidence of both employer and employee.

P. C. P.

OUR STRENUOUS PIONEERS.

"Do you think it will go now, Robbie?"
"Nay; tha'll nivver get a welling heat on that"

THE RETURN TO THE BILLETS.

A shaft of moonlight falls athwart the darkling road
   And lights the scene; a straggling knot of men
Who stagger on 'mid curses rude and broad;
   Some fall, some rise and struggle on again.

And some lay where they, fell, and blessed sleep
   Lets fall her magic cloak and wraps them round;
And angels up above look down and weep,
   As sprawled about they slumber on the ground.

O'er many a hard tense face there breaks a smile,
   And quivering lips form many a gigic name,
The dreamers see their loved ones for a while,
   And find their sweet caresses just the same.

For eight long days and nights they've held the line,
   And kept the wily German foe at bay;
They've stuck like death and held on rain or shine,
   They've earned their rest, and who dare say them Nay?

So let them sleep; on guard the silver moon,
   Whose gentle beams on war-worn faces shine,
Sleep on, brave men, enjoy the soldier's boon,
   You lion-hearts who held the British line.
                                          - E. S.

France, 1916.

Lieutenant Crowther, M.C., D.C.M.

WHY DO THEY CALL HIM CHARLIE
And Why Does He Sing "On Ilkley Moor Baht Hat?"

APPENDIX 1

THE TYKE 15

STRETCHER BEARERS OF THE FIRST BRADFORD "PALS"

Names, (left to right) Top rank: Pte. J. Howarth, Pte. T. Topham Pte. F. Hewitson, Pte W. Stubbs, Pte. T. W. Ingledew, Pte. S. Beardmore, Pte. H. Leeming, Second row: Pte. W. Greenhow, Corpl. W. S. Wood, Captain C. H. Roche, M.C., R.A.M.C., Corpl. H. Crossland, Pte. F. Thornton, Pte. E. Stead, Bottom row: Pte. G. Edmondson, Pte. H. Tankard, Pte. A. R. Midgeley. Pte. S. M. Moon, Pte. A. Edmondson. They are all "somewhere in France."

WHEN I COME HOME.

My life will wear a richer hue,
The sky will shine a brighter blue,
The friends I loved in days of yore,
I hope to greet them all once more.
And when I see my home again,
Despite the darkness and the pain
Of days that will be past and gone,
It will repay for all I've done.
              When I come home.

In all the places that I've been,
In all the sights my eyes have seen.
The fairest picture yet to me
Is loved ones far across the sea.
Who'll meet me with a loving smile,
And there my heart will rest awhile;
But even now I understand,
The beauty of my own Homeland.
              When I come home.

The memory of the dead who're gone.
Their Battle fought, their Victory won,
Will help me in the days to be,
To show their sacrifice for me

Was not in vain, and that I stand
Their guardian, by my own right hand
To keep the land they died for free,
The champion of liberty.
              When I come home.

And if in God's great better scheme,
My fancy proves to be a dream,
And I am called to cross the sea,
Which hides His Blessed Face from me,
And have to meet Him face to face,
And see the glories of His grace,
I shall more fully understand
The glory of the last Homeland.
              If God should call me home.
                    -H. L.

THE MADDING CROWD.

Newcomer (at resort): "Is this a restful place?"
Native: "Well, it used to be until folks began comin' here for a rest."

★ ★ ★ ★ ★

QUICK WORKER.

Hicks. "She married in haste."
Wicks: "And repented in leisure, I suppose."
Hicks: "No, she repented in haste, too."

MAJOR McCAVIN GRIEG.

THE LATE LORD KITCHENER.

It is no desire of ours to enter into controversial matters which are of no concern to us in any shape or form. But we do not think it right or fair to let the opportunity pass of registering our emphatic protest against the dirty and malicious statements which have been flung at the late Commander-in-Chief.

It is a cheap way to notoriety, slinging innuendoes at dead men.

We hold no brief on behalf of Lord Kitchener. His works and his record are the best monument to his memory. But we do feel that in the hurly-burly of controversy, when men are prone to say things they afterwards regret, that care should be taken not to besmirch the character of men who have left the arena.

When a man is dead the scales wherein he was weighed are broken. The years to come bring weights and measures of their own. To the England of the future days can well be left the place in history which Lord Kitchener will occupy. But we must lodge our protest that these attacks on the memory of a great soldier are lacking both in taste and judgement, and as such merit the condemnation of all right-thinking people.

OBSERVER.

TO THE ARM CHAIR CRITIC.

I reads all the papers out 'ere at the Front,
'Cos I'm one of the boys 'as is bearing the brunt,
And I've some questions to ask of the man over there,
Who could win fifty wars from the depth of his chair.

'Ave yer done a fifteen mile wearin' Tommy Atkins' pack?
Why, if yer tried to lift it, it 'ud break yer bloomin' back.
'Ave yer slept in draughty billets, where the rats go chasing round?
Or where there ain't no billets, just on the cold wet ground?
'Ave yer ever seen the trenches, and the miseries wot's there?
'Ave yer seen a badly wounded man a-tearin' of his 'air?
'Ave yer seen a shell come over, and been near where it bust,
And maybe blown yer own best pal to particles of dust?
'Ave ye ever been out wirin' on a dark and rainy night?
'As the gas-alarm gong ever made yere 'air stand up with fright?
'Ave yer cowered on the fire-step when the sky's been rainin, shell,
Expecting every minute to find yourself in 'ell?
'Ave yer seen a stream of wounded agoin' to the base,
And 'ave yer seen the silent tears run down a strong man's face?
'Ave yer dug a grave at midnight, for 'im as was yer mate?
'Ave yer hoped and prayed that "Blighty" would be yer lucky fate?
I'd like to ask a lot more things, but 'avn't got the time.
Them bloomin' 'Uns 'ave been and gone an' sprung a bloomin' mine;
Just remember these last words - Don't sit down there and yelp,
But don the bloomin' khaki, and come out 'ere and 'elp.

-E. S.

* * * * *

INDIRECT TAXATION.

Brinker: "Yes, your wife's clothes have cost me a good bit of money."
Tinker: "My wife's clothes! What do you mean?"
Brinker: "Why, every time your wife gets a new gown, my wife must have one just as expensive."

APPENDIX 1

THE TYKE

PARLEZ VOUS?

Buckley had been at his best. Dump said he had done his worst, but it was certain he had had his fling, and had gone through the whole gamut. Simcoe's, Machonochies, the Fray Bentos people, not to mention Symingtons, owe him something for he had so nicely blended the whole of their respective products into one homogeneous whole that it was impossible for the most epicurean taste to detect that the regimental meat had gone over with the regimental vegetables to grace the Sergeants' Mess table instead of contributing to the "thick" part of the stew.

It was after pondering over the probable after-effects of a liberal portion of the stew. and after taking, solely as a stomachic, a demi's worth of Marthe's best, that I sat down to try and sneak forty winks, and, just as I reached a somnolent condition, in burst Dump.

"Just the fellow I'm seeking," he commenced. "I want to learn French, and I want to learn it badly." "You know it badly," I remarked, "otherwise you would not make the howlers you do, but, if you want to learn it, well, try Hugo's system." "Now you know what I mean," he continued. "I've backed another loser - a woman asked me if I'd like a drink of coffee, and I replied 'merci,' and bless me if she didn't put the coffee pot away. What I want to know is, if 'merci' doesn't mean 'thanks' what does it mean? Of course, you can sit there and grin, but I want to be 'in the know.' I've been many a time in a 'staminet and have had to sit as quiet as a fried egg while you have been exchanging a nice bit of 'back chat' with the old dear over the counter, and having a drop of something free, and saying 'Bon swanky' or something like it, and bumping your glasses together and having a nice old time of it. Now, my lad, I want to be in the know, and I don't want you to push me off with any book like 'What the British Soldier Would like to Say in French' or anything like it."

"Because that's not the tack at all."

"Fancy me going up to some nice 'mam' selle' and saying from the book, 'Good morning, miss, are there any Germans in the neighbourhood? Which road leads to the hospital? I am hungry. The man I met yesterday is the son of the man who left to-day.' A nice sort of conversation that. I don't think. She'd gas, scream, call for the police, and I'd find myself in the 'mush.', Now what I want is something like. 'Good morning, Miss; pleasant day, what? Nice day for a turn at the cinema, I'm sure you don't mind? Oh, no; I'm not married by any means, I'm too young to suffer.' and so on.

"Now there was a bit of sense in old Mohammed's book, 'Curse words, and how to use them,' the one we bought in Egypt. Anyone could soon get the hang of that, and I learnt 'Himshy Yalla' in no time. Now the blooming kids out here don't *compris* 'Himshy Yalla' or even 'Taala Hina.' A nice lot of ignorant blokes, I think. Any darned kid in Egypt knew 'Himshy Yalla.'

"But Egypt's not France, and what I want is to get a real hang of the 'bat' and blow this 'compris!' business. A nice sort of a carry on it is and not 'arf. 'Compris eggs, madame? Oui? Then quatre eggs.' Old Sowden killed the 'compris' game with his usual 'me come back in half an hour for oofs and chips, beaucoup, madame, compris?' and when she said 'No, compris' he'd look at you and say in disgust 'Well, I'm blowed, they don't understand their own bloomin' lingo.'

" No, what I want is to give it to them, in their own style, hot and strong, thick and heavy, and you call tell me a few good cuss words as well, when we get going, and I think we'll start straight away, d'yer compris?"

" No compris," I replied.

" I see, a sort of frightened I'm going to do you out of the business affair, I guess; and you call yourself a friend of the poor, and you can't teach a chap a bit of French, so that he can help to keep up the 'Entente Cordiale.' It is mean, that's what it is, and I've a good mind to write home and tell your parents and all of 'em what sort of a carry-on you're having, a'clinking yer glasses and saying 'Bon Swanky,' and if I knew what you were talking about to 'em I'd tell 'em that as well. I'd put a spoke in the wheel, and you can sit there and smile, but I'd stir 'em up, and it would take a ton of writing and a month of Sundays to settle it. But, then, it's no use worrying; the poor must always be put on, I expect, and I fancy if I did know a bit of French I'd land myself in the cart and soon be in the 'mush.' D'yer compris?"

"I compris," I replied. DUX.

OUR CONCERT.

Amid the stress of these days of strenuous warfare there are those occasional times-always welcome - when one can stay and rest awhile,and for a short period put on one side the cares and-worries of the campaign and give one's self up torecreation and enjoyment . On these occasions,whenever possible, concerts are held, and before going any further one must pay tribute to the unbounded enthusiasm and untiring efforts of Pte.W. Guilfoyle in the organisation and management of these pleasing functions. Such an event took place on Easter Saturday evening in the Cinema Theatre of the little village in which we were billeted. The chair was occupied by Regimental-Sergeant-Major A. E. Oddy, who made a most efficient and genial M.C. of the proceedings, which were opened by a selection from the band (under the conductorship of Drum-Major Allison) entitled the "Bin-Boys," which received a most enthusiastic welcome from a crowded and appreciative audience. The next item was a song by Pte. Core, of the Stretcher Bearer Section, who gave an accomplished rendering of " Two eyes of grey." Pte. North, in an impersonation of Mr. Bransby Williams as Fagin the Jew, from Charles Dickens's "Oliver Twist," created a most excellent impression. Pte. R. Bell followed with an old favourite, "Down by the old mill stream," the chorus of which was lustily taken up by all the assembly. After this we had something rather out of the ordinary for a concert programme in this part of the world. Pianos are not, as a rule, part of a fighting Battalion's kit, and consequently the use of one is somewhat rather of a luxury. Pte. Midgley - a pianist of no mean order - delighted the company with a beautifully-played pianoforte selection. We hope the opportunities of hearing Pte. Midgley will be more frequent in the future. Following this came a delightful duet by Ptes. Core and Peel, entitled " The larboard watch," which was very tastefully given. The next item was a selection by the band, entitled "Joyland," and comprised the latestchoruses of the all the popular songs of the day - "Big blue eyes," "While the Angelus is ringing," " At the fox trot ball," "A little bit of heaven," "Baby doll," and "Virginia" were among the items rendered, and they received prompt and lusty support from the audience, who let themselves go to the full extent of their vocal powers. In fact, the selections by the band were easily the most appreciated items of the programme, and we have never heard them to better advantage than on this occasion. After this we had the privilege of hearing one of our Artillery friends, in the person of Bombdr. Alderton, who gave a very sweet and impressive rendering of " Thora," and, to satisfy the demands of his audience, sang the "Blind boy" as an encore. One of the most popular items of the evening was Pte. Beasley, who sang very effectively "Delecie," and in response to a persistent demand for an encore gave an old favourite, "Mother," in which an audience heartily joined. Our next item was by another visitor, Lieut. Hawkins, of Manchester, who sang "Somerset" in a manner most pleasing to his audience, and in response, by way of encore, gave us" The little Irish girl." Pte. Stevenson followed with "Let Stammering Sam sing," and Pte. Raynor most effectively gave a very pleasing item, "Some-where in Sunset Land," for which he was recalled, and gave "When you come home." Pte. Whaller brought the programme to a close with a most pleasing effort entitled "The old sexton," and the evening's entertainment finished with the National Anthem.

R. S. M. Oddy made a most effective chairman, and the thanks of the Battalion are due to all the artistes, to the Band, and to all who in any way helped to make up a most pleasant and enjoyable evening.

"MUSICIAN."

"SPARE PARTS."

He is a noble beast. He stand s fully 12 hands in his stocking feet, and dozes peacefully while the shells rip hairs from his tail, and playfully flick his ears. His is a calm temperament; nothing disturbs his serenity. His neck is beautifully arched, and the Arab strain in his blood is plainly discernible in his action. He is undoubtedly a high stepper, and in every movement of his supple limbs the muscles roll and quiver in a manner characteristic of his noble sire. His pedigree you will see is beyond question - Bloomsbury Ranker, out of Flatulent Flora, twice removed.

His eye is clear, very clear, when it is open, but it is seldom open. He has been known to slumber while on the trot, and you will gather from this that he has been known to trot. In fact, he once executed quite a small gallop, when a groom put a hot potato under his tail. His name is "Spare Parts," and never was a name so well deserved. He has been the charger of the L. G. O. and together they are a wonderful pair.

To-day there is not a dry eye in the Battalion. "Spare-Parts" has received his movement orders. He is reclaimed by his old fighting unit in the cavalry. It was a great sight to see him receive the news. His splendid chest heaved convulsively, the veins stood out on his forehead like those of a Derby Winner. His mane bristled, and his tail oscillated like the rudder of a canal barge ... Now I see one glorious eye open. His withers and shoulders quiver in ecstasy, and his noble frame is still. Hush; "Spare Parts" is asleep.

J. M. B

* * * * *

The statement that President Wilson has gone to war owing to the increased cost of paper making it impossible for him to continue writing notes is not confirmed in Official Circles.

APPENDIX 1

THE TYKE 19

OVERHEARD IN NO MAN'S LAND. (An Actual Fact).
Last Draft (as "Dud" Shell splashes in shell hole full of water): Say, mate! Was that one of those "Tear Shells" they talk about ?

"OVERHEARD."

Scene: Hotel Luxuria, W., when Jinks and Binks, after a far from scanty lunch, are enjoying a well conditioned cigar. Jinks owns a munitions factory, and Binks has property.

Jinks (unfolding the Times): " Well, we are doing quite well now."

Binks (looking up from his Daily Mail): "Rather .I think we've got 'em."

Jinks (contentedly drawing at his cigar): I really think we are going to get things quite our own way. I see the Daily Mail says troops are asking not to be taken out of the line."

Binks (sipping his liqueur): "We must throw every man in and push for all we are worth. Every man under 46 ought to be in the firing line now," (Binks is 47.)

Jinks: " Everyone under 50 should be there. Splendid thing for development of character." (Jinks is 51.)

Binks (aggressively): " We must preserve the nation's leaders, else our property and principles will suffer after the war. (Somewhat sarcastically) Still after what you say, even bachelors over 50 might be spared. (Jinks is a bachelor).

Jinks (rather huffily) : " That depends (adding, as an apparent afterthought). " By the way, are your boys still busy ? "

Binks (testily) : " Yes, sir, they are." (Returns to his paper hurriedly). (Binks's elder son (24) married a Bishop's daughter, is private secretary to the Minister for the Suppression of Amusements for Soldiers on Leave, thereby becoming indispensable. The other son (22) has married a Peer's daughter, and this, after a dismal attempt at " business" has naturally qualified him for the post of Manager and Organiser of the Trench Weapons Department for the "Timbuctoo" contingent. He is therefore carefully preserved for home use).

A short silence ensues, when each looks up at the sound of movement. A khaki figure is seen leaving, who smiles somewhat grimly, and recollects that in two days he will be on his way back to the Western Front, for the "further development of his character."

-H. R. W.

* * * * *

Perhaps now we shall have some Yankee Do instead of so much "Yankee Doodle." We guess some .

Things We Want to Know.

If "Fatty" is still suffering from Hebuterneitis?

If he can supply the depth of the deepest dug-out in that village?

Who the Sergeant was who was photographed in a bearskin coat and steel helmet and full marching order?

If the photographer's shop was about as near the trenches as he is ever likely to get?

Who the Officer's servant was who, when home on pass, got his spurs mixed up with a lady tram conductor's skirt on the top of the car, and what came of it?

When the Canteen will have something to sell again?

Who the cook was who tried to brew tea with stew the other day?

If the same man did not one day sweeten the tea with salt?

Who sent two limbers for the mail when there was none?

What Company's Field Kitchen was it that sent four Mess Tins full of stew to "D" company to keep warm, as they wanted to get done?

What did Corporal Buckley say? "A" Dear me.

What Company Cooks sent for some eggs and then refused to allow the obliging one to cook his own? Oh "B" careful.

Why we never hear the "Company orderly men for washing water" as in Egypt?

And if in these days the man who used to shout it would still be a success at it if he tried again?

Where all those people have got to who promised us contributions?

The name and number of the man who, on seeing an Observation Balloon for the first time, asked "Is that a Zeppelin?"

Who stayed in bed until 10 o'clock, and caused a Battalion parade at 7 a.m. the next day in consequence?

If he would like to attach himself permanently to a Rest Camp?

If the next time the "Bing Boys are Here" the Band will kindly take them down the "Long Long Trail"?

Who the man was in a recent night alarm to parade in battle order and had to come back for his rifle?

If he generally goes to meet the Bosche in that fashion?

Whose Field Kitchen it was that had such nasty things said about it on the ten days' march that it broke down on the road? Wait and "C."

If the Regimental Stores were not lucky to be able to ride all the way?

If the "Star Spangled Banner" is the Kaiser's favourite selection?

Why they will call him "Charlie"?

If the L.G.O. did not find it difficult to "Stand to"?

And what was he looking for in the bucket?

Why Charlie insisted upon leaning against his superior officer?

If the C/O. is not an expert in the Terpsichorean Art?

Why the Major is so fond of Village Reconnaisance?

And if his heart is now in France, South Africa, or the wilds of Scotland?

Why the M.O. lunches occasionally with his French fellow practician, and if Madame is not the attraction?

INQUIRER.

For terms as to advertisements please write.
EDITOR: 2/Lt. J. JOHNSON, 16th West Yorkshire Regiment.
SECRETARY: Sergt. DRAKE, 16th West Yorkshire Regiment.
MSS. and Drawings to be submitted to Pte. L. HARDAKER, 16th West Yorkshire Regiment.

Printed and published by WILLIAM BYLES & SONS LTD., Kirkgate, Bradford.

APPENDIX 1

THE TYKE

Sometimes it is better to say little and think a lot. Some statesmen we know just now have said too much. A seat on the front bench is sometimes hard riding.

* * * * *

If cleanliness is next to godliness, the British army is well on the way to heaven.

* * * * *

The brewers now tell us beer is a food. A kind of soothing syrup, we presume. But if we can have meatless days, a good few beerless ones might shift the public-house Empire-builders on. A sort of stewing in their own juice.

* * * * *

An optimist is a man who can eat Army Stew and say he has had a good dinner. In our opinion he is also something else.

* * * * *

A pessimist is one of those persons who always see the black side of a bright achievement. Chiefly found in "Blighty."

* * * * *

A clean Field Kitchen does not always mean a good cook, but a good cook keeps one all the same.

AWFUL EXPERIENCE.

"How dreadful it must be," exclaimed Mrs Twickenbury, "to be sailing along quietly and suddenly see a peristyle pop out of the water."

* * * * *

Austria wishes to talk peace. The time is rapidly coming when the Allies will be talking of "Pieces." Austria will probably be one of these.

* * * * *

"Uneasy is the head that wears a crown" We should imagine the German Emperor has a pretty bad headache. He might even lose it yet.

* * * * *

Russian soldiers under the new Government will be allowed to smoke in the streets, travel inside trains, visit clubs and attend political meetings. There is also a very strong rumour that they will be allowed to go on fighting. - *Punch*.

* * * * *

If the great British public would think less about its stomach and more about its duty this war would soon be over. But some folk have apparently for their motto "No food, no fight." Our will would be turn it round. "No fight, no food."

APPENDIX 2: DOCUMENTS RELATING TO THE COURTS MARTIAL OF HERBERT CRIMMINS AND ARTHUR WILD

There are a number of documents in the Public Record Office which relate to the trial and conviction of these two soldiers. Some of the correspondence relates to delays resulting from difficulties in procuring witnesses. It should be remembered that these were the weeks immediately after the Somme Offensive. It should also be remembered that both the accused were volunteers. Reproduced here are the charge sheets for the two men, transcripts of the hand-written record of both trials, statements (seemingly conflicting) about their characters, the schedules of the proceedings (both of which contain recommendations for mercy), examples of some of the memos which recommended that the sentences be carried out, and reports from the Medical Officer that the executions had taken place.

APPENDIX 2

Documents relating to Field General CM25, Loisne Chateau, 21st August, 1916: the Court Martial of Private Herbert Crimmins

1. Charge Sheet for Private Herbert Crimmins

The accused, No. 18/313 Private Herbert Crimmins, 18th (Service) Battalion West Yorkshire Regiment, is charged with: - When on Active Service, deserting His Majesty's Service, in that he, at BUS-LES-ARTOIS, on the 30th day of June, 1916, after being warned for duty as a Ration Carrier, absented himself from his Battalion until 1 p.m. on the 4th day of July, 1916, when he gave himself up to the Military police at VIGNACOURT.
(Signed) H.Carter, Major, Commanding 18th (S) Bn. West Yorkshire Regt.

2. Transcript of the trial of No18/313 Pte H. Crimmins 18th (S) Bn W. YORK R.

Prosecution

1st Witness: 2nd Lieutenant J.R.Thornton, 18th (S) Bn W York R. sworn states:
On June 10th 1916 at BUS LES ARTOIS I was detailed to take charge of the ration dump in the assembly trenches and of the ration carriers. The accused Pte Crimmins was one of the ration carriers detailed.
From this date until June 30th we were continually taking stores, water ammunition etc from EUSTON dump to the ration dump in the Assembly trenches. Each man including the accused was duly instructed by me in his duties on July 1st the day of the attack. About noon on June 30th the ration party were issued out with extra ammunition. The accused Pte Crimmins was present. The ration party were then warned not to leave camp.
At 4 pm on June 30th I received orders to parade at 6 pm to proceed to the trenches. I sent the orderly Sergeant - Sergeant Breen - round to warn the ration party and subsequently received a report from him.
At 6 pm on the same date I was present at the roll call of the ration carriers and the accused Pte Crimmins was absent. The roll call was actually called by Corporal Wise. I did not see the accused Pte Crimmins again until late in the month of July.
Sergeant Breen was wounded on July 1st and is no longer with the Regiment.
The accused declined to cross examine the witness.

2nd Witness: No. 18/1128 Corporal T. Wise. 18th (S) Bn W. YORK R. sworn states:
About 12 noon on June 30th 1916 at BUS LES ARTOIS I personally warned the ration carriers including the accused Pte Herbert Crimmins to parade for the trenches at 5.45 pm thatnight.
At this parade I issued the accused with extra ammunition.
At 5.45 pm on the same date I called the roll of the ration carriers and the accused Pte Crimmins was absent.
I did not see the accused again until after the attack some days later when he was in the guard room.
The accused did not desire to cross examine this witness.
3rd Witness
No. 739 Sergeant H. Reader. Military Mounted Police, sworn states: -
About 1 pm on the 4th July 1916 I was on duty at VIGNACOURT when the accused Pte Crimmins gave himself up to me and stated that he was absent from 2 pm 30th June 1916. I detained him. The accused had no rifle equipment or ammunition when he gave himself up.
The accused declines to cross examine this witness.

Defence
1st Witness: The accused states on oath: -
On June 30th 1916 about 11 am at BUS LES ARTOIS I and my friend Pte Wild went out

to the estaminet and had something to drink. I then returned to camp for dinner about 12 noon, and afterwards returned to the same estaminet where we had more drink and stayed until closing time. We then wandered along a road three or four miles and went into a cornfield and there fell asleep.

When we woke up it was dusk and we were afraid to go back, and so went on to the village called BEAUQUESNE.

We eventually reached VIGNACOURT where Private WILD thought he had a brother. We intended to ask his advice. On enquiry we found he was not there so we gave ourselves up to the military police.

I am very sorry for what I did. I had not the slightest intention of deserting. My father has been in the Army twenty seven years and I have five brothers now serving abroad. I have been in the trenches both before and after this occurrence and tried to do my best.

Cross examined

Q. Did the drink you had so affect you that you did not know what you were doing from the time you left the Estaminet until you reached the cornfield ?
R. A. We could walk but the drink was in us.

2nd Witness for Defence: No. 18/1128 Corporal T. Wise 18th (S) Bn W. YORK. R., examined on his former oath states: -
The accused has been in my section since November 1915 and during that time has given no trouble whatever with me. He has been a very good soldier and very good in his work.

3rd Witness for Defence: 2nd Lieut J. R. Thornton. 18th (S) Bn, W. York. R., examined on former oath states: -
The accused is in my Company and I have known him for the last three months as a good character. I know of nothing against him. He has always worked well and on a recent tour in the trenches went out on wiring parties and did his work satisfactorily.

After the finding

2nd Lt. H. L. Dalley. 18th (S) Bn W. York. R. sworn states: -
I produce certified true copy of A.F.B122 of the accused and also manuscript A.F.B296 signed by the President and attached to the proceedings.
The accused declines to cross examine this witness.

3. Character statements

There are two statements as to the character of the accused Private Crimmins signed H. Carter, Commanding 18th Battn West Yorks, Regt.

A hand-written one with no date states: "I certify that the character of the accused, No. 18/313 Pte H. Crimmins, has been very good during his 16 months' service. There are no entries on his Field Conduct Sheet prior to this charge. The accused has been in custody since 4th day of July, 1916."

A typed one dated "22/8/16" states: "Reference Circular Memorandum on Courts-Martial, Part III, Section 1, Para. (b), Sub-Para. (i), the character of this man from a behaviour point of view is good; from a fighting point of view, indifferent. From evidence gathered from his Company Sergt-Major, he was of a nervous disposition in the trenches, and not of much use. He has served with the M.E.F. (Egypt) from 6th December, 1915, to 9th March, 1916, and with the B.E.F. (France) from 10th March, 1916, to the present time.
Reference Sub-Para. (iii), this soldier is a weak man, and as far as I can gather he has, in my opinion, been ledaway (possibly under the influence of drink) by Pte Wild. I think the crime was committed deliberately, nevertheless, as he has shown himself to be of a nervous disposition when in the trenches."

APPENDIX 2

4. Schedule of Court Martial No. 25

Date 21st August 1916. No. CM25
Name of Alleged Offender: No18/313 Herbert Crimmins 18th W. York. R.
Offence charged: "Sec: 12 I(a) When on Active Service deserting His Majesty's Service.
Plea: Not guilty
Finding, and if Convicted, Sentence: Guilty. To suffer death by being shot. With a strong recommendation to mercy on account of his exceptionally good character.

The Schedule is signed By J.D.Ingles, Convening Officer, and by H.H.Kennedy, President [of the Court]. Lower down in the column headed "Finding, and if Convicted, Sentence" appears the word: "Confirmed", *the signature:* "D. Haig", *the date:* "1 Sep:16".

5. Memo, dated 23rd August 1916, from Brigadier General J. D. Ingles, Commanding 93rd Infantry Brigade:

"The state of discipline of the 18th Battn West Yorkshire Regt is good. I recommend that the extreme penalty be inflicted in that the crime was committed deliberately."

6. Memo from Captain H. E. Yorke, RAMC, Medical Officer

I certify that No. 18/313 Private H. Crimmins of 18th West Yorkshire Regiment was executed by shooting at 5.51 a.m. on September 5th 1916 at LESTREM. Death was instantaneous.

Transcript of documents, reference WO71/495, from the Public Record Office. Reproduced with their kind permission.

Documents relating to Field General CM26, Loisne Chateau, 21st August, 1916: the Court Martial of Private Arthur Wild

1. Charge Sheet for Private Arthur Wild

The accused, No. 18/356 Private Arthur Wild, 18th (Service) Battalion West Yorkshire Regiment, a soldier of the regular Forces, is charged with: - When on Active Service, deserting His Majesty's Service, in that he, at BUS-LES-ARTOIS, on the 30th day of June, 1916, after being warned for duty as a Ration Carrier, absented himself from his Battalion until 1 p.m. on the 4th day of July, 1916, when he gave himself up to the Military police at VIGNACOURT.
(Signed) H.Carter, Major, Commanding 18th (S) Bn. West Yorkshire Regt.

2. Transcript of the trial of 18/356 Private Arthur Wild

Prosecution

1st Witness: J.R.Thornton, 2nd Lieutenant 18th (S) Bn W York R. sworn states: -
On June 10th, 1916, at BUS LES ARTOIS I was detailed to take charge of the ration dump in the Assembly Trenches and of the ration carriers. The accused Pte Arthur Wild was one of the ration carriers detailed.
From this date until June 30th we were continually taking stores, water, ammunition etc fron EUSTON Dump to the ration dump in the Assembly trenches.
Each man including the accused was duly instructed by me in his duties on July 1st the day of the attack.
About noon on June 30th the ration party were issued out with extra ammunition. The accused Pte Wild was then present. The ration party were then warned not to leave camp. At 4 pm on June 30th I received orders to parade at 6 pm to proceed to the trenches. On sending the Sergeant - Sergeant Breen - round to warn the ration party, he reported to me the absence of the accused Pte Wild.

At 6 pm on the same date on calling the roll of the ration carriers the accused Pte Wild was still absent. I was present at the roll call which was actually called by Corporal Wise. I did not see Pte Wild the accused again until late in the month of July.
The accused declined to cross examine the witness.

2nd Witness: No. 18/1128 Corporal T. Wise. 18th (S) Bn W. YORK R. sworn states: About 12 noon on June 30th 1916 at BUS LES ARTOIS I personally warned the ration carriers including the accused Pte Arthur Wild to parade for the trenches at 5.45 pm that night.
At 5.45 pm on that date I called the roll of the ration carriers and the accused Pte Arthur Wild was absent.
The accused declined to cross examine the witness.

Examined by the Court:

I issued the accused Pte Wild with extra ammunition at 12 noon that day on the same parade as that on which he was warned.
I did not see the accused Pte Wild again until after the attack some days later when he was in the guard room.
The accused did not desire to ask any questions.

3rd Witness: No. 739 Sergeant H. Reader. Military Mounted Police, sworn states: About 1 pm on the 4th July 1916 I was on duty at VIGNACOURT when the accused Pte Arthur Wild gave himself up to me and stated that he was absent from 2 pm 30th June 1916. I detained him.
The accused did not desire to ask any questions.

Examined by the Court:

The accused Pte Wild was not in possession of equipment rifle or ammunition when he gave himself up.
The accused declines to ask any questions on this.

Defence

1st Witness: The accused states on oath: -

Early in June 1916 when my battalion were in the trenches at COLINCAMPS, I was working in a sap leading out from the front line trench at night, when a "coalbox" landed alongside me and exploded. I was severely shaken by this and taken out of the sap to a dugout of the Company Commander, when after being given tea I was sent to my dugout to rest.
I was excused after that from going into the front line trench for the rest of the battalion's tour in the trenches. On returning to hutments I was excused working parties in the front trenches by my Company Commander. I did see the Medical Officer who gave me some pills and said I should be better in a few days.
I saw the Medical Officer owing to being unable to stand the noise of shellfire when going up to the trenches.
I am very sorry for what I have done. I had no intention of deserting. I and my friend went out on the 30th June 1916 and had something to drink about 11 am.
We returned to camp for dinner and then went back to the Estaminet where we had been in the morning and stopped there until closing time. We wandered along a road into a cornfield and there fell asleep. We did not wake up till it was getting dark. We saw a village which we went to and found it was BEAUQUESNE.
I had a brother stationed at VIGNACOURT so I intended to go there, tell him everything and then give myself up.
On arrival there I found that my brother had moved so I gave myself up.

APPENDIX 2

Cross examination by the Prosecutor
I did not report sick after the explosion of the "coalbox" as I was allowed to rest by my Company Commander.
Q. Did you on any occasion after being made a member of the ration party have occasion to report to the Medical Officer?
A. No.
Q. How far do you think the cornfield where you slept was from BUS?
A. About 3 or 4 miles, I think.
Q. Why did you on waking up when it was getting dark not return to BUS?
R. Because I was frightened of the consequences of my absence and also thought I should not be able to stand the noise of guns.

2nd Witness for the Defence: No. 47. Private C Onam. 18th (S) Bn W. York. R., sworn states:

On one occasion in June 1916 I was in a working party along with the accused Pte Wild near EUSTON dump when heavy shelling commenced. I then noticed the accused Pte Wild was bad with shellshock so I reported him to the Officer in Charge who told me to take him straight back to camp which I did. By shellshock I mean that he was all of a shake and ducked and quivered at every shell.

3rd Witness for the Defence: No. 1267 Sergeant Hustwick. 18th (S) BnW.York. R., sworn states:
Early in June 1916 the accused was working under me in a sap at night in the front line trenches at COLINCAMPS, when the Enemy sent over three minenwerfers which landed wery close. I had to send the accused Pte Arthur Wild out of the sap as he was so shaken with shellshock and I did not see him again that night.

4th Witness for the Defence: 2nd Lieut J. R. Thornton. 18th (S) Bn, W. York. R., examined on former oath states: -
Early in June 1916 the accused Pte Wild was in the front trenches at COLINCAMPS when some "coalboxes" landed near him. He was taken out with shellshock and I assisted to get him out.
On another occasion on a later date whilst going up on a working party to the assembly trenches from EUSTON dump, shelling was going on and the accused Pte Wild, who was on of the party of which I was in charge, gave way completely and I sent him back to camp at BUS. I reported the matter to the Company Commander but do not know what steps he took.
I have known the accused Pte Wild for nearly three months and he has never given any trouble except on the occasion in question. Recently he has been in the trenches again. He behaved alright in the support trench and on one occasion formed one of a wiring party when he did his job as well as anyone else.

5th Witness for the Defence: No. 18/1128 Corporal T. Wise. 18th (S) Bn W. York R., examined on former oath states:
The accused Pte Wild is in my section and has been since we were in FOVANT in November 1915. And during the whole of that time I have found him a good worker and a good soldier.

After the finding

2nd Lt. H. L. Dalley. 18th (S) Bn W. York. R. sworn states: -
I produce certified true copy of A.F.B122 of the accused Pte Wild and manuscript A.F.B296 signed by the President and attached to the proceedings. The accused Pte Wild has been in custody since 4th July 1916.
The accused declines to cross examine the witness.

3. Character statements

There are two statements as to the character of the accused Private Wild signed H. Carter, Commanding 18th Battn West Yorks, Regt.

A hand-written one with no date states: "I certify that the character of the accused, No. 18/356 Pte A. Wild, has been very good during his 16 months' service. There is one entry on his Field Conduct Sheet, dated 22.11.15, for: Late on Company Parade. The accused has been in custody since 4th day of July, 1916."

A typed one dated "22/8/16" states: "Reference Circular Memorandum on Courts-Martial, Part III, Section 1, Para. (b), Sub-Para. (i), this man has always been of a rather lazy disposition, and one who needs driving the whole time to get the full amount of work out of him. Of his previous conduct in action I know nothing, except that he has never done anything exceptionally good. The case of shell-shock which is mentioned in the evidence was nothing serious, as I happened to be in the front line trench myself at the time. He has served with the M.E.F. (Egypt) from 6th December, 1915, to 9th March, 1916, and with the B.E.F., (France) from 10th March, 1916, to the present time. Ref. Sub-Para. (iii), in my opinion, of the two men Crimmins and Wild, Wild was the stronger character, and I think undoubtedly deserted deliberately, with the sole object of avoiding further active service."

4. Schedule of Court Martial No. CM26

Date 21st August 1916. No. 26
Name of Alleged Offender: No18/356 Arthur Wild 18th W. York. R.
Offence charged: "Sec: 12 I(a) When on Active Service deserting His Majesty's Service
Plea: Not guilty
Finding, and if Convicted, Sentence: Guilty. To suffer death by being shot. With a strong recommendation to mercy on account of the nervous condition of the accused due to the explosion of the trench mortar projectile in the near vicinity of the sap in which he was working in the front line trench in the COLINCAMPs section in the early days of June 1916.

The Schedule is signed by J.D.Ingles, Convening Officer, and by H.H.Kennedy, President [of the Court]. Lower down in the column headed "Finding, and if Convicted, Sentence" appears the word: "Confirmed", *the signature:* "D. Haig", *the date:* "1 Sep:16".

5. Memo, dated 23rd August 1916, from Brigadier General J. D. Ingles, Commanding 93rd Infantry Brigade:

"The state of discipline of the 18th Battn West Yorkshire Regt is good.
I recommend that the extreme penalty be inflicted in that the crime was committed deliberately."

6. Memo from Captain H. E. Yorke, RAMC, Medical Officer

I certify that No. 18/356 Private A. Wild of 18th West Yorkshire Regiment was executed by shooting at 5.51 a.m. on September 5th 1916 at LESTREM. Death was instantaneous.

Transcript of documents, reference WO71/496, from the Public Record Office. Reproduced with their kind permission.

APPENDIX 3 : MAPS

MAP 1: 93rd Infantry Brigade objectives, July, 1916: Page 26 onwards.
MAP 2: British positions facing Serre, July, 1916: Page 26 onwards.
MAP 3: Neuve Chapelle, July/August, 1916: Page 50 onwards.
MAP 4: Givenchy, September, 1916: Page 54.
MAP 5: Hebuterne & Rossignol Wood, February, 1917: Page 57 onwards.
MAP 6: Gavrelle, May, 1917: Page 73 onwards.
MAP 7: Arleux, July, 1917: Page 89 onwards.
MAP 8: Mericourt, August, 1917: Page 92 onwards.

Notes on Map References:

At the time of the First World War, British Army maps were divided into large squares bearing large letters, A, B. C, D, etc. These squares were sub-divided into small squares numbered 1 to 30 or 1 to 36, depending on the scale. These squares were further sub-divided into four minor squares identified, left to right a, b, c, d, the sides of which were then divided by ten.

Thus, to find the location of map reference C30b 6.9, one found the large square 'C', then the small square 30, then the sub-division 'b'. Finally, counting six-tenths west to east and eight-tenths south to north, one arrived at the exact location on the map.

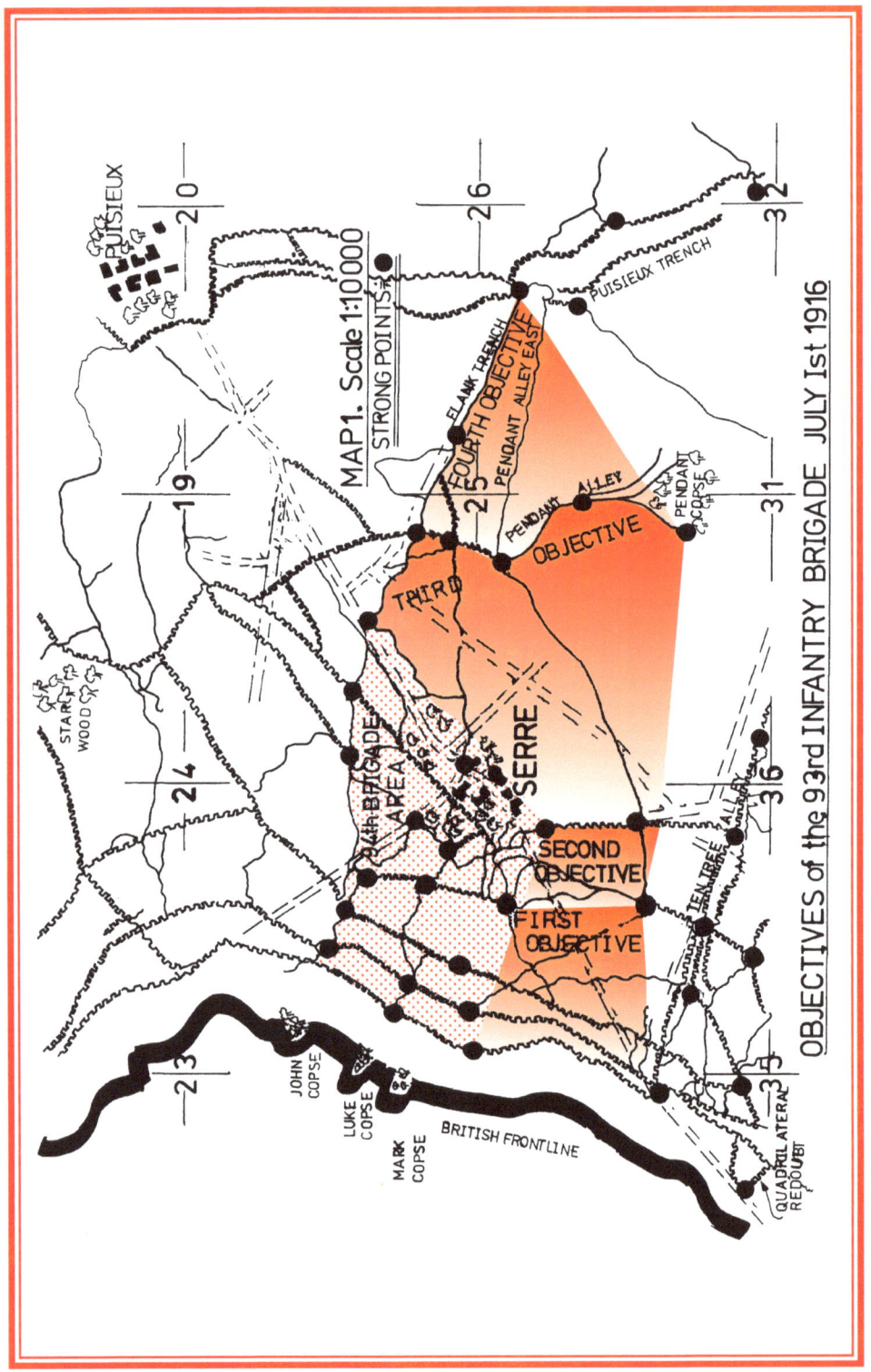

APPENDIX 3

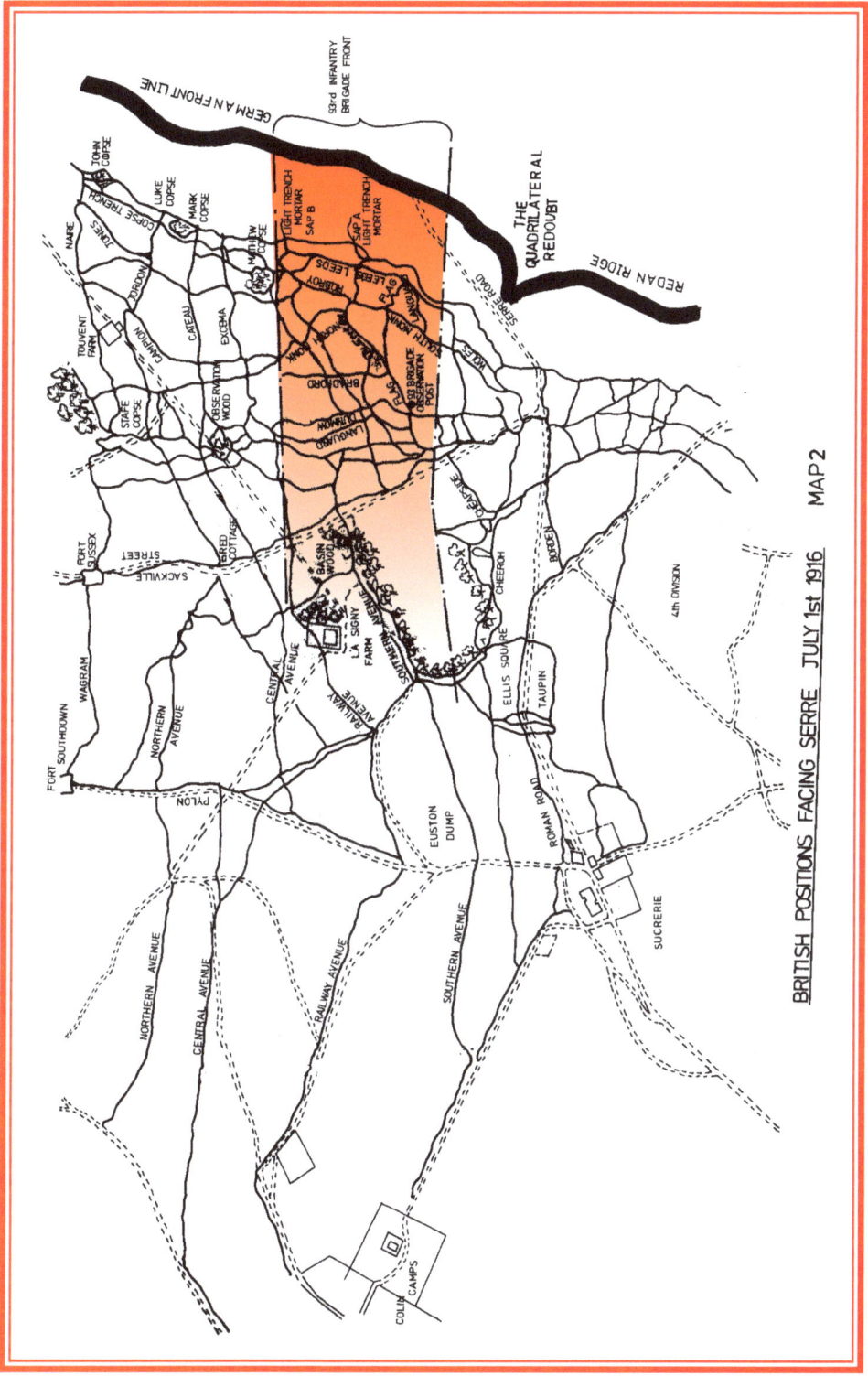

BRITISH POSITIONS FACING SERRE JULY 1st 1916   MAP 2

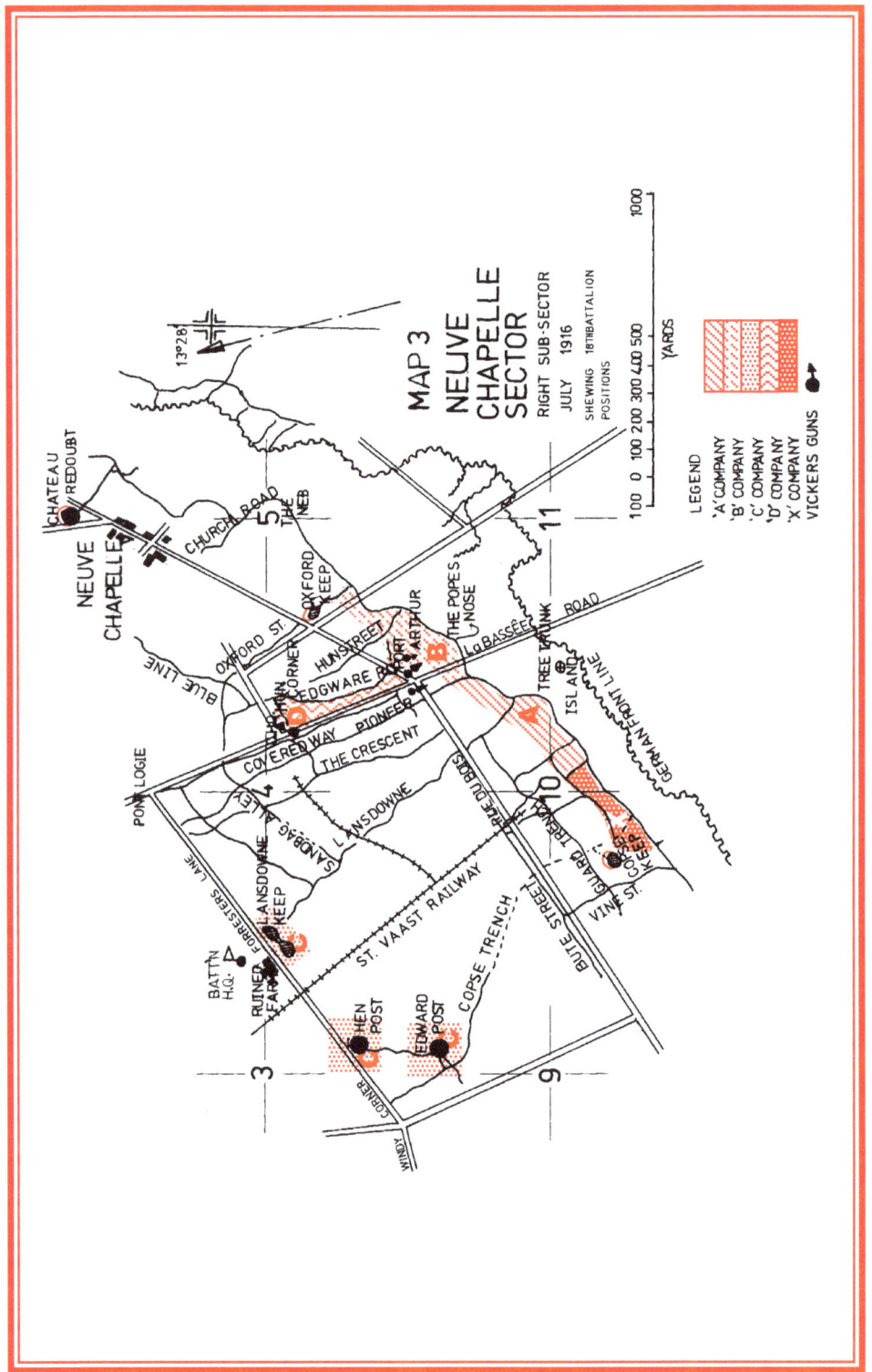

APPENDIX 3

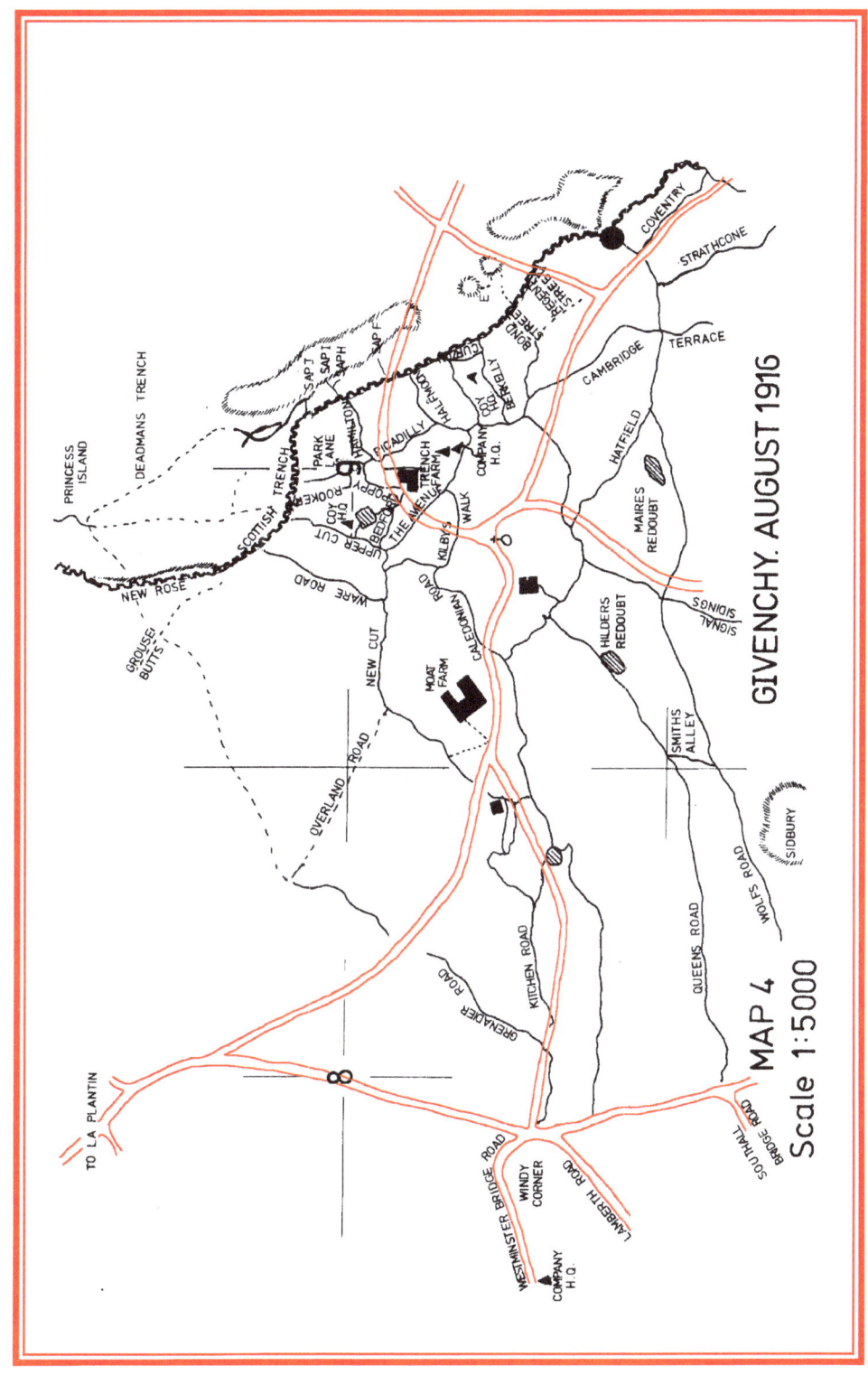

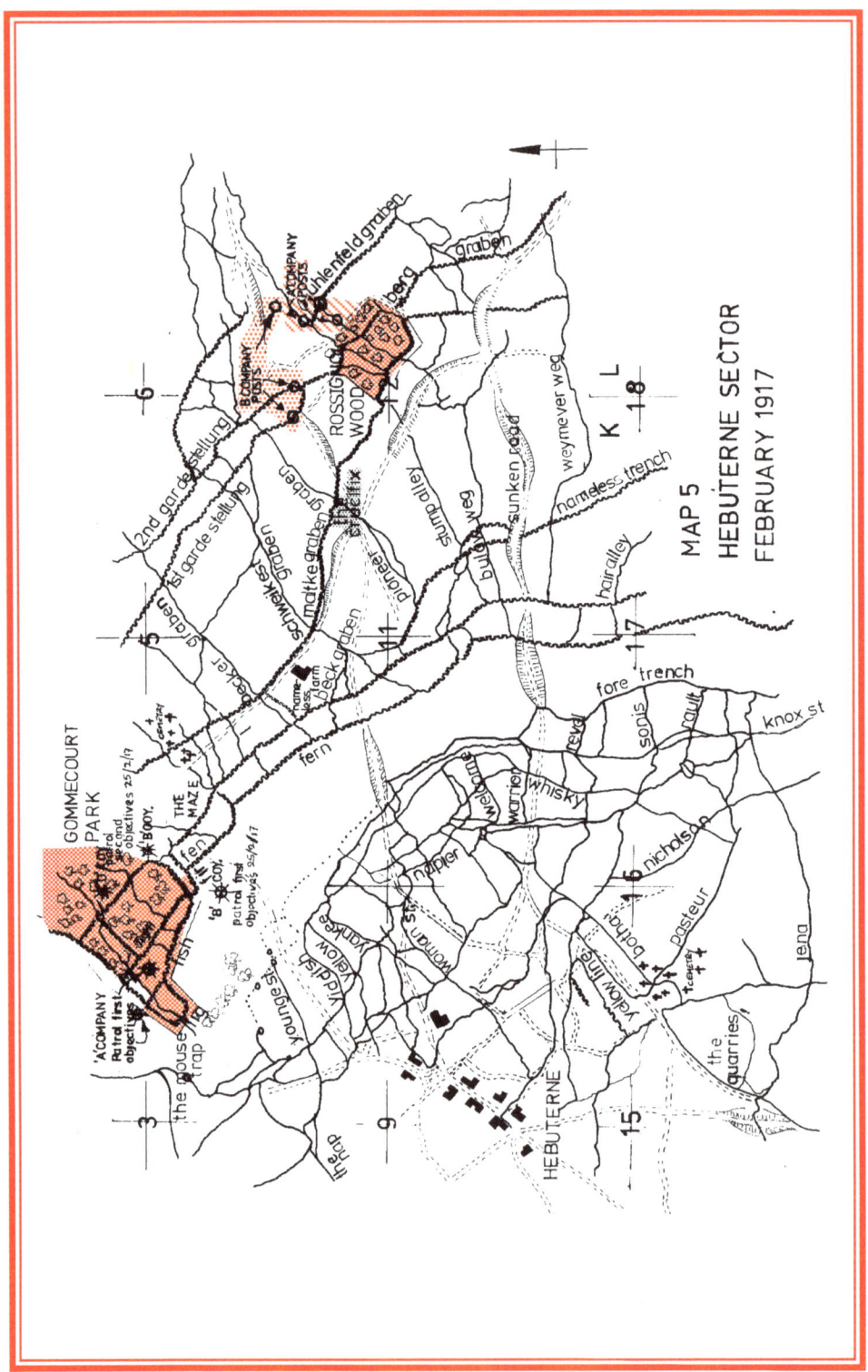

APPENDIX 3

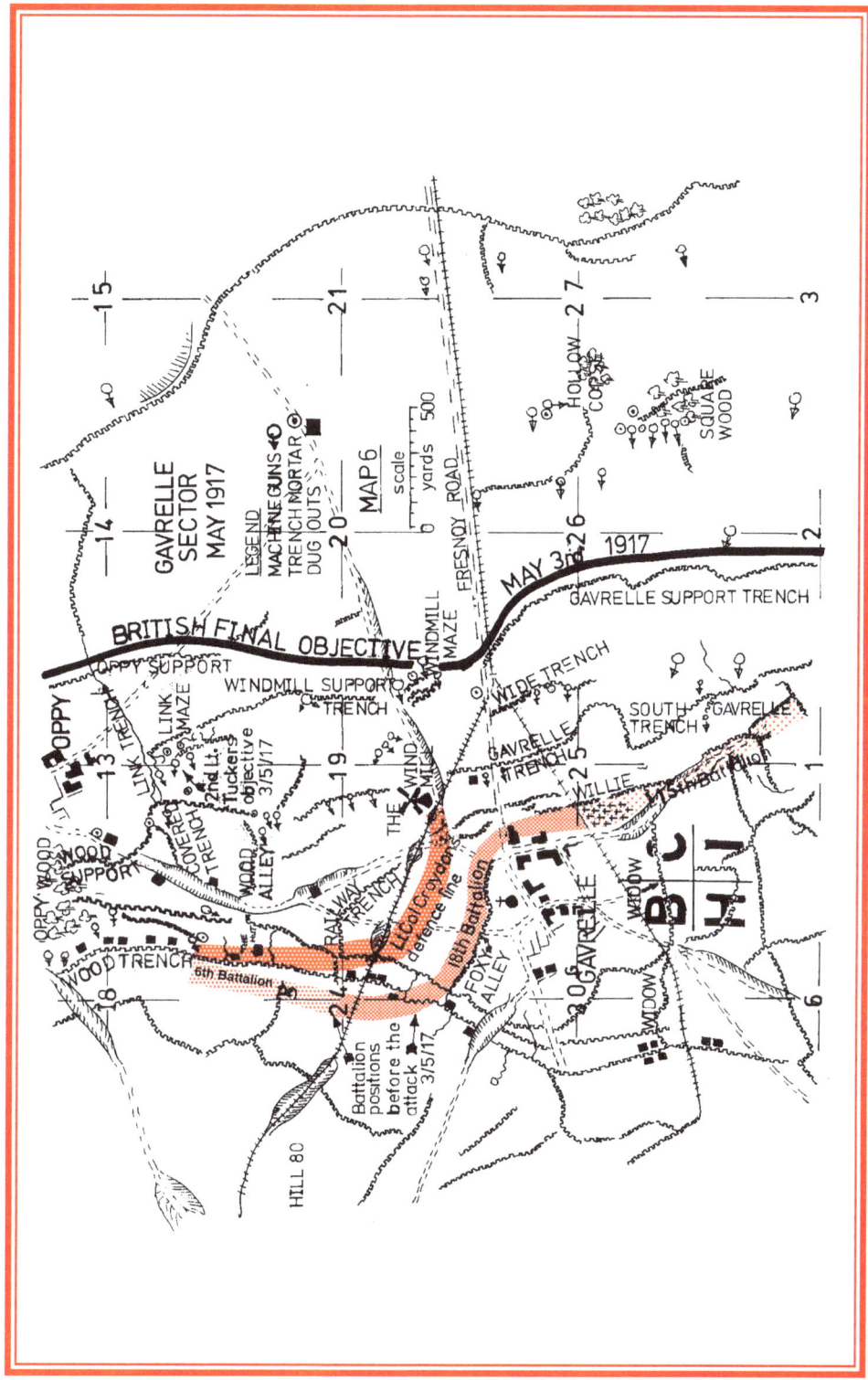

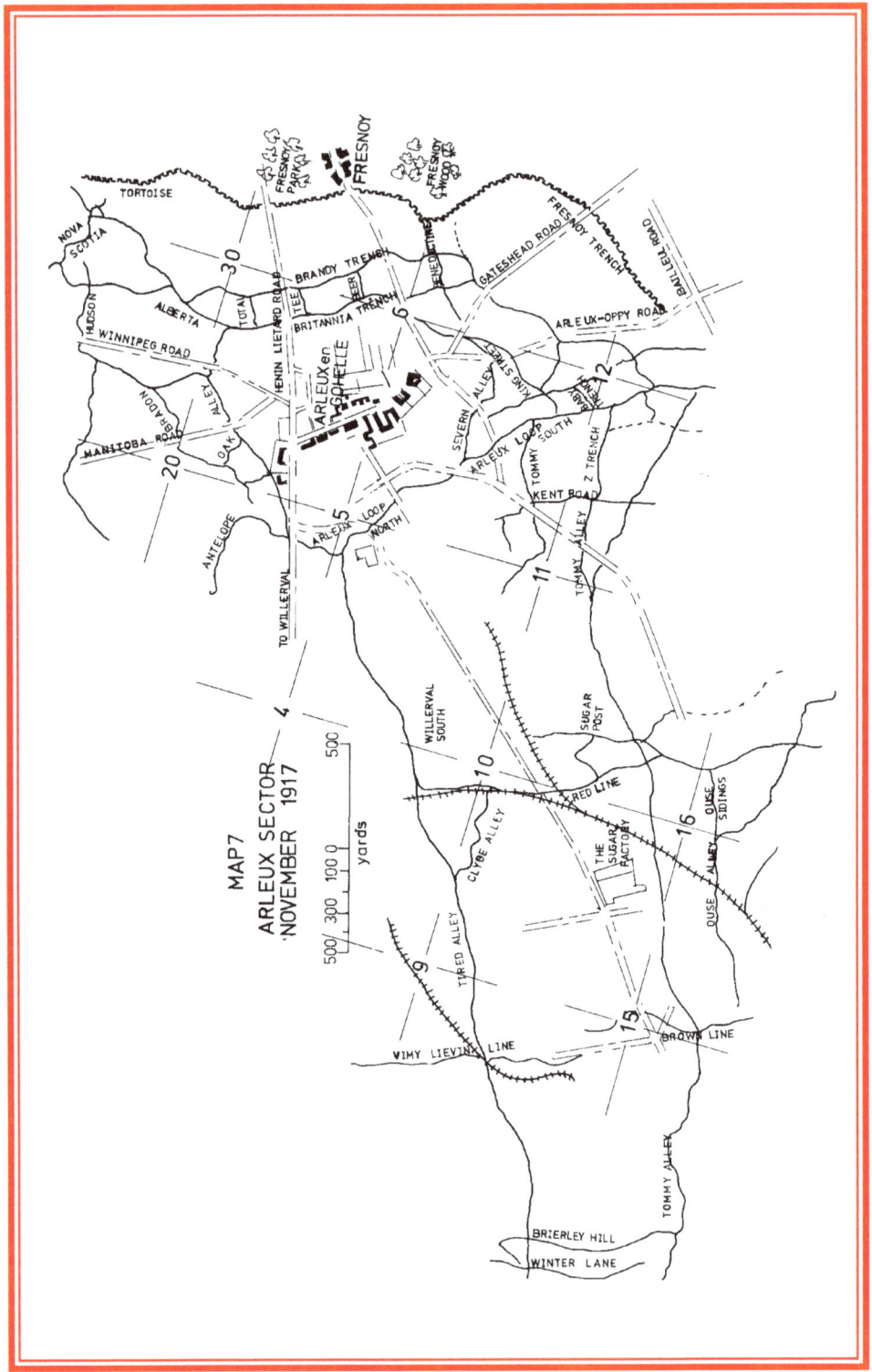

APPENDIX 3

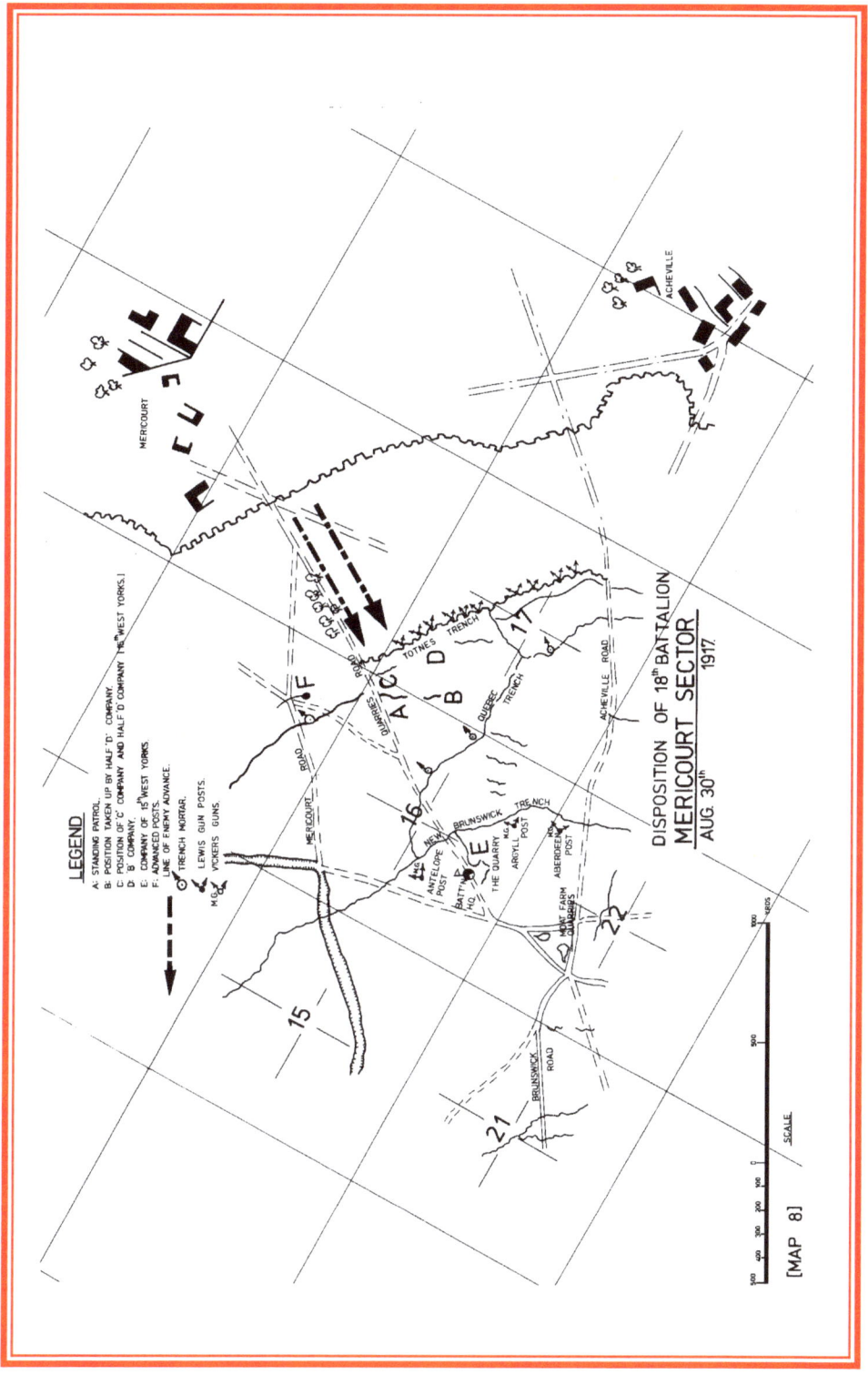

APPENDIX 4 : OFFICERS AND MEN WHO DIED IN THE GREAT WAR : EXTRACTS OF THE ENTRIES FOR THE 16TH AND 18TH BATTALIONS.

British Crown Copyright, 1991 MoD, reproduced with permission from the Controller of HMSO. Explanation of abbreviations: "b." - "born"; "e." - "enlisted"; "d." - "died"; "d. of w." - "died of wound"; "k. in a." - "killed in action"; "F. & F." - "France & Flanders (including Italy).

"To the world you were a soldier,
To me you were the world".
The father of Bradfordien Pte. Frederick Rowland Wade, First Lancs Regiment,
stands behind his son's headstone in a Somme cemetery.

APPENDIX 4

16th Battalion

Commissioned officers:
Armitage, Geoffrey Ambler, Capt. (Tp.), k. in a., 27/2/17.
Blagbrough, George Stanley, Major (Tp.), k. in a., 11/12/16, (att. from East Yorks. Regiment).
Clough, Alan, Temp. Capt., k. in a., 1/7/16.
Greville, David Onslow, 2/Lt., k. in a., 3/5/17.
Hyde, Charles Stuart, T/2/Lt., k. in a., 1/7/16.
Jackson, Robert William, M.C., 2/Lt., k. in a., 23/10/18 (att. from 1st Bn.).
Knight, Walter Foster, T/Lt., k. in a., 27/2/17 (att. from 14th Bn.).
Laxton, Reginald Earl,, T/2/Lt., k. in a., 10/6/16.
Long, Bernard Wilfrid, T/2/Lt., k. in a., 16/8/17.
Morant, Gerald Alexander Mackay, M.C., T/Capt., k. in a., 15/4/18 (att. 2/5th Bn)
Newlands, Sidney Barron, T/2/Lt., k. in a., 1/7/16.
Paus, Oscar Lionel, T/2/Lt., d. of w., 29/7/17.
Platnauer, Leonard Maurice, 2/Lt., d. of w., 3/5/17.
Pringle, Robert William Hey, T/Capt., k. in a., 1/7/16.
Ransome, Cecil Talbot, T/Lt., k. in a., 1/7/16.
Robb, John, 2/Lt., (Tp.) k. in a., 21/7/17.
Robinson, John Holdsworth, 2/Lt., k. in a., 1/7/16.
Russell, Henry, Capt., (Tp.) d. of w., 10/6/16.
Smith, Donald, Temp. Capt., k. in a., 1/7/16.
Stead, Ralph, 2/Lt. (Tp.) k. in a., 1/7/16.
Sutcliffe, Robert, 2/Lt., d. of w., 5/7/16.
Symonds, Frank James, Temp. 2/lt., k. in a., 1/7/16.
Tweedale, Eric, 2/Lt., (Tp.), K. in a., 1/7/16 (att. from 13th Bn.).
Webster, Michael Harold, Lt. (Tp.), k. in a., 1/7/16 (att. from 13th Bn.).

Non-commissioned officers and men:
Abrey, Charles Frederick, b. West Ham, London, e. Stratford, 9440, Pte, 27/2/17.
Ackroyd, George, b. Matlock, Derbyshire, e. Matlock, 19281, Pte, d. of w, F. & F., 1/3/17.
Ackroyd, Willie, b. Bradford, e. Bradford, Yorks, 16/682, Pte., k. in a., F. & F., 27/7/16.
Airton, George Beecroft, b. Yeadon, Yorks, e. Bradford, Yorks, 16/1343, Sgt., k. in a., F.& F., 1/7/16.
Aked, Clement, b. Cleckheaton, e. Bradford, (Eccleshill), 16/858, Pte., k. in a., F. & F., 1/17/16.
Alcock, William, b. Bradford, e. Bradford, Yorks, 33530, Pte., k. in a., F. & F., 3/5/17.
Alderson, Henry, b. Leeds, e. North Shields (North Shields), 19821, Pte., d. of w., F. & F., 1/3/17.
Ambler, Victor, b. Eccleshill, Bradford, Yorks, e. Bradford, 16/739, Sgt., k. in a., F. & F., 1/7/16.
Anderson, George, b. Ripon, e. Ripon, Yorks, 25060, Pte, d. of w., F. & F., 11/9/17.
Arkley, John, b. Sunderland, e. Sunderland, 4/8145, L/Cpl., k. in a., F. & F., 3/5/17.
Arnold, Edmund Gilyard, b. Eccleshill, Bradford, e. Bradford, 16/1264, Pte., k. in a., F. & F., 1/7/16.
Arundel Percy, b. Leeds, e. Leeds, 37527, Pte., d. of w., F. & F., 28/'8/17.
Arthington Ernest Harry, b. Bradford, e. Bradford, Yorks, 16/1/41. Pte., k. in a., F. & F., 1/7/16.
Aveyard, John Hodgson, b. Bradford, e. Bradford, Yorks, 16/1140, k. in a., F. & F., 1/7/16.
Backhouse, Sidney, e. Wetherby, Yorks, 31999, Pte., k. in a., F. & F., 13/11/16.
Baldock, Claude Henry, b. Nottingham, e. Nottingham, 41713, Pte., k. in a., F. & F., 3/5/17, formerly 49311, K.O.Y.L.I.
Balme, Benjamin, b. Clayton, Bradford, Yorks, e. Bradford, 16/736, Pte., k. in a., F. & F., 1/7/16.
Bannister, William, b. Bradford, e. Bradford, Yorks, 16/438, Pte., k. in a., F. & F., 24/4,/16.
Barker, Alfred, b. Goole, e. Bradford, Yorks, 16/188, Pte., k. in a., F. & F., 1/7/16.
Barker, Herbert, b. Bradford, e. Bradford, Yorks, 16/543, Pte., k. in a., F. & F., 1/7/16.
Barstow, Rawden, b. Cleckheaton, e. Bradford, (Cleckheaton), 16/1547, Pte., d., Home, 13/12/16.

THE BRADFORD PALS

Barton, Fred, b. Kippax, Yorks, e. Leeds, 19382, Pte., k. in a., F. & F., 3/5/17.
Bastow Frank, b. Bradford, e. Bradford, Yorks, 16/1244, Pte., k. in a., F.& F., 1/7/16.
Batchelor, James, b. Croydon, Surrey, e. London, 10612, Cpl., d. of w., F. & F., 28/2/17.
Batley, Bernard Walton, b. Dewsbury, Yorks, e. Bradford, 16/1228, Pte., d. of w., Home, 8/8/16.
Beanland, Joe, b. Bradford, e. Bradford, Yorks, 38323, Pte., d. of w., F.& F., 3/5/17.
Beard, Joseph, b. Bradfield, Sheffield, e. Sheffield, 11981, Pte., d. of w., F. & F., 10/11/16.
Bell, Clifford, b, Calcutta, India, e, York, 38333, Pte., k. in a., F. & F., 27/2/17.
Bell, Edward, b. Bradford, e. Bradford, Yorks, 16/1065, Cpl., k. in a., F. & F., 1/7/16.
Bellarny, Frank, b. Handsworth, Sheffield, e. Sheffield, 41705, L/Cpl., k. in a, F. & F, 3/5/17, formerly 27942, K.O.Y.L.I.
Bentley, Sargent, b. Low Moor, Bradford, e. Bradford, Yorks, 16/312, Pte., d. of w., F. & F., 4/7/16.
Bimrose, Alfred, e. Leeds (Leeds), 300105, Pte., k. in a., F. & F., 3/5/17.
Blackwell, Arthur, b. Bradford, e. Bradford, Yorks, 16/1147, Pte., d. of w., F. & F., 9/8/16.
Blakeborough, William Herbert, b. Bradford, e. Bradford, Yorks, 16/369, Pte., d. Home, 14/5/15.
Blakey, Percy, b. Bradford, e. Bradford, Yorks, 16/820, Pte., d. of w., F. & F., 24/4/16.
Bond, William, b. Bradford, e. Bradford, Yorks, 16/68, Cpl., k. in a., F. & F., 27/2/17.
Booth, William Crane, b. Valetta, Malta, e. Bradford, Yorks , 16/1029, Pte., d. of w., F. & F. 6/7/16.
Bottomley, Wilfred Norman, b. Halifax, e. Halifax, Yorks, 38370, Pte., k. in a., F. & F., 3/5/17.
Bowden, Joseph Frederick, b. Bradford, e. Bradford, Yorks, 16/925, Pte., k. in a., F. & F., 3/5/17.
Bower, John Arthur, b. Low Moor, Bradford, e. Bradford, Yorks, 16/263, k. in a., F. & F., 1/7/16.
Brabant, Edwin Walter, b. America, e. Leyton, London (Uxbridge), 52419, Pte., k. in a., F. & F., 12/4/18, formerly M./282462, A. S. C.
Braithwaite, Massee, b. Leeds, e, Leeds, 35628, Pte. k. in a, F. & F., 3/5/17.
Bramley, William, b. Halifax, e. Halifax, Yorks, 29291, Pte., k. in a., F. & F., 3/5/17.
Brayshaw, William Alan, b. Rylstone Skipton, e. Bradford, 16/1391, Pte., d., Home, 20/10/15.
Briggs, Albert, b. Clayton, Bradford, e. Bradford, Yorks, 16/1040, Pte., k. in a. F. & F., 1/7/16.
Broady, Michael, b. Staincliffe, Batley, Yorks, e. Bradford, 16/1628, Pte., k. in a. F. & F., 1/7/16.
Brook James, b. Elland, Yorks, e. Halifax, Yorks, 40194, Pte., k. in a., F & F., 13/11/16.
Buckborough, James Ernest, b. Bradford, e. Bradford, Yorks, 16/104, Pte, k. in a., F. & F., 1/7/16.
Buckley, Albert, b. Manningham, Bradford, Yorks, e. Bradford, 16/410, Pte., k. in a., F. & F., 1/7/16.
Bunclark, Walter Ernest, b. Torquay, Devon, e. Bradford, Yorks, 16/622, Sgt., k. in a., F. & F., 27/2/17.
Burnley Arthur, b. Idle, Bradford, e. Bradford, Yorks, 16/1585, Pte., k. in a., F. & F., 1/7/16.
Burrows, John, b. Bradford, e. Bradford, Yorks, 16/920, Sgt., d. of w., F.& F., 7/5/16.
Busfield, Whitehead, e. Pateley Bridge, Yorks, 32002, Pte., k. in a., F. & F., 13/11/16.
Calvert, Albert, b. Bradford, e. Bradford, Yorks, 16/381, Pte., d., F. & F., 28/11/18.
Carter, Jabez, b. Gomersal, Yorks, e. Liversedge, Yorks, 38796, Pte., k. in a., F. & F., 3/5/17.
Cartwright, Ned, b. Heckmondwike, Yorks, e. Bradford, 16/1572, Pte., k. in a., F. & F., 27/2/17.
Catlow, James William, b. Bingley, Yorks, e. Bradford, 16/1627, Pte. k. in a., F. & F., 27/2/17.
Cawthra, Arthur, b. Bradford, e. Bradford, Yorks, 26102, Pte., k. in a., F. & F., 9/11/16.
Chapman, Ernest, b. Bradley, Yorks, e. Huddersfield, 38308, Pte., k. in a., F. & F., 27/2/17.
Chilton, James, b. Kirby Fleetham, Yorks, e. York, 28145, Pte., d. of w., F. & F., 14/6/17.
Clayton, Ernest, b. Featherstone, Yorks, e. Doncaster, 40857, Pte., k. in a., F. & F., 29/7/17.
Clement, John Henry, b. Sheffield, e. Leeds, 24533, Pte., k. in a., F. & F., 13/11/16.
Clough, Squire, b. Bradford, e. Bradford, Yorks, 16/707, Cpl., k. in a., F. & F., 1/7/16.
Cockroft, William, b. Bradford, e. Bradford, Yorks, 16/1170, Pte., k. in a., F & F., 1/7/16.
Coe, Harold Glover, b. Pudsey, Yorks, e. Bradford, 16/130, Pte., k. in a., F. & F., 1/7/16.
Coles, Gerald Irvin, b. York, e. York, 37461, Pte., k. in a., F. & F., 3/5/17.
Constable, Alfred, b. Bradford, e. Bradford, Yorks, 16/514, L/Cpl., d. of w., F. & F., 27/6/16.
Cooper, Ernest, b. Elvington, Yorks, c, York, 32301, Pte., d., F. & F., 17/6/17.
Cooper, George, b. Bradford, e. Bradford, Yorks, 16/1443, Pte., k. in a. F & F., 1/7/16.
Cope, Edward, b. Queensbury, Bradford, Yorks, e. Bradford, 16/249, Sgt., k. in a., F. & F., 3,/5/17.
Core, Arthur, b. Skipton, Yorks, e. Keighley, Yorks, 28746, Pte., k. in a., F. & F., 3/5/17.

APPENDIX 4

Cording, John, b. Featherstone, Yorks, e. Featherstone, 43073, Pte., k. in a., F. & F., 21/7/17.
Cousins, Arthur, b. Sherburn-in-Elmet, Yorks, e. York, 19212, Pte., k. in a., F. & F., 27/7/16.
Crabtree, Leonard, b. Halifax, e. Bradford, Yorks, 16/609, Pte., k. in a., F. & F., 1/7/16.
Craig, Archibald, b. Stornaway, Ross, e. Fort George, Scotland, 16/1734, Pte., k. in a., F.& F., 3/5/17.
Craven, George Willie, b. Saddleworth, Yorks, e. Bradford, 16/806, Pte., k. in a., F. & F., 1/7/16.
Creek, Clifford, b. Leeds, e. Leeds, 38812, Pte., k. in a., F. & F., 5/12/17.
Creek, Luther, b. Keighley, Yorks, e. Bradford, 16/1240, Pte., d. of w., F. & F., 7/7/16.
Cromwell, Garfield, b. Bradford, e. Bradford, Yorks, 16/475, Pte., k. in a., F. & F., 1/7/16.
Crossland, Harry b. Bradford, e. Bradford, Yorks, 16/991, L/Cpl., k. in a., F. & F., 3/5/17.
Cryer, John Henry Ernest, b. Halifax, Yorks, e. Bradford, 16/863, Pte., k. in a., F. & F., 1/7/16.
Culling, William Alfred, b. Bradford, e. Bradford, Yorks, 16/904, Sgt., k. in a., F. & F., 27/7/16.
Cummins, George Henry, b. Whitby, e. Whitby, Yorks, 17168, Pte., k. in a., F. & F., 3/5/17.
Dadswell, Hugh Cecil, b. Wallingford, e. Bradford, Yorks, 16/397, Sgt., k. in a., F. & F., 1/7/16.
Dane, James Arthur, b. Liverpool, e. Bradford, Yorks, 16/821, Sgt., k. in a., F. & F., 3/5/17.
Dargue, Herbert, b. Dewsbury, e. Bradford, Yorks, 16/1043, L/Cpl., d. F.& F., 6/5/17.
Davies, Emest Jones, b. Pontefract, e. Bradford, Yorks, 16/177, Pte., k. in a., F. & F., 13/8/16.
Davis, Ernest Warr, b. Enfield, Middlesex, e. Pontefract, Yorks, 41667, Pte., d. of w., F. & F., 5/5/17, formerly 39625, K.O.Y.L.I.
Dawson, Thomas, b. Easby, Gt. Ayrton, Yorks, e. York, 38079, Pte., k. in a., F. & F., 3/5/17.
Day, Ernest, b. Leeds, e. Leeds, 37521, Pte., k. in a., F. & F., 21/7/17.
Deakin, Albert john, b. Kempsey, Worcs, e. Bradford, 20/96, Cpl.. k. in a., F. & F., 27/2/17.
Dearden, Ernest, b. Birdwell, Barnsley, e. Bradford , 16/283, Pte., d. of w., F. & F., 21/8/16.
Dixon, Parrington, b. Dent, Yorks, e. Bradford, Yorks, 16/391, Pte., k. in a., F. & F., 1/7/16.
Douglas, Charles, b. South Shields, e. Piccadilly, London, 38591, Pte., k. in a., F. & F., 27/2/17.
Dowson, John, b. Whitby, Yorks, e. Bradford, Yorks, 16/1198, Pte., k. in a., F. & F., 1/7/16.
Duce, Walter b. Bradford, e. Bradford, Yorks, 16/1084, Pte., k. in a., F. & F., 1/7/16.
Duncan, Thomas Thompson, b. Middlesborough, e. Bradford, 16/462, Pte., k. in a., F. & F., 1/7/16.
Durkin, Martin, b. Bradford, e. Bradford, Yorks, 20/219, Pte., d. of w., F. & F., 29/7/16.
Eades, William, b. St. Peters, Birmingham, e. Birmingham, 14344, Pte., k. in a., F. & F., 19/8/17.
Easterby, Albert, b . Bradford, e. Bradford, 16/745, Pte., k. in a., F. & F., 1/7/16.
Edmondson, Willie, b. Bradford, e. Bradford, (Manningham), 16/902, Pte., d. of w., Home, 11/11/16.
Ellis, Francis Wilfred, b. Bradford, e. Bradford, Yorks, 16/1591, Pte., k, in a., F.& F., 27/6/16.
Ellis, John Cyril, b. Bradford, e. Bradford, (West Bowling), 16/954, Pte., d. of w., F. & F., 5/7/16.
Elson, Charles Robert, b. Burton-on-Trent, e. Bradford, 16/1484, Pte., d. of w., F. & F., 12/6/16.
Emery, John William, b. Fenton, Staffs, e. Lichfield, 23721, Pte., d. of w., F. & F., 22/7/16.
Endersby, Harold, b. Farsley, Yorks, e. Leeds, 15/1518, Pte., k. in a., F. & F., 3/5/17.
England, William, b. Leeds, e. Leeds, 21435, Pte., k. in a., F. & F., 3/5/17.
Essex, Henry, b. Hull, e. Leeds, 31963, Pte., k. in a., F. & F., 10/11/16.
Fallon, Charles Henry, b. Bradford, e. Bradford, Yorks, 18/554, Pte., k. in a. F. & F., 3/5/17.
Farrar, Charles, b. Bradford, e. Bradford, Yorks, 16/ 637, Sgt., d, of w. F. & F., 2/3/17, D.C.M.
Fawthorpe, Harold, b. Bradford, e. Bradford, Yorks, 16/642, Pte., k. in a., F. &.F., 1/7/16.
Feather, Henry, b Keighley, e. Bradford, Yorks, e, 16/387, Cpl., k. in a., F. & F., 27/2/17.
Fenton, Arthur, b. Bradford, e. Bradford, Yorks, 16/239, Pte., k. in a., F. & F., 1/7/16.
Fenwick, Richard, b. Hull, e. York, 6130, Pte., k. in a, F. & F., 3/5/17.
Fethney, Harry, b. Bradford, e. Bradford, Yorks, 18/1420, L/Cpl., k. in a., F. & F., 1/7/16.
Fielden, John, b. Todmorden, Yorks, e. Halifax, 40225, Pte., k. in a., F. & F., 3/5/17.
Flatters, John Crowther, b. Wombwell, e. Thorne, Doncaster, 28497, Pte., k. in a., F. & F., 3/5/17.
Forder, Alfred, b. King's Lynn, Norfolk, e. Bradford, 16/921, Pte., k. in a., F. & F.,1/7/16.
Foster, Edwin, b. Halifax, Yorks, e. Bradford 16/530, Pte., k. in a., F. & F., 1/7/16.
Foster, William, b. Birstall, Yorks, e. Bradford (Batley, Yorks), 20/93, Cpl., k. in a., F. & F., 5/2/17.
Fowler, George Haugbton, b. Bradford, e. Bradford, Yorks, 16/1354, Pte., k. in a., F. & F., 1/7/16.
Fox, John Henry, b. Holbeck, Leeds, e. Huddersfield, Yorks, 38362, Pte., k. in a., F. & F., 3/5/17.

THE BRADFORD PALS

Friend, Albert Edward, b. Shorncliffe, Kent, e. York (York), 32815, Pte k. in a., F.& F., 13/5/17.
Frost, James William, b. Barnsley, Yorks, e. Cleckheaton, 16/1666, Pte., k. in a., F. & F., 1/7/16.
Fuller, George, b. Bradford, e. Bradford, Yorks, 16/1434, Pte., k. in a. F. & F., 1/7/16.
Galley, Alfred, b. Leeds, e. Leeds, 17124, Pte., k. in a., F. & F., 27/2/17.
Garbutt, Alfred Welburn, b. Leeds, e. York, 38675, Pte., k in a., F. & F., 27/2/17.
Garbutt, William, b. York, e. Bradford, Yorks, 16/1629, Pte., k. in a. F & F., 21/2/16.
Gatehouse, Fred, b. Leeds, e. Huddersfield, Yorks, 16/1577, Pte., d. of w. F. & F., 3/7/16.
Gaunt, Jonas. b. Leeds, c Leeds, 33435, Pte" k. in a., F.& F., 27/2/17.
Gee, Fred, b. Drighlington, Bradford, Yorks, e. Bradford, 16/1674, L/Cpl. k. in a., F.& F., 1/7/16.
Gibson, Albert, b. Wakefteld, Yorks, e. Leeds, 29529, Pte., k. in a. F. & F., 12/5/17.
Gibson, John Robert, b. Leeds, e. Leeds, 31965, Pte., k. in a., F. & F., 31/11/16.
Gilgan, James, b. Bradford, e. Bradford, Yorks, 16/947, Pte., d. of w. F.& F., 31/1/16.
Gledhill, John Taylor, b. Golcar, Yorks, e. Huddersfield, 40858, Pte., F.& F., 24/7/17,
        formerly 29/706, Northumberland Fusiliers.
Grainge, Edmund, b. Bradford, e. Bradford, Yorks, 16/834, Pte., d. of w. F. & F., 13/6/16.
Granger, William, b. York, e. York, 36533, Pte., d., F. & F., 15/3/17.
Gratwick, Albert, b. Osbaldwick, Yorks, e. York, 38619, Pte., d. of w. F. & F., 18/8/17.
Graves, Cecil, b. Horsforth, Yorks, c, Bradford, Yorks, 16/424, Cpl., k. in a., F.& F., 27/2/17.
Gray, Gerald, b. Bradford, e. Bradford, Yorks, 16/886, Pte., d., Home, 18/1/15.
Green, Albert Edward, b. Leeds, e. Leeds, 37480, Pte., k. in a., F. & F., 27/2/17.
Green, Thomas, b. Mitcham, Surrey, e. Huddersfield, Yorks, 38307, Pte., k. in a., F. & F., 27/2/17.
Greenhough, Frank, b. Bradford, e. Halifax, Yorks, 40195, Rflmn., d. of w., F.& F., 6/3/17.
Greenwood, Arthur, b. Manningham, Bradford, e. Bradford, 16/953, Pte., k. in a., F. & F., 1/7/16.
Greenwood, Bernard, b. Cornholme, Lancs, e. Todmorden, 38022, Pte., k. in a., F. & F., 27/2/17
Gregory, Norman Knight, b. Saltaire, Yorks, e. Bradford, 16/1288, A/Sgt., k. in a., F.& F., 12/5/17.
Grist, Charles, e. Sheffield, 16201, Pte., d., F. & F., 3/5/17, formerly 15190, East Yorks Regt.
Hainsworth, Leonard, b. Farsley, Leeds, e. York, 15481, Pte., k. in a., F. & F., 25/2/17.
Hale, Walter, b. Yeadon, Bradford, e. Bradford, Yorks, 16/828, Pte., k. in a., F. & F., 3/5/17.
Hall, Arthur, b. Leeds, e. Leeds, 37316, Pte., k. in a., F. & F., 27/2/17.
Hall, Joseph, b. Oakworth, Yorks, e. Keighley, Yorks, 16/1684, Pte., k. in a. F. & F., 1/7/16.
Halmshaw, Joseph, b. Cleckheaton, e. Cleckheaton, Yorks, 16/1474, Pte., k. in a., F. & F., 1/7/16.
Hamp, Frederick John, b. East Claydon, Winslow, Bucks, e. Harrogate, 12621, L/Cpl., k. in a., F. & F., 21/7/17.
Hand , Edgar, b. Bradford, e. Bradford, Yorks, 16/868, Pte., k. in a., F. & F., 3/7/17.
Hannan, Arthur, b. Leeds, e. Leeds, 35277, Pte., k. in a., F. & F., 27/2/17.
Hanson, Albert, b. Barnsley, Yorks, e. Bradford, Yorks, 16/1490, Pte., k. in a., F. & F., 1/7/16.
Hanson, Albert, b. Halifax, e. Halifax, Yorks, 32516, Pte., d. of w., F.& F., 12/5/17.
Hanson, Brinton, b. Bradford, e. Bradford, Yorks, 16/824, Sgt., k. in a., F. & F., 9/11/16.
Harbron, Albert, b. Bradford, e. Bradford, Yorks, 16/1145, Pte., k. in a., F. & F., 1/7/16.
Hardwick, Eldred, b. Halton, Leeds, e. Leeds, 14061, Pte., k. in a., F. & F., 3/5/17.
Hardy, Herbert, b. Bradford, e. Bradford, Yorks, 16/1161, Pte., k. in a., F. & F., 27/2/17.
Hargrave, Charles, b. Leeds, e. Leeds, 32840, Pte., d. of w., F. & F., 2/5/17.
Hargreaves, Thomas Edward, b. Bradford, e. Bradford, Yorks, 16/1568, Pte., k. in a., F. & F., 1/7/16.
Harris, Frederick, b. St. Pancras, London, e. London, 35957, Pte., d., Home, 29/12/16.
Harrison, George Tate, b. Bradford, e. Bradford, Yorks, 16/1233, L/Cpl., k. in a., F.& F., 13/11/16.
Harrison, Philip James, b. Tealby, Lincs. e. Bradford, Yorks, 16/1001, Pte., k. in a., F.& F., 1/7/16.
Harrison, Willie, b. Bradford, e. Bradford, Yorks, 16/804, Sgt., k. in a., 27/2/17.
Hart,Ted. Edward, b. Hackney, London, e. Finsbury Park, London, 20/302, Pte., k. in a., F. & F., 3/5/17,
        formerly 22180, Suffolk Regt.
Hartley, George Thomas, b. Hebden Bridge, Yorks, e. Halifax, Yorks, 38102, Pte., k. in a., F.& F., 27/2/17.
Hartley, James, b. Oswaldtwistle, Lancs, e. Halifax, (Barnoldswick), 38110, Pte., k. in a., F. & F., 27/2/17.
Hartley, Walter, b. Bradford, e. Bradford (Clayton-le-Moors, Accrington), 16/232, Pte., k. in a., F.& F. , 1/7/16.
Hatfield, Herbert, b. York, e. York, 37533, Pte., k. in a., F. & F., 3/5/17.

APPENDIX 4

Hawkesworth, Richard, b. Hunslet, Leeds, e. Bradford, 16/167, Sgt., k. in a., F. & F., 1/7/16.
Haxby, Lofthouse, b . Armley, Leeds, e. Leeds, 12722, Pte., k. in a., F. & F., 3/5/17.
Heyes, Nathan, b. Leeds, e. Leeds, 3/9260, Pte, k. in a,, F. & F., 3/5/17.
Hirst, John Wade, b. Leeds, c, Bradford, Yorks (Bradford), 16/1452, Pte., d. of w., F.& F., 5/7/16.
Hodgson, Alfred, b. Clayton, Bradford, e. Bradford, Yorks, 16/926, Pte., k. in a., F.& F., 1/7/16.
Hodgson, James Frederick, b. Bradford, e. Bradford Yorks, 16/733, Pte., k. in a., F.& F., 11/8/16.
Holdsworth, Arthur, b. Lincoln, e. Lincoln, 40423, Pte., k. in a., F. & F., 3/5/17, formerly, 3228, 4th Lincs Regt.
Holdsworth, Harry, b. Bradford, e. Halifax, Yorks, 32158, Pte., k. in a., F. & F., 27/2/17.
Holgate, William Arthur, b. Sawley, Clitheroe, Yorks, e. Keighley, 28522, Pte., d., F. & F., 29/12/18.
Holmes, Clough, b. Bradford, e. Bradford, Yorks, 16/1121, Pte., k. in a., F. & F., 1/7/16.
Holmes, Wilfred, b. Addingharn, Yorks, e. Bradford, 16/713, Pte., k. in a., F. & F., 1/7/16.
Horn, Dawson, b. Leyburn, Northallerton, e. Bradford, 16/865. Pte. k. in a., F.& F., 1/7/16.
Horsfall, Fred, b. Saltaire, Yorks, e. Bradford, Yorks, 16/1442, Pte., k. in a., F. & F., 27/2/17.
Horsfall, Tom, b. Shipley, Yorks, e. Bradford, Yorks, 16/535, Pte., k. in a., F. & F., 1/7/16.
Howard, Ernest, b. Bowling, Bradford, Yorks, e. Bradford, 16/998, L/Cpl., k. in a., F. & F., 1/7/16.
Howarth, George, b. Bradford, e. Bradford, Yorks, 16/1016, Pte., k. in a., F. & F., 1/7/16.
Howden, Sidney, b. Liverton, Lincs, e. Holbeach, 40426, Pte., k. in a., F. & F. , 27/2/17, formerly 4682, Lincs Regt.
Hunt, William Denis, b. Garforth, Leeds, e. Bradford, 16/420, Pte., d. of w., F. & F., 13/11/16.
Hurp, Edward, b. Bradford, e. Bradford, Yorks, 16/47, Sgt., k. in a., F. & F., 27/2/17.
Hutchison, Louis, b. Leeds, e. Leeds, 24815, Pte., d. of w., F. & F., 16/11/16.
Illingworth, Henry, b. Bradford, e. Bradford, Yorks, 16/95, Pte., d., Home, 30/12/14.
Irving, Frank, b. Bradford, e. Bradford, Yorks, 16/152, Pte., d. of w., F. & F., 10/11/16.
Irving, Wilfred, b. Little Woodhouse, Yorks, e. Halifax, 40215, Pte., k. in a., F. & F., 9/11/16.
Ives, Mark Mountain, e. Leeds, (Bramley, Yorks), 40203, Pte., k. in a., F. & F., 27/2/17.
Jackson, Horace, b. St. Mary's, Lincoln, e. Birmingham, 15515, Pte., k. in a., F. & F., 27/2/17.
Jackson, Wilfred, b. Bradford, e. Bradford, Yorks, 16/195, Pte., d. of w., F. & F., 12/7/16.
Jagger, Wilfred, b. Leeds, e. Leeds, 28892, Pte., k. in a., F. & F., 27/12,/17.
James, John, b. Cheadle, Staffs, e. Pontefract, Yorks, 14796, L/Cpl., d. of w., F. & F., 6/6/17.
Jarvis, Arthur William, e. Spalding, Lincs, 40427, Pte., k. in a., F. & F., 3/5/17, formerly 4303, 4th Lincs Regt.
Jarvis, Charles, b. Rotherham, e. Chapeltown (Eccleseld, Sheffield), 18477, Pte., d. of w., F. & F. , 30/7/17.
Jeffery Thomas Frederick, b Plymouth, Devon, e. Bradford, 40824, Pte., k: in a., F. & F., 3/5/17.
Johns, Samuel, b. Leeds, e. Leeds, 23798, Pte., k. in a., F. & F., 27/2/17.
Johnson, Alfred, b. Barrow-on-Humber, e. Bradford, Yorks, 16/217, Pte., k. in a., F. & F., 1/7/16.
Johnson, Henry Martin Finch, b. Highbury, London, e. Bradford, (Eccleshill), 16/362, Cpl., k. in a., F. & F., 1/7/16.
Jones, George, b. Salford, Lancs, e. Manchester, 10193, L/Cpl., k. in a., F. & F. , 27/10/16.
Jones, Tom Lancelot, b. Liverpool, e. Liverpool, 37651, Pte., k. in a., F. & F. , 3/5/17, formerly 117979, R.F.A.
Jordan, Waiter, b. Leeds, e. Bradford, Yorks, 16/1186, Pte., k. in a., F. & F., 1/7/16.
Jowett, Charles, b. Leeds, e. Leeds, 38783, Pte., k. in a., F. & F., 3/5/17.
Jowett, Harry, b. Howarth, Yorks, e. Bradford, 16/1368, Pte., k. in a., F. & F., 1/7/16.
Keighley, Clifford, b. Leeds, e. Leeds, 24199, Cpl., k. in a., F. & F., 27/2/17.
Kelsey, Percy, b. Peak Forest, Derbyshire, e. Chapel-en-le-Frith (Dove Holes), 40400, LiCpl., k. in a., F. & F., 25/2/17, formerly 53475, Lincs Regt.
Kellett, James, b. Gildersome, Yorks, e. Leeds, 300077, Pte., d. of w., F. & F., 6/5/17.
Kendrick, Fred., b. Dewsbury, Yorks, e. Bradford (Shipley), 16/1262, Pte., k. in a., F. & F., 1/7/16.
Kenningham, Edgar, b. Bradford, e. Bradford, Yorks, 18/771, L/Cpl., k. in a., F. & F., 1/7/16.
Kenny. William, b. Bradford, e. Bradford, Yorks, 16/336, Pte., d. of w., F. & F., 7/7/16.
Kershaw Frederick Percy, b. Bradford, e. Bradford, Yorks, 16/415, Pte., k. in a., F. & F., 1/17/16.
Kilvington, Charles, b. York, e. Leeds (Leeds), 32298, Pte., k. in a., F. & F., 27/2/17.
King, Herbert, b. Wakefield, Yorks, e. Leeds, 32307, Pte., k. in a., F. & F., 9/11/16.
Kirkman, Harry, b. Bradford, e. Bradford, Yorks, 16/1189, Pte., d., F. & F., 20/ 11/16.
Kitchingman, Norris, b. Ripon, Yorks, e. Bradford, 16/248, Pte., k. in a., F. & F., 19/5/16.
Knight, Rowland Hebden, b. Allerton, Bradford, e. Bradford, 16/737, Pte., k. in a., F. & F., 1/7/16.

THE BRADFORD PALS

Ladley, Charles William, b. Sowerby Bridge, Yorks, e. Leeds, 38678, Pte., k. in a., F. & F., 27/2/17
Lamberton, John Thomas, b. Felling, Gateshead, e. Newcastle-on-Tyne (Windy Nook, Durham), 16007, Pte., k. in a., F. & F., 3/5/17.
Lassey, Willie b. Bradford, e. Bradford, Yorks, 16/29, Pte., d. of w, F. & F., 16/5/16.
Latham Percy George, b. Bradford, e. Bradford, Yorks, 16/156, C.S.M., k . in a., F.& F., 1/7/16.
Laycock, Harry, b. Manningham, Bradford, e. Bradford, 16/550, Pte., k. in a., F. & F., 3/5/17.
Leach, Ernest, b. Bradford, e. Bradford, Yorks, 16/198, Pte., k. in a., F. & F., 1/7/16.
Leach, Eddy, b. Bradford, e. Bradford, Yorks, 16/531, Pte., k in a., F. & F., 1/7/16.
Ledger, Joseph Henry, b. Carbrook, Sheffield, e. Attercliffe, Sheffield, 22587, Pte., k, in a., F. & F., 1/7/16, formerly 24906 K.O.Y.L.I.
Leech, George Edward, b. Bradford, e. Bradford, Yorks, 16/749, Pte., k. in a., F. & F., 1/7/16.
Leeming, Henry Richard, b. Giggleswick, Yorks, e. Keighley, 20/146, Pte., k. in a., F. & F., 29/7/16.
Leeming, Jonas Manasseh, b. Eceleshill, Bradford, e. Bradford, Yorks, 16/1511, Pte., k. in a., F. & F., 1/7/16.
Leigh, Ernest Kirkham, b. Darwin, Lancs, e. BarnowIdswick, 20/188, Pte., k. in a., F. & F., 29/7/16.
Leonard, Harry, b. Huddersfield, e. Huddersfield, 38358, Pte., k. in a., F. & F., 3/.5/17.
Lightowler, Willie, b. Bradford, e. Bradford, Yorks, 20/24, Pte., k. in a., F. & F., 1/7/16.
Lingard, Thomas, b. Bradford, e. Bradford, Yorks, 16/175, Pte., k. in a., F. & F., 1/7/16.
Linley, Abraham, b. Leeds, e. Bradford, Yorks, 16/1677, Pte., k. in a., F. & F., 1/7/16.
Little, Henry Arnold, b. Bradford, e. Bradford, Yorks, 16/413, L/Sgt., k. in a., F. & F., 27/2/17.
Lockett, John, b. Bradford, e. Bradford, Yorks, 16/199, Pte., k. in a., F. & F., 1/7/16.
Longster, Thomas George, e. Leeds (Leeds), 300118, Rfln., d. of w., F. & F., 14/5/17.
Lowe, Bertie, b. Workington, Cumberland, e. Bradford, 16/1673, Pte., k. in a., F. & F., 1/7/16.
Lumb, Mark, b. Batley, e. Batley, 43764, Pte., k. in a., F. & F., 3/5/17, formerly 28326, K.O.Y.L.I.
Lumb, Matthew, b. Halifax, e. Halifax, Yorks, 41309, Pte., k. in a., F. & F., 3/5/17.
Lynch, Joseph, b. Leeds, e. Leeds, 34004, Pte., d., F. & F., 7/10/17.
McConnell, William, b. Kirkinner, Wigtownshire, e. Bradford, 16357, L/Cpl., k. in a., F. & F., 27/7/16.
McCormack, George Alexander, b. Bradford, e. Bradford, Yorks, 16/318, Cpl., k. in a., F. & F., 3/5/17.
McDermott, Frederick, b. Wooburn, Bucks, e. Bradford (Bradford), 16/560, Pte., k. in a., F. & F., 1/7/16.
McGuire, Thomas Osbourne, b. Boston, e. Boston, 40414, L/Cpl., k. in a., F. & F., 27/2/17, formerly 4586, Lincs Regt.
McIntyre, Arthur, b. Filey, Yorks, e. Bradford (Long Preston), 16/229, Cpl., k. in a., F. & F., 27/2/17.
McMahon, John Thomas, b. Batley, Yorks, e. Bradford, 16/1509, Pte., k. in a., F. & F., 1/7/16.
McMurrough, Robert, b. Sunderland, e. Sunderland, 4/8176, Pte., d. of w., F. & F., 28/2/17.
Mackay, Edford, b. Wibsey, Bradford, e. Bradford, Yorks, 16/908, Pte., d. of w., F. & F., 10/5/16.
Mair, Fred Sutherland, b. Leeds, e. Leeds, 32407, L/Cpl., k. in a., F. & F., 27/2/17.
Mallinson, Albert, b. Bradford, e. Bradford, Yorks, 16/704, Pte., k. in a., F. & F., 1/7/16.
Manley, John, b. Bradford Moor, Bradford, e. Bradford, 16/913, Sgt., k. in a., F. & F., 3/5/17.
Mann, Albert James, b. Spa, Norfolk, e. York, 36570, Pte., d., F. & F., 28/5/17.
Marsden, Ben, b. Bradford, e. Bradford, Yorks, 16/1241, Pte., k. in a., F. & F., 1/7/16.
Marston, James, b. Bradford, e. Bradford, Yorks, 16/1277, L/Cpl., k. in a., F. & F., 1/7/16.
Martin, Albert, b. Wickham Skeith, Eye, Suffolk, e. York, 4/8150, Pte., k. in a., F. & F., 29/7/17.
Martin, John, b. Richmond, Yorks, e. Richmond, 22010, Pte., k. in a., F. & F., 27/2/17.
Martindale, Irvin, b. Bradford, e. Bradford, Yorks, 16/1297, Pte., k. in a., F. & F., 1/7/16.
Martindale, Maurice, b. Manningham, e. Bradford, (Heaton), 16/319, Pte., k. in a., F. & F., 1/7/16.
Mason, Riley, e. Pontefract, Yorks, (Morley, Yorks), 41708, Pte., d. of w., F.& F., 13/5/17.
May, Clement, b. Keighley, Yorks, e. Leeds, 32857, Pte., d. of w., F. & F., 13/11/16.
May, William, b. Bradford, e. Bradford, Yorks, 16/1437, Pte., d. of w., Home, 9/7/16.
Metcalfe, Thomas William, b. Shipton, Yorks, e. York (York), 38332, Pte., k. in a., F. & F., 27/2/17.
Midgley, Verity, b. Bradford, e. Bradford, Yorks, 16/518, L/Cpl., k. in a., F. & F., 1/7/16.
Midgley, Walter, b. Keighley, e. Keighley, Yorks, 32633, Pte., k. in a., F. & F., 3/5/17.
Miller, Frederick Harold, b. Markington, Yorks, e. Ripon, 40827, Pte., k. in a., F. & F., 3/5/17.
Mills, John William, b. Bradford, e. Bradford, Yorks, 16/399, Pte., k. in a., F. & F., 1/7/16.
Moffatt, Seth Shaw, b. Newcastle, e. Newcastle (Benwell), 41707, Pte., k. in a., F. & F., 27/2/17, formerly 40960, 3rd K.O.Y.L.I.

APPENDIX 4

Mooney Joseph, b. Bradford, e. Bradford, Yorks, 16/735, Sgt., k. in a. F. &F., 13/11/16.
Moore, Ernest, b. Derby, e. Doncaster, 41670, Pte., d. of w., Home, 5/5/17, formerlv 34262, K.O.Y.L.I.
Moore, John, 6. Bradford,'e. Bradford, Yorks, 16/1423, Pte., k. in a., F. & F., 1/7/16.
Moore, Joe, b. Bradford, e. Bradford, Yorks, 16/892, Pte., k. in a., F. & F., 27/7/16.
Morgan, William, b. Bradford, e. Bradford, Yorks, 16/8, Sgt., k. in a,, F. & F., 1/7/16.
Morritt, Walter, b. Leeds, e. Leeds, 32852, Pte,, k. in a., F. & F., 3/5/17.
Morton, James, b. Heckmondwike, Yorks, e. Bradford, 16/1488, Pte., k. in a., F. & F., 27/2/17.
Mosley, William. Arthur, b. Bradford, e. Bradford, Yorks, 16/133, Cpl., k. in a., F. & F., 1/7/16.
Mountain, John Edwin, b. York, e. Acomb, Yorks, 35063, Pte., k. in a., F. & F., 27/2/17.
Mountain, John William, b. Leeds, e. Leeds, 24708, L/Sgt., d. of w., F. & F., 28/2/17.
Muff. Herbert, b. Bradford, e. Bradford, Yorks, 16/1291, Pte., k. in a., F. & F., 28/8/16.
Murgatroyd, William, b. Baildon, Yorks, e. Baildon, 38351, Pte., k. in a., F. & F., 3/5/17.
Musgrave, Frank, b. Bradford, e. Bradford, Yorks, 16/762, Pte,, k. in a., F. & F., 1/7/16.
Myers, Thomas Henry, b. Leeds, e. Leeds, 35187, Pte., k. in a., F. & F., 27/2/17.
Naughton, Francis William, b. York, e. York, Pte., 32947, k, in a., F. & F., 27/2/17.
Naylor, Arthur, b. Leeds. e. Leeds, 40206, Pte., k, in a., F. & F., 27/2/17.
Naylor, Herbert, b. Leeds, e. Leeds, 36807, Pte., k. in a., F. & F., 3/5/17.
Naylor, Reginald Bolton, b. Leeds, e. Leeds, 36772, Pte., d. of w., Home, 8/6/17.
Needham, William Henry, b. Sheffield, e. Sheffield, 36347, Pte., k. in a., F. & F., 27/2/17.
Nelson, Fred, b. Bradford, e. Bradford, Yorks, 16/180, Sgt., k. in a., F. & F., 29/7/17.
Nettleton, Ernest, b. Idle, Bradford, Yorks, e. Bradford, 16/1172, L/Cpl., k. in a., F. & F., 27/2/17.
Newman, Herbert Beaumont, b. Bradford, e. Bradford, 16/1100, Pte., k. in a., F. & F., 1/7/16.
Newsholme, Arthur William, b. Bradford, e. Bradford, 16/781, L/Cpl., k. in a., F. & F., 27/2/17.
Newton, Alfred Ernest, b. Bingley, Yorks, e. Bradford, 16/524, Cpl., k. in a., F. & F., 1/7/16.
Newton, James, e. Leeds, 36849, Pte., d., Home, 8/5/17.
Nurse, Herbert Edward, b. Chorlton-on-Medlock, Manchester, e. Bradford, 16/967, Pte., d. of w., F. & F., 3/7/17.
Packett, Donald, b. Cullingworth, Bradford, e. Bradford, 16/659, Cpl., k. in a., F. & F., 1/7/16.
Palmer, John William, b. Leeds, e. Leeds, 17/1584, Pte., k. in a., F. & F., 27/2/17.
Parker, Tom, b. Bradford, e. Bradford, Yorks, 16/1258, Pte., k. in a., F. & F., 1/7/16.
Parker, Willie, b. Clayton, Bradford, e. Bradford, Yorks, 16/725, Pte., k. in a., F. & F., 1/7/16.
Parkinson, Walter, b. Bradford, Yorks, e. Matlock, Yorks, 19249, Pte., k. in a., F. & F., 2/12/16.
Paterson, Malcolm Bruce, b. Shipley, Yorks, e. Bradford, 16/687, Pte., k. in a., F. & F., 1/7/16.
Pearson, Alexander Frederick, b. London, e. Leeds, 40834, Pte., k. in a., F. & F., 27/2/17.
Pearson, James Arthur, b. Bradford, e. Bradford, Yorks, 20/131, Pte., k. in a., F. & F., 29/7/16.
Pearson, Maurice, b. Bradford, e. Bradford, Yorks, 16/1433, Pte., k. in a., F. & F., 1/7/16.
Pearson, Stephen, b. Bradford, e. Bradford, Yorks, 16/1420, Pte., k. in a., F. & F., 1/7/16.
Peck, John William Rowley, b. Bradford, e. Bradford, Yorks, 28690, Pte., k, in a., F. & F., 27/2/17.
Peel, Joseph Edward, b. Heckmondwike, e. Liversedge, 28679, Pte., k. in a., F. & F., 12/5/17.
Perray, Percy, b. Leeds, e. Leeds, 27850, Pte., k. in a., F. & F., 2/12/16.
Pickup, James Edwin, b, Horton, Bradford, e. Bradford, 16/521, L/Cpl., k. in a., F. & F., 1/7/16.
Poole, Samuel, b. Bradford, e. Bradford, Yorks, 16/1037, L/Cpl., k. in a., F. & F., 1/7/16.
Porter, Fred, b. Dudley Hill, Bradford, e. Bradford, Yorks, 16/632, Pte., k. in a., F. & F., 1/7/16.
Potts, Joseph, b. Bradford, e. Bradford, Yorks, 16/1336, Pte., k. in a., F. & F., 1/7/16.
Powell, Ernest, b. Darfield, Barnsley, Yorks, e. Bradford 16/509, Pte., k. in a., F. & F., 27/2/17.
Pratt, Ernest, b. Leeds. e. York, 32843, L/Cpl., k. in a., F. & F., 27/2/17.
Prentice, Arthur, b. Tockwith, Yorks, e. Pudsey, 40835, Pte., d., Home, 21/2/18.
Quirk, Thomas, b. Bradford, e. Bradford, 20/114, Pte., d, of w., F. & F., 1/8/16.
Raine, George, b. Shipley, Yorks, e. Bradford, Yorks, 16/691, Pte., k. in a., F. & F., l/7/16.
Ramsden, Herbert, b. Pudsey, Yorks, e. Bradford, 16/731, Pte., k. in a., F. & F., 1/7/16.
Ratcliffe, Sid, b. Halifax, e. Halifax, Yorks, 40196, Pte., d. of w., F. & F., 8/5/17.
Rawnsley, Herbert Vincent, b. Clayton, Bradford, e. Bradford, 16/1133, Pte., k. in a., F. & F., 1/7/16.

THE BRADFORD PALS

Renshaw, Ernest, b. Shipley, Yorks, e. Bradford, Yorks, 16/513, Pte., k. in a., F. & F., 1/7/16.
Reveley, Gordon Reginald, b. St. Stephens, Bradford, e. Bradford, 16/837, Pte., k. in a., F. & F., 18/5/16.
Rhodes, Albert, b. Leeds, e. Leeds, 38782, Pte., d., F. & F., 9/5/17.
Rhodes, Charles, b. Frizinghall, Bradford, e. Bradford, Yorks, 16/964, Pte., k. in a., F. & F., 1/7/16.
Rhodes, Thomas, b. Thackley, Bradford, e. Bradford, Yorks, 16/1247, Pte., k. in a., F. & F., 1/7/16.
Rice, Lawrence, b. Bradford, e. Bradford, Yorks, 16/1344, Pte., k. in a., F. & F., 1/7/16.
Ridley, Fred, b. York, e. Bradford, Yorks, (Bradford), 16/1428, Pte., k. in a., F. & F., 1/7/16.
Ridley, Frederick Birkett, b. Aspatria, Cumberland, e. Leeds (Armley), 35294, Pte., k. in a., F. & F., 27/2/17.
Roach, Thomas, e. Leeds (Leeds), 300076, L/Cpl., k. in a., F. & F., 3/5/17.
Roberts, John, b. Leeds, e. Yorks, 38643, Pte., k. in a., F. & F., 30/4/17.
Robertson, John Bright, b. Stirling, Scotland, e. Bradford, 16/123. Pte., d. of w., F. & F., 3/7/16.
Robinson, Emest, b. Bradford, e. Bradford, Yorks, 16/874, Pte., d. of w., F. & F., 12/5/17.
Robinson, Frederick William, b. Burley-in-Wharfedale, e. Bradford (Manningham), 16/1326, Pte., d. of w., F. & F. ,10/7/16.
Robinson, Horace, b. Wakefield, Yorks, e. Bradford, 16/1242, Pte., k. in a., F. & F., 3/5/17.
Robinson, James William, e. Shipley, Yorks, 38293, Pte., d. of w., Home, 3/4/17.
Robinson, Sam, b. Leeds, e. Leeds, 40836, Pte., k. in a., F. & F., 30/4/17.
Robshaw, Charles, b. Barwick-in-Elmet, e. Garforth, Leeds, 33220, Pte., k. in a., F. & F., 27/2/17.
Rogers, Henry Lawrence, b. Bradford, e. Bradford, Yorks, 16/340, Pte., k. in a., F & F., 1/7/16.
Rogers, Joseph, b. Skipton, Yorks, e. Skipton, 28740, Pte., d. of w., F. & F., 2/5/17.
Rowland, Robert, b. Bradford, e. Bradford, Yorks, 16/1398, Pte., k. in a., F. & F., 1 /7/16.
Rudd, Joseph, b. Bradford, e. Bradford, Yorks, 16/663, Pte., k. in a., F. & F., 2/12/16.
Rudd, Percy b. West Bowling, Bradford, e. Bradford, Yorks, 16/307, Pte., d. F. & F., 22/10/18.
Rushworth, William, b. Bradford, e. Bradford, Yorks, 16/246, Pte., k. in a., F. & F., 15/8/16.
Rust, Walter, b. Bradford, e. Bradford, Yorks, 19/130, Pte., d., F. & F., 9/11/16.
Ryan, Bernard, b. Leeds, e. Leeds, 14930, Pte., k. in a., F. & F., 3/9/16.
Saunders, James, Henry, b. Bradford, Yorks, e. Bradford, 16/701, Pte., d. of w., F. & F., 7/8/16.
Sayers, John James, b. Bradford, Yorks, e. Bradford, Yorks, 16/1293, Pte., k. in a., F. & F., 1/7/16.
Scarth, George, b. Leeds, e. Leeds, 37014, Pte., F. & F., 12/2/17.
Schofield, Fred, b. Brighouse, Yorks, e. Halifax, Yorks (Bradford), 40218, Pte., k. in a., F. & F. 3/5/17.
Scott, George, b. York, e. York, 11662, Pte., d. of w., F. & F. 12/5/17.
Scott, Harry, b. Shipley, Yorks, e. Bradford, Yorks 16/1289, Pte., k. in a., F. & F. 1/7/16.
Selby, Christopher, b. Bradford, e. Bradford, Yorks, 16/1399, Pte., d. of w., F. & F. 5/7/16.
Senior, Charles, b. Leeds, e. Leeds, 37716, Pte., k. in a., F. & F. 3/5/17.
Senior, Thomas Edward, b. Leeds, e. Leeds, 32405, Pte., k. in a., F. & F. 27/2/17.
Setterington, Thomas, b. Leeds, e. Tadcaster, Yorks, 33040, Pte., d. of w., F. & F. 7/3/17.
Shackleton, Ernest, b. Bradford, e. Bradford, Yorks, 16/825, Pte., k. in a., F. & F. 1/7/16.
Sharman, Charles Victor, b. Bradford, e. Bradford, Yorks, 16/370, Pte., d. of w., F. & F 1/8/16.
Sharp, Harold, b. Leeds, e. Leeds, 27214, Pte., k. in a., F. & F. 27/6/17.
Sharpe, Fred, b. Thornton, Yorks, e. Bradford, Yorks, 38291, Pte., d. of w., F. & F. 2/3/17.
Shaw, Albert, b. Horton, Bradford, Yorks, e. Bradford, 16/879, Pte., d. of w., F. & F 4/9/16.
Sheldon, Tom, b. Ripon, e. Ripon, Yorks, 23363, L/Cpl., k. in a., F. & F. 3/5/17.
Shooter, James Robert, b. Low Moor, Yorks, e. Bradford, 16/1048, Pte., k. in a., F. & F. 1/7/16.
Shouksmith, Harold Wilson, b. York, e. Leeds, 40845, Pte., k. in a., F. & F. 3/5/17.
Sircom, Harry Innerdale, b. Bradford, Yorks, e. Bradford, 16/732, Pte., d. of w_ F. & F. 19/6/16.
Skirrow, Harry Edmundson, b. Bradford, Yorks, e. Bradford, 16/914, Pte., d. of w., F. & F. 13/12/16.
Slingsby, Fred, b. Windhill, Bradford, York., e. Bradford, 16/350, Pte., k. in a., F. & F. 23/4/16.
Smales, Joe, b. Rothwell, Leeds, e. Wakefield, Yorks, 28511, Pte., d., F. & F. 3/8/18.
Smith, Arthur, b. Leeds, e. Leeds, 40853, Pte., k. in a., F. & F. 27/2/17.
Smith, Charles, b. Leeds, e. Leeds, 25323, Pte., k. in a., F. & F. 27/2/17.
Smith, Ernest Marsden Conrad, b. Leeds, e. Leeds, 37233, Pte., k. in a., F. & F. 27/2/17.
Smith, Frederick Arthur, b. Shipley, Yorks, e. Bradford, 16/1416, Pte., k. in a., F & F. 1/7/16.
Smith John William, b. Nottingham, e. Nottingham, 43844, Pte., k. in a, F. & F. 3/5/17, formerly 30560, Sherwood Foresters.

APPENDIX 4

Smith, Raymond, b. Bradford, Yorks, e. Bradford, 16/21, Pte., k. in a., F. & F. 1/7/16.
Smith, Tom, b. Keighley, e. Keighley, Yorks, 16/1674, Pte, k. in a., F. & F. 3/5/17.
Smith, Victor, Denholme, Yorks, e. Bradford, 16/269, Pte., k. in a., F. & F. 23/4/16.
Smith, Walter, b. Cleckheaton, Yorks, e. Bradford, 16/451. Pte., d. of w., F. & F. 9/7/16.
Smith, Willie, b. Leeds, e. Leeds. 24153, Pte., k. in a., F. & F. 28/10/16.
Speight, Albert, b. Dewsbury, Yorks, e. Bradford, 16/1430, Pte., k. in a., F. & F. 1/7/16.
Spence, Alfred Brightrick, b. Heaton, Bradford, e. Bradford, 16/823, Sgt., k. in a., F. & F. 1/7/16.
Spence, Eric, b. Bradford, Yorks, e. Bradford, 16/466, L/Cpl., k. in a., F. & F. 1/7/16.
Spencer, Francis William, b. Bradford e. Bradford, Yorks, 16/165, Sgt., k. in a., F. & F. 3/5/17.
Spire, Henry Osbourne, b. Bradford, e. Bradford, Yorks, 16/726, L/Cpl., k. in a., F. & F. 1/7/16.
Stables, Walter, b. Horsforth, Yorks, e. Leeds, 24248, Pte., k. in a., F. & F. 3/5/17.
Stakersmith, Wilfred Raymond, e. Selby (Micklefield, Yorks), 38680, Pte., k. in a., F. & F. 27/2/17.
Stamp, Edward John, b. Leeds, e. Leeds, 17198, A/Cpl. k in a., F. & F. 1/7/16.
Stancomb, Bryan Mortimer, b. Bradford, e. Bradford, Yorks, 41317, Pte., F & F. 22/2/17.
Stanney, Thomas, Richard, b. Brentford, e. Brentford, Mddlesex. 20/323, Pte., d., Home, 25/4/17, formerly 22870, Suffolk Regt.
Stead, John William, b. Goole, e. Wakefield, 41711, Pte., k. in a., F. & F. 27/2/17, formerly 33952, K.O.Y.L.I.
Stell, Joseph, b. Keighley, e, Keighley, Yorks, 18/1046, L/Cpl., k. in a., F. & F. 1/7/16.
Stephenson, Charles William, b. Leeds, e. Leeds, 37458, Pte., k. in a., F. & F. 3/5/17.
Stephenson, William David, b. Hunslet, Leeds, e. Harrogate 4/8430, L/Cpl., k. in a., F. & F., 9/11/16.
Stobart, Fred, b. Lemington, Northumberland, e. Whitley Bay, 59695, Pte. (Accident), F. & F., 6/2/18.
Stockton, Charles, b. Hull, e. Hull, 13944, Pte., k. in a,. F. & F. 3/5/17.
Strawson, Harold, e. Horncastle, 40441, Sgt., k. in a., F. & F. 3/5/17. formerly 3805, Lincoln Regt.
Sugden, Arnold, b. Halifax e. Halifax, Yorks, 28324, Pte., d. of w., F. & F. 22/l1/16.
Sutcliffe, Herbert, b. Pudsey, e. Pudsey, Yorks, 32422, Pte., k. in a., F. & F. 9/11/16.
Swinbank, James Allan, b. Bradford, e, Bradford, Yorks, 16/314, Pte., k. in a., F. & F. 9/11/16.
Sykes, Arthur, b. Bradford, e. Bradford, Yorks, 16/1706, Pte., d. of w., F. & F. 1/8/16.
Sykes, Arthur Edward, b. Halifax, Yorks, c., Bradford, Yorks, 16/1448, L/Cpl., k. in a., F. & F., 1/7/16.
Tankard, Herbert, b. Listerhills, Bradford, e. Bradford, Yorks, 16/96, Pte., k. in a., F. & F., 3/5/17.
Tarrant, George, b. Portsmouth, e. Bradford, Yorks, 16/455, L/Cpl., d. of w., F. & F., 12/6/1(?).
Tasker, Douglas, b. Bradford, e. Bradford, Yorks, 16/1274, Pte., k. in a., F. & F., 1/7/16.
Taylor, Allan, b. Leeds, e. Leeds, 35568, Pte., k. in a., F. & F., 3/5/17.
Taylor, George Stead, b. Bradford, e. Bradford, Yorks, 16/505, Pte., k. in a., F. & F., 1/7/16.
Taylor, Pearson, b. North Rigton, Pannel, Harrogate, e. Knaresborough, 33030, Pte., d. of w., F. & F., 5/5/17.
Thackray, Thomas, b. Bradford, e. Bradford, Yorks, 26127, Pte., k. in a., F. & F., 29/7/16.
Thrippleton, Austin, b. Stanningley, Leeds, e. Bradford, 16/1266, Pte., k. in a., F. & F., 1 /7/16.
Tillett, Henry, b. Tadeaster, e. Tadcaster, Yorks, 32356, Pte., d., F. & F., 3/5/17.
Todd, Walter, b. York, e. York, 28171, Pte., k. in a., F, & F., 3/5/17.
Tolson, Percy, b. Birkenshaw, Bradford, Yorks, e. Bradford, 16/1024, Pte., d. of w., F. & F. ,29/'9/16.
Tomlinson, Denis, b. Halifax, e. Bradford, 16/734, Pte.. k. in a. F. & F., 1/7/16.
Townend, James Arthur, b. Bradford, e. Bradford, Yorks, 16/120, L/Cpl., k. in a., F. & F., 1/7/16.
Towse, Albert, b. Pannel, Yorks, e. Harrogate, 23837, Pte., d., F. & F., 12/3/17.
Underwood, Harry. b. Girlington, Bradford, e. Bradford, 16/31, Cpl., k. in a., F. & F., 1/7/16.
Valentine, George Henry, b. Northampton, e. Leeds, 37459, L/Cpl., k. in a., F. & F., 3/5/17.
Waddilove, Norman, b. Bradford, e. Bradford, Yorks, 16/313, Pte., k. in a., F. & F., 1/7/16.
Wadsworth, Alfred, b. Leeds, e. Leeds, 32981, Pte., k. in a., F. & F., 3/5/17.
Waite, Wilfred, b. Guiseley, Yorks, e. Bradford (Bradford), 16/1036, Pte., k. in a. F. & F., 1/7/18.
Walker, Ernest, e. Chesterfield, 41717, Pte., k. in a., F. & F., 27/2/17, formerly 34315, Sherwood Foresters.
Walker, Harry, b. Leeds, e. Leeds, 32894, Pte., d., F. & F., 9/8/17.
Walker, Joseph, b. Hebden Bridge, e. Halifax, 41673, Pte., k. in a., F. & F,3/5/l7, formerly 39607, K.O.Y.L.I.
Walker, Percy, b. Manningham, Bradford, e. Bradford, 16/169, L/Sgt., k. in a., F. & F., 1/7/16.

Walmsley, Arthur, b. Bradford, e. Bradford, Yorks, 16/380, L/Cpl., k. in a., F. & F., 1/7/16.
Watkinson, John, b. Leeds, c Leeds, 31806, k. in a., F. & F., 3/5/17.
Watson, Charles Arthur, b. Baildon, Yorks, e. Bradford, 16/73, e. C. S. M. k. in a., F. & F., 1/7/16.
Weaver Charles, b. Witney, Oxfordshire, e. Bradford, (Heckmondwike), 16/1631, Pte., k. in a., F. & F., 1/7/16.
Whitaker, Gordon Stanley, b. Wakefield, e. Leeds, 37457, Pte., k. in a. F. & F., 30/4/17.
Wightman, Alfred Affleck, b. Leeds, e. Leeds, 35629, Pte., k, in a., F. & F., 13/5/17.
Wilks, Waiter, b. Leeds, e. Leeds, 33061, Pte., d., F. & F., 11/5/17.
Will, John William, b. Leeds, e. Bradford, Yorks, (Bradford), 16/87, Pte., k. in a., F. & F., 3/5/17.
Williams, William, b. Bradford, e. Bradford, Yorks, 28726, Pte., k. in a., F. & F., 2/12/16.
Willis, Edgar, b. Bradford, e. Bradford, Yorks, 16/614, Pte., k. in a., F. & F., 1/7/16.
Wilson, George, b. Bradford, e. Bradford, Yorks, 16/82, L/Cpl., k. in a., F. & F., 1/7/16.
Wilson, Norris, b. Wistow, Selby, Yorks, e. Selby, 31986, Pte., k. in a., F. & F., 9/11/16.
Wood, James Preston, b. Bradford, e, Bradford, Yorks, 19983, Pte., d. of w., F. & F., 10/11/16.
Wood, Thomas Stanley, b. Scarborough, e. Bradford (Beeston Hill, Leeds), 16/355, Pte., k. in a., F. & F., 1/7/16.
Woodhead, Ernest. b. Bradford, e. Bradford, Yorks, 16/469, Pte., k. in a., F. & F., 26/6/16.
Woodhouse, Francis John, b. Pontefract, e. Bradford, 16/106, L/Sgt., d. of w., F. & F., 22/7/16.
Woodhouse, Norman, b. Bradford, e. Bradford, Yorks, 16/1435, Pte., k. in a., F. & F., 1/7/16.
Woodhouse, Walter, b. Bradford, e. Bradford, Yorks, 16/69, Pte., k. in a., F. & F., 1/7/16.
Woodrow, William, b. Bradford, e. Bradford, Yorks, 16/1397, Pte., k. in a., F. & F., 1/7/16.
Woods, Gilbert, b. Leeds, c, Leeds, 31968, Pte., k. in a., F. & F., 10/11/16.
Woodward, Samuel, b. Leeds, e. Leeds, 32895, Pte., k. in a., F. & F., 3/5/17.
Wormald, Walter, b. Leeds, e. Leeds, 23317, L/Cpl., d. of w., F. & F., 13/5/17.
Worth, Rowland, b. Leeds, e. Leeds, 40863, Pte., k. in a., F. & F., 27/2/17.
Wright, Samuel Horsley, b. York, e. York, 37506, Pte., d. of w., F. & F., 5/5/17.
Wright, Walter, b. Nun Monkton, York, e. Ripon, Yorks, 41305, Pte., d., F. & F., 5/8/17.
Young, John William, b. Cawood, York, e. York, 38635, Pte., k. in a., F. & F., 27/2/17.

APPENDIX 4

18th Battalion.

Commissioned officers:

Akam, James Rhodes, Lt., k. in a., 1/7/16.
Baker, Frederick Gerald, 2/Lt., (Tp.), k. in a., 17/4/18.
Clough, Morris, Capt., k. in a., 25/4/18.
Colley, Harold, 2/Lt., k. in a., 1/7/16.
Cross, Ronald Sidney, Capt., (Tp.) k. in a., 27/7/16.
Dalton, Richard Gregory, T/2/Lt., k. in a., 31/8/17.
De Lacy, John Matthew, 2/Lt., k. in a., 23/9/17 (and R.F.C., 57 Sqn.).
Derwent, Robert Ivor, 2/Lt. k. in a., 1/7/16.
Duckitt, Charles Stanley, T/Capt., k. in a., 3/5/17.
Foizey, Harold Egbert, Lt. (Tp.), K. in a., 1/7/16.
Gill, Daniel, T/2/Lt., k. in a., 24/10/16.
Gray, John, 2/Lt., died, 26/11/18.
Holt, Wifrid, 2/Lt., k. in a.,3/5/17.
Hummel, Raymond, T/2/Lt., k. in a., 19/5/16.
Humphries, Walter Rawleigh, 2/Lt. (Tp.) k. in a., 27/7/16.
Jones, Robert Henry, T/2/Lt., k. in a., 29/6/16 (att. from 13th Bn.).
Keevil, Cecil Horace Case, T/Capt., killed, 13/6/17 (and R.F.C.).
Kennard, Maurice Nicholl, T/Lt.-Col., k. in a., 1/7/16.
King, John Rose, M.C., Lt. (Tp.), k. in a., 22/4/18 (att. 10th Bn.).
Mansfield, Harold Lawrie, 2/Lt., d. of w., 3/5/17.
Moulson, Samuel, T/2/Lt., k. in a., 4/9/18.
Nowell, Francis Percival, T/2/Lt., d. of w., 2/7/16.
Robinson, Frank Victor, Lt. (Tp.), k. in a., 3/5/17.
Sleigh, William Ward, Lt., (Tp.), k. in a., 25/2/17.
Smith, John Taylor, Temp. 2/Lt., d. of w., 29/3/18 (att. 2nd Bn.).
Tooke, Bernard, Temp. Capt., k. in a., 3/5/17.
Walton, Francis John George, 2/Lt., (Tp.), k. in a., 1/7/16.
Warner, William James, 2/Lt., k. in a., 3/5/17.
Watson, Frank, Lt., k. in a., 1/7/16 (att. 03 T.M.B.).
Williams, Eric, Lt., k. in a., 27/3/18, (att. 2nd Bn.).
Worsnop, John William, 2/Lt., k. in a., 30/6/16.

Non-commissioned officers and men

Abey, Henry, b. Sunderland, e. York, 34991, Pte., k. in a., F. & F., 12/5/17.
Abbott, William Edwin, b. Wistow, Yorks, e. Bradford, (Bowling), 18/625, A/Sgt., k. in a., F. & F., 30/6/16.
Alderton, Harry, b. Bradford, e. Bradford, (Manningham), 18/454, Pte., k. in a., F. & F., 1/7/16.
Allatt, Thomas Henry, b. Bradford, e. Bradford, Yorks, 18/248, Pte., k. in a., F. & F., 16/9/16.
Allerton, John William, b. Selby, Yorks, e. York, 17921, Pte., k. in a., F. & F., 10/5/17.
Allott, James, b. Pudsey, Yorks, e. Pudsey, Yorks, 33101, Pte., d. of w., F. & F., 25/10/16.
Ambler, Frederick Brammer, b. Sheffield, e. Bradford, Yorks, 18/1409, Pte., d., F. & F., 22/4/16.
Anderson, John William, b Burley-in-Wharfedale, e., Hull, 34286, Pte., k. in a., F. & F., 3/5/17.
Applin, Harry Warren, b. Laisterdyke, Yorks, e. Bradford, 18/1410, Pte., d. of w., F. & F., 15/7/16.
Arundale, George Amos, b. Seamer, Yorks, e. Yorks, 33327, Pte., k. in a., F. & F., 3/5/17.
Atkinson, William, b. Bradford, e. Bradford, Yorks, 18/1458, Pte., d. of w, F. & F., 25/10/16.
Auker, Frank, b. Bradford, Yorks (Laisterdyke, Yorks), 18/1569, Pte., k. in a., F. & F., 30/6/16.
Austin, William, b. Heanor, Derbyshire, e. Barnsley, Yorks, 22677, Pte., d. of w., F. & F., 24/5/16.
    formerly 23 York & Lancs Regt.

THE BRADFORD PALS

Barber, Edward, b. Batlev, Yorks, e. Bradford, Yorks, 18/744, Pte., k. in a., F. & F., 1/17/16.
Barber, George Arthur, b. Chatham, Kent, e. Bradford, (Frizinghall), 18/876, L/Sgt., d. of w., F. & F., 1/7/16.
Barker, Willie, b. Scholes, Yorks, e. Bradford, Yorks, 18/1164, Pte., d. of w., F. & F., 27/7/16.
Barnes, Charlie, b. Queensbury, Yorks, e. Bradford, Yorks, 18/1391, Pte., k. in a., F. & F., 1/7/116.
Barraclough, Norman, b. Buttershaw, Yorks, e. Bradford, 18/1097, Pte., d. of w., F. & F. , 25/10/16.
Barraclough, William, b. Bradford, e. Bradford, Yorks, 18/123, Pte., k. in a., F. & F., 24/4/16.
Barran, Morris, b. Farsley, Yorks, e, Bradford, (Rodley, Leeds), 20/136, Pte., k. in a., F. & F., 1/7/16.
Bateman, Percy, b. Wibsey, Yorks, e. Bradford, Yorks, 18/104, Cpl., d. of w., Home, 8/7/16.
Beaumont, Albert, Knottingley, e. Pontefract, 40774, Pte. d. of w., F. & F., 11/5/17, formerly, 28334, K.R.R.
Beck, Henry, b. Bradford, e. Bradford, Yorks, 18/81, Pte., k. in a., F. & F., 1/7/l 6.
Bell, William Frederick, b. Middlesbrough, e. Middlesbrough, 16361, Pte., d., F. & F., 10/4/17.
Betts, Ross, b. Scarborough, e. Scarborough, Yorks, 10375, Pte., F. & F., 27/7/16.
Biggins, Laurence Lyons, b. Hull, e. Bradford, Yorks, 18/71, L/Cpl., k. in a., F. & F., 27/5/16.
Binns, John Richard, b. Leeds, e. Leeds, 33111, Pte., k. in a., F. & F., 3/5/17.
Binns, Thomas, b. Hunslet, Yorks, e. Bradford, (Shipley), 18/874, Pte., k. in a.. F. & F., 30/6/16.
Birkill, Charles, b. Bradford, e. Bradford, Yorks, 18/875, C.S.M., k. in a., F. & F., 20//7/18.
Blow, John Thomas, b. Spalding, (Cowbit), 457, Pte., d. of w., F. & F., 26/5/17, formerly 24914, Lincs Regt.
Booth, Edmund, b. Bradford, e. Bradford, Yorks, 18/190, Pte., k. in a., F. & F., 1/7/16.
Booth, George Herbert, b. Pudsey, Yorks, e. Bradford, 18/296, Pte., k. in a., F & F., 1/7/16.
Bowskill, Arthur William, b. Mansfield, Notts, e. Bradford, 18/1119, Pte , d. of w., F. & F., 1/7/16.
Bramhill, Thomas, e. Louth, Lincs, 40459, Pte.. k. in a., F. & F., 3/5/17, formerly 25293, Lincs. Regt.
Brayshaw, John, b. Bradford, e. Bradford, Yorks, 41283. Pte., k. in a., F. & F., 3/5/17.
Brewer Albert, b, Bradford, e. Bradford, Yorks, 20/155, Pte., k. in a., F. & F., l/7/16.
Briggs, George, b. Leeds, e. Leeds, 33102, Pte., d. of w., F. & F., 1/5/17.
Briggs, Arthur. b. Bradford, e. Bradford, Yorks, 18/456, Pte., k. in a. F. & F., 24/4/16.
Britton, Charles, b. North Bierley, Yorks, e. Bradford, Yorks, 18/603, Pte., k. in a., F. & F., 3/5/17.
Broadley John Ernest, e. Leeds (Leeds), 41287, Pte., k. in a., F. & F., 3/5/17.
Brock, James Edgar, b. Bradford, e. Bradford, Yorks, 18/993, Pte., k. in a., F. & F., 1/7/16.
Brogden, Thomas Blakey, b. Bradford, e. Bradford, Yorks, 18/950, Pte., k. in a., F. & F., 1/7/16.
Brown, Alfred, b. Retford Notts., e. Bradford, Yorks, 18/431, Pte., d. of w., F. & F., 3/7/16.
Brown, Ernest, b. Bradford, e. Bradford, Yorks, 18/243, Pte., k. in a., F. & F., 3/7/17.
Brown, Frank Raper, b. Leeds, e. Leeds. 34209, Pte., k. in a., F. & F., 29/6/17.
Brown, Harold, b. Tong, Bradford. e. Bradford, Yorks, 18/952, L/Cpl., k. in a., F. & F., 3/5/17.
Brown, John, b. Castleton, Yorks, e. Bradford, 18/1487, Pte., k. in a., F. & F., 1/7/16.
Brown, Thomas, b. Mitford, Northumberland, e. Newcastle-on -Tyne, 47987, Pte., k. in a., F. & F., 3/5/17,
            formerly 32865, Yorkshire Regt.
Brunt, Arnold Vincent, b. Poole, Otley, Yorks, e. Bradford, 18/ 1331, Pte., k. in a., F. & F., 3/5/17.
Bryan, Joseph Henry, b . Bradford, e. Bradford, Yorks, 18/523, Pte., k. in a., F. & F., 3/5/17.
Burgoyne, Cyril Percival, a. Hull, e. Bradford, Yorks, 18/78, Cpl., k. in a., F. & F., 23/6/17.
Burley, Charles William, b. Grimsby, e. Bradford, Yorks, 18/1320, Pte., k. in a., F. & F., 30/4/17.
Burton, Norman, b. Clayton West, Yorks, e. Bradford, 18/378, Pte., k. in a., F. & F., 1/7/16.
Burton, Samuel, b. Birkenhead, Cheshire, e. Bradford, 18/1242, L/Cpl., d. of w., F. & F., 17/6/17.
Buswell, Ernest Victor, e. Leicester, 40453, L/Cpl., d., F. & F., 3/5/17. formerly 30987, Leicestershire Regt.
Bywater, Walter, b. Low Moor, Yorks, e. Bradford, Yorks, 18/1460, Pte., k. in a., F. & F., 3/5/17.
Caley, Ernest William, b. Butley, Suffolk, e, Keighley, 40329, Pte., d. of w., F. & F., 25/10/16.
Calvert, Herbert, b. Leeds, e. Leeds, 34482, Pte., k. in a., F. & F., 3/5/17.
Carter, Guy Ripley, e. Bradford (Bradford, Yorks), 40327, Pte., k. in a., F. & F., 13/11/16.
Cawthome, Herbert, b. Bradford. e. Bradford, Yorks, 18/449, Pte., k. in a., F. & F., 1/7/16.
Caygill, Percy, e. York (Garforth, Yorks). 40304, Pte., k. in a., F. & F., 3/5/17.
Chambers, Arthur, e. Leeds (Hunslet, Yorks), 40252, Pte., d. of w., F. & F., 25/10/16.
Cheshire, Norman, b. Bradford, e. Bradford, Yorks, 18/697, Pte., k. in a., F. & F., 1/17/16.
Clark, John Robert, b. Nottingham, e. Nottingham, 47969, Pte., k. in a., F. & F., 3/5/17.

APPENDIX 4

Clarke, Edward, b. Rossington, Yorks, e. Mexborough, 27553, Pte., k. in a., F. & F.,2/3/17, formerly 22182, York & Lancs.
Clarkson, George, b. Masham, Yorks, e. Masham, Yorks, 33090, Pte., d. of w., F. & F., 12/5/17.
Clayburn, Joe, b. Bradford, e. Bradford, Yorks, 18/1415, Pte., k. in a., F. & F., 12/5/17.
Clayton, Horace, b. Luton, Beds., e. Bradford, Yorks, 18/844, Pte., k. in a., F. & F., 1/7/16.
Clegg, Joseph, b. Normanton, Yorks, e. Bradford, 18/879, Cpl., d. of w., F. & F., 1/7/16.
Clough, George, b. Bradford, e. Bradford, 18/507, Pte., k. in a., F. & F., 1/7/16.
Cockshott, Frank, b. Bradford, e. Bradford, Yorks, 18/902, Pte., k. in a., F. & F., 30/7/16.
Collinson, John Edward, b. Bradford, e. Bradford, Yorks, 18/1491, Pte., k. in a., F. & F., 25/2/17.
Cooke, Williamson, b. Leeds, e. Leeds, 29497, Pte., k. in a., F. & F., 19/5/17.
Coulson, George, b. Rothwell, Yorks, e. Leeds, 26275, Pte., d., F. & F.,15/9/17.
Craven, James, b. Bradford, e. Bradford, Yorks, 18/152, Pte., k. in a., F. & F., 1/17/16,
Craven, Wilfred, b. Bradford, e. Bradford, Yorks, 18/878, Pte., k. in a., F. & F., 30/6/16.
Craven, William Allen, b. Bradford, e. Bradford, Yorks, 18/667, Pte., k. in a., F. & F., 1/7/16.
Crerar, John, b. Bradford, e. Bradford, Yorks, 18/997, Pte., d. of w., F. & F., 29/9/16.
Crimmins, Herbert, 18/313, Pte., k, F. & F., 5/9/16.
Croft, Stanley, b. Bradford, e. Bradford, Yorks, 18/35, L/Cpl., k. in a., F. & F., 27/7/16.
Crossley, Herbert, b. Bradford, e. Bradford, Yorks, 18/683, Pte., k. in a., F. & F., 13/11/16.
Crossley, John William, b. Bradford, e. Bradford, Yorks, 18/17, Pte., d. of w., F. & F., 19/5/16.
Crotch, Ernest, b. Bradford, e. Bradford, Yorks, 18/525, Pte., k. in a., F. & F., 1/7/16.
Crowe, Norman, e. York (Bulmer, Yorks), 40269, Pte., k. in a., F. & F., 13/11/16.
Crowther-Clarance, b. Bradford, e. Bradford, Yorks, 18/672, Pte, k. in a., F. & F., 1/7/16.
Cullum, Harold, b. York, e. Bradford, Yorks, 18/1055, Pte., k. in a., F. & F., 18/8/16.
Cure, Vincent, b. Bradford, e. Bradford, Yorks, 18/1211, Pte., d. of w., F. & F., 3/7/16.
Darling, Horace, b Bradford, e. Bradford, Yorks, 18/1264, Pte., k. in a., F. & F., 13/11/16.
Davies, Henry, b. Aberystwyth, e. Hammersmith, 48007, Pte., k. in a., F. & F., 3/5/17,
    formerly PM2/230451, R.A.S.C. (M.T.).
Daybell, Arthur, b. Bradford, e. Bradford, Yorks, 18/187, Pte. k. in a., F. & F., 1/7/16.
Denton, Thomas William, b. Bradford, e. Bradford, Yorks, 18/148, L/Sgt., k. in a., F. & F., 3/5/17.
Dixon, Fred, b. Bradford, e. Bradford, Yorks, 18/479, Pte., k, in a., F. & F., 1/7/16.
Dixon, Wilfred, b. Morton, Yorks, e. Bradford, Yorks, 18/375, Pte., d. of w., F. & F., 20/5/16.
Donovan, William, b. Hillsborougb Bks., Sheffield, e. Sheffield, 7252, Pte., k. in a., F. & F., 3/5/17.
Driver, Herbert, b. Bingley, Yorks, e. Keighley, Yorks, 18/1480, L/Cpl., k. in a., F. & F., 27/9/16.
Duggan, John, b. Greenock, Lanarks, e. Bradford, 18/624, Pte., d. of w., F. & F., 30/9/16.
Dunn, John, b. Leeds, e. Leeds, 33364, Pte., k. in a., F. & F., 3/5/17.
Dutton, Henry Frederick, b. Leicester, e. Leicester, 40462, Pte., d. of w., F. & F., 26/11/16,
    formerly 31024, Leicestershire Regt.
Dyson, Herbert, b. Bradford, e. Bradford, Yorks, 18/261, Sgt., k. in a., F. & F., 1/7/16 M.M.
Eccles, Harry, b. Woodley, e. Bradford (Bradford, Yorks), 18/1463, Pte., k. in a., F. & F., 10/6/16.
Ellis, Leslie, e. Pudsey, Yorks, (Bramley, Yorks), 41291, Pte., k. in a., F. & F., 3/5/17.
Fawcett, John, b. Castle Bolton, Yorks, e. Halifax (Skipton), 40330, Pte., d. of w., F. & F., 16/6/17.
Fawcett, Joseph Robert, b. Bradford, e. Bradford, Yorks, 18/176, Pte., k. in a., F, & F., 1/7/16.
Fearnside, William Edward, e, Bradford (Bradford, Yorks), 40271, Pte., k. in a., F. & F., 3/5/17.
Ferguson, John, b. Sunderland, e. Leeds, 12870, L/Cpl, k. in a., F. & F., 3/5/17.
Ferrand, Claude Ernest, b. Bradford e. Bradford, Yorks, 18/252, Pte., k. in a., F. & F., 22/5/16.
Firth, Arthur, b. Bradford, e. Bradford, Yorks, 18/1076, Pte., k. in a., F. & F., 30/6/16.
Firth, Herbert, b. Birstall, Yorks, e. Bradford, Yorks, 18/1244, Cpl., d. of w., F. & F., 7/5/17.
Firth, Joseph, b. Baildon, Yorks, e. Bradford, Yorks, 20/169, Pte., d. of w., F. & F. , 1/7/16.
Firth, Lewis, b. Bradford, e. Bradford, Yorks, 18/1167, Pte., d. of w., F. & F., 1/7/16.
Fisher, Alfred, e. Leicester, 40467, Pte., k. in a., F. & F. 3/5/17, formerly 31009, Leicestershire Regt.
Forryan, Thomas, e. Leicester (South Knighton), 40468, Pte., d. of w., Home, 7/7/17,
    formerly 30997, Leicestershire Regt.
Fry, James, b. Bradford, e. Bradford, Yorks, 18/68, Pte., k. in a., F. & F., 28/4/16.
Garbutt, John, b. Southport, e. Bradford, 18/638, L,/Cpl., k. in a., F. & F., 1/7/16.

THE BRADFORD PALS

Garside, Ratcliffe, b. Bradford, e. Bradford, Yorks, 18/882, Pte., k. in a., F. & F., 27/8/16.
Gaunt, Joseph William, b. Bradford, e. Bradford, Yorks, 18/526, Pte., k. in a. F. &.F., 3/7/17
Gaunt Leonard, b. Bradford, e. Bradford, Yorks, 18/405, Pte., k. in a., F. & F., 1/7/16.
Geeves, George, b. Bradford, e. Bradford, 47992, Pte., d. of w., F. & F., 13/5/17, formerly 28960, Yorkshire Regt.
Gentle, Thornas Henry, b. Birmingham, e. Birmingham, 47926, Pte., k. in a., F. & F., 3/5/17,
    formerly M2/267871, R.A.S.C. (M.T.).
George, Edward Sydney, b. Birmingham, e. Birmingham, 47927, Pte., k. in a., F. & F., 3/5/17,
    formerly 229811, R.A.S.C.
Giles, Henry Edward, b. Ashford, e. Ashford, Kent, 325156, Pte., k. in a., F. & F., 28/1/18.
Gill, John, b. Silsden, Yorks, e. Keighley, Yorks, 18/836, Pte., d. of w., F. & F., 1/7/16.
Gill, Sam, b. Bradford, e. Bradford, Yorks, 18/783, Pte, d. of w., F. & F., 3/7/16.
Gillett, Herbert Elijah, b. Bradford, e. Bradford, Yorks, 20/26 Pte., k. in a., F. & F., 30/6/16.
Gledhill, Herbert, b. Bradford, e. Bradford, Yorks, 18/614, Pte., k. in a., F. & F., 1/7/16.
Gledhill, John, b. Adwalton, Bradford, e. Bradford, Yorks, 19/133, Pte., k. in a., F. & F., 3/5/17.
Goddard, Tom, b. Leicester, e. Leicester, 27329, Pte., k. in a., F. & F., 12/5/17.
Godridge, William Henry, b. New Wombwell, Yorks, e. Bradford, 18/520, Pte., k. in a., F. & F., 3/5/17.
Goldthorpe, Walter, b. Sowerby Bridge, e. Bradford, 18/784, Pte., d. of w., F. & F., 1/7/16.
Gough, George Albert, b. Wolverhampton, Staffs, e. Bradford, 18/555, Pte., d. of w., F. & F., 15/11/16.
Grant, Albert, b. Leeds, e. Leeds, 33377, Pte., d., F. & F., 11/12/16.
Grant, Richard, b. Leeds, e. Leeds, 48806, Pte., k, in a., F. & F., 8/2/18.
Grayson, Randolph, e. Leeds, 40302, Pte., k. in a., F. & F., 24/10/16.
Greasley, Joseph James, e. Leicester (Birstall), 40475, Pte., k. in a., F. & F., 3/5/17,
    formerly 31129 Leicestershire Regt.
Green, Harry Charles, e. Bradford, Yorks, 18/193, Sgt., d. of w., F. & F., 22/6/16.
Green, Walter, b. Huddersfield, e. Halifax, Yorks, 32178, Pte., k, in a., F. & F., 13/11/16.
Greenwood, Henry Bernal, b. Bradford, e. Bradford, Yorks, 18/9, Sgt., k. in a., F. & F., 30/6/16.
Greenwood, Percival, b. Bradford, e. Bradford, Yorks, 18/906, Sgt., d. of w., F. & F., 5/5/17, M.M.
Gresswell, William Wood, e. Bradford, Yorks, 16/1728, Pte., k. in a., F. & F., 26/10/16.
Hackford, Frank, b. Martin, Doncaster, e. Bradford, Yorks, 18/413, Pte., d. of w, F. & F., 6/7/16.
Hague, Harold, b. Sheffield, e. Sheffield, 9071, Pte, k. in a., F. & F., 1/7/16.
Haigh, Ernest Willie, b, Halifax, e. Halifax, Yorks, 40241, Pte., k. in a., F. & F., 12/5/17.
Haigh, Morris, b. Batley, Yorks, e. Bradford, Yorks, 18/1105, Pte., k. in a, F. & F., 27/7/16.
Haines, Walter B., b. Leeds, e. Leeds, 26277, Pte., d. of w., F. & F., 7/5/17.
Hallam, George b. Leeds, e. Leeds, 300070, Pte., k. in a., F. & F., 15/6/17.
Halliday, Samuel, b. Windhill, Yorks, e. Bradford, Yorks, 18/80, L/Cpl., d., Home, 10/11/15.
Hamblin, Hubert Charles, b. St. Albans, Herts, e. Bradford, 18/196, C.S.M., k. in a., F. & F., 1/7/16.
Hamilton, William, b. Carrington, New South Wales, Australia, e. Newcastle-on-Tyne (Sunderland),
    20269, Pte., k. in a., F. & F., 3/5/17.
Hammond, Percy, b. Farnley, Leeds, e. Bradford, Yorks, 18/206, Pte., k.. in a., F. & F., 1/7/16.
Hanson, George James, b. Selby, e. Selby, Yorks (Cawood), 33422, Pte., k. in a., F. & F., 3/5/17.
Hardwick, William Cyril, b. Leeds, e. Colsterdale, Yorks, 15/1269, L/Cpl., k. in a., F. & F., 3/5/17.
Hargreaves, Richard, b. Wyke, Yorks, e. Bradford, Yorks, 18/1107, Pte., d. of w., F. & F., 17/5/16.
Harper, John Abbotson, b. Giggleswick, Yorks, e. Keighley, 20/145, Pte., k. in a., F.& F., 1/7/16.
Harriman, Elisha Horn, b. Hogsthorpe, Lincs, e. Spilsbly, Lincs, 40482 Pte., d., F & F., 5/2/17.
Harrison, Thomas Henry, b. Pudsey, Yorks, e. York, 41280, Pte., k. in a., F. & F., 3/5/17, M.M.
Hawkridge, James, b. Hopperton, Yorks, e. Harrogate, (Starbeck), 33402, Pte., d., F. & F., 5/5/17.
Hayes, Walter, b. Leeds., e. Leeds, 24254, L/Cpl., d. of w., F.& F., 27/10/16.
Haylock, Arthur, e. Bradford, Yorks, 40303, Pte., k. in a,, F. & F., 13/11/16.
Haynes, John Edward, b. Kirkstall, Yorks, e. Bradford, Yorks, 18/940, Pte., k. in a., F. & F., 1/7/16.
Haynes, Robert William, b. Armley, Leeds, e. Leeds, 33112, Pte., k. in a., F. & F., 3/5/ 17.
Haywood, Bertie, b. Waxham, Norfolk, e. Leeds (West Hartlepool), 40258, L/Cpl., k. in a., F. & F., 26/10/16.
Hazlewood, Harry, b. Doncaster, e. Bradford, Yorks, 18/25, Pte., k. in a., F. & F., 3/9/16.

APPENDIX 4

Heathcote, Dennis, b. Countesthorpe, Leicestershire, e. Leicester, 40479, Pte., k. in a., F. & F., 10/5/17, formerly, 31131, Leicestershire Regt.
Heeley, Robert, b. Bradford, e. Bradford, Yorks, 18/639, Pte., k. in a., F. & F., 3/5/17.
Hefford, Wilfred, b. Kettering, Northants, e. Leeds, 33183, Pte., k. in a., F. &F., 13/5/17.
Helliwell, Albert, b. Bradford, e. Bradford, Yorks, 18/1475, Pte., d. of w., F. & F., 6/7/16.
Helliwell, Maurice, b. Bradford, e. Bradford, Yorks, 18/279, Pte., k. in a., F. & F., 1/7/16.
Hill, Harry, b. Bradford, e. Bradford, Yorks, 18/1424, Cpl., k. in a., F. & F., 1/7/16.
Hill, John Henry, b. Bradford, e. Bradford, Yorks, 18/95, Pte., d. of w., F. & F., 27/4/16,
Hill, Norman, b. Bradford, e. Bradford, Yorks, 19/98, Pte., d. of w., F. & F., 6/7/16.
Hill, Thomas, b. Bradford, e. Bradford, Yorks, 18/1106, Pte., k. in a., F. & F., 1/7/16.
Hills, Harry, b. Bradford, e. Bradford, Yorks, 18/295, Pte., k. in a., F. & F., 1/7/16.
Hodgson, Joseph, b. Bradford, e. Bradford, Yorks, 18/1498, Pte., k. in a., F. & F., 1/7/16.
Hogan, William, b. Bradford, e. Bradford, Yorks, 18/1464, Pte., k. in a., F. & F., 17/6/17.
Holdsworth, Harry, b. Low Moor, Bradford, e. Bradford, 18/126, Cpl., k. in a., F. & F., 1/7/16.
Hollingdrake, Walter, b. Bradford, e. Bradford, Yorks, 18/709, Pte., k. in a., F. & F., 3/5/17.
Holmes, John, b. Bradford, e. Bradford, Yorks, 18/1625, Pte., k. in a., F. & F., 1/7/16.
Homsby, Joseph Edmund, b. Leeds, e. Leeds, 38687, Pte., d., F. & F., 21/2/17.
Horrocks, George, b. Bolton Woods, Yorks, e. Bradford, 18/374, Pte., k. in a., F. & F,. 1/7/16.
Houghton, John William, b. Metheringham, Lincs, e. Lincoln, 40481, Pte., k. in a., F. & F., 3/5/17, formerly 24931, 3/4 Lincs Regt.
Housecroft, Vincent, b. Drighlington, Yorks, e. Leeds, 26196, Pte., k. in a., F. & F. 3/5/17.
Hughes, Hughie, b. Beaumaris, Anglesey, e. Manchester, 20012, Cpl., k. in a., F. & F. 1/7/16, formerly 25081, 10th Hussars.
Hughes, Joseph Holmes, b. Whitby, Yorks, e. Leeds, 300040, Pte., k. in a., F. & F., 3/5/17.
Humphreys, Stanley, b. Bradford, e. Bradford, Yorks, 18/1132, Pte., k. in a. F. & F., 1/7/16.
Hurley, Herbert, b. Bradford, e. Bradford, Yorks, 18/1201, Pte., k. in a., F. & F. , 3/5/17.
Hutchinson, Harrison, b. Bradford, e. Bradford, Yorks, 18/1594, Pte., d. of w., F. & F., 27/7/16.
Ingleson, Harvey Dixon, b. Leeds, e. Leeds, 300057. Pte., k. in a., F. & F., 15/6/17.
Jackson, Fred, b. Bradford, e. Bradford, Yorks, 18/1427, Pte., k. in a., F. & F., 1/7/16.
Jackson, James, b. Scarborough, e. Scarborough, Yorks, 12969, Pte., k. in a. F. & F., 3/5/17.
Jagger, George William, b. Bradford, e. Bradford, Yorks, 18/942, Pte., d. of w., F. & F. 1/7/16.
Jary, Robert Eldred, e. Boston, 40484, Pte., d., F. & F. 15/1/17.
Jeffery, Arthur, b. Blackheath, Kent, e. Lewisham, Kent, 40786, Pte., k. in a., F. & F., 3/5/17, formerly 26153, K.R.R.
Johnson, Arthur, b. Bradford, e. Bradford, Yorks, 18/975, L/Cpl., k. in a, F. & F., 1/7/16.
Johnson, Charlie, b. Bradford, e. Bradford, Yorks, 18/60, Sgt., k. in a., F. & F., 3/5/17.
Johnson, Herbert, b. Staveley, Westmorland, e. Keighley, 18/838, L/Cpl., k. in a., F. & F., 1/7/16.
Jones, William Harold, b. Llanrhaiardi, Denbighshire, e. Bradford, 18/1269, Pte., k. in a., F. & F., 1/7/16.
Jordan, Arthur, b. Bradford, e. Bradford, Yorks, 18/1585, Pte., k. in a., F.& F., 1/7/16.
Jordon, William, b. Alnwick, Northumberland, e. Newcastle-on-Tyne, 47994, Pte., k. in a., F. & F., 3/5/17, formerly 32862, Yorks Regt.
Jowett, Frederick, b. Darlington, c, Bradford, 18/450, Pte., d. of w,, F. & F., 27/7/16.
Jowett, Thomas Lund, b. Pudsev, Yorks, e. Bradford, Yorks, 18/943, Pte., k. in a., F. & F., 1/7/16.
Joyce, Michael Henry, b. Bradford, e. Bradford, Yorks, 18/1523, L/Cpl., d. of w., F. & F., 3/7/16.
Kay, William Henry, e. Grantharn, 40486, Pte., k. in a., F. & F., 29/4/17, formally 25204, 3/4th Lincs Regt.
Kellett, Walter Arnold, b. Wibsey, Yorks, e. Bradford, 18/1343, Pte., k. in a., F. & F., 23/6/17.
Kendall, Harry, b. Queensbury, Yorks, e. Keighley, 18/634, Drmr., k. in a., F. & F., 1/7/16.
Krause, Frederick Lewis, b. Nottingham, e. Nottingham, 27367, Pte., d. of w., F. & F., 1/3/17.
Langdale, Thomas, b. Welburn, Yorks, e. Beverley, Yorks, 23057, Pte., k. in a., F. & F., 25/2/17, formerly 19313, East Yorks Regt.
Lapish, Fred, b. Shipley, Yorks, e. Bradford, Yorks, 19/103, Pte., k. in a., F. & F., 13/11/16.
Larvin, James, e. York (York), 40266, Pte., d. of w., F. & F., 12/5/17.

THE BRADFORD PALS

Leckenby, Mark, b. Bramham, Yorks, e. York, 34478, Pte., d., F. & F., 3/5/17.
Lee, Arthur, b. Leicester, e. Leicester, 40489, Pte., k. in a., F. & F., 3/5/17, formerly 31165, Leicestershire Regt.
Lee, Joseph, b. Glenfield, Leicester, e. Leicester, 40488, Pte., k. in a., F. & F., 3/5/17,
       formerly 31165, Leicestershire Regt.
Lee, Willfred, b. Liversedge, Yorks, e. Cleckheaton, Yorks, 18/1155, Pte., k. in a., F. & F., 12/5/17.
Lister, William Edward, b. Bradford, e. Bradford, Yorks, 18/1300, Pte, k. in a., F. & F. 1/7/16.
Littlewood, Tom Crowther, b. Skelmanthorpe, e. Huddersfield, 28457, Pte., d. of w., F. & F., 30/4,/17.
Lockwood, Arthur Harling, e. Bradford, (Laisterdyke), 18/61, Pte., k. in a., F. & F. 17/12.17.
Lowndes, Sam, b. Holmfirth, Yorks, e. Keighley, Yorks, 18/713, L/Cpl., k. in a., F. & F. 1/7/16.
McCaffrey, James, b. Leeds, e. Leeds, 19/229, Pte., d. of w., F. & F., 25/10/16.
McDonald, Joseph, b. Bradford, e. Bradford, Yorks, 18/1346, Pte., k. in a., F. & F., 1/7/16.
Macaulay, Kenneth, b. Keighley, e. Keighley, Yorks, 18/835, Pte., k. in a., F. & F., 30/6/16.
Mann, Thomas, b. Bradford, e. Bradford, 18/629, Pte., k. in a., F. & F., 28/8/17.
Margerison, John, b. Bradford, e. Bradford, Yorks, 18/49, Drmr., k. in a., F. & F., 1/7/16.
Marsden, Charles, b. Bradford, e. Bradford, Yorks, 18/1271, Pte., k. in a., F & F., 1 /7/16.
Marshall, Leonard, b. Wibsey, Yorks, e. Bradford, Yorks, 18/335, Pte., k. in a., F. & F., 3/5/17.
Massen, Thomas, e. Bradford, Yorks (Bradford), 18/1010, Cpl., k. in a., F. & F, 1/7/16.
Mayne, John George, b. Walworth, London, e. Bradford, 18/700, Sgt., d. of w., F. & F, 5/7/16.
Meays, Harry, b. Ackworth, Yorks, e. Bradford, 18/650, Pte., k. in a., F. & F., 30/6/16.
Melia, Patrick Franice, b. Wednesbury, Staffs, e. Middlesbrough, 21330, Pte., d. of w., F. & F, 22/8/16.
Metcalfe, David, b. Bradford, e. Bradford, Yorks, 18/698, L/Cpl., k. in a., F. & F., 3/5/17.
Metcalfe, John, e. York (Wetherby, Yorks), 201568, Pte., k. in a., F. & F., 31/8/17.
Metcalfe, Willie, b. Bradford, e. Bradford, Yorks, 18/446, Pte., k. in a., F. & F., 1/7/16.
Midgley, Mark, b. Bilton, Yorks, e. Poppleton, (Rufforth Grange, York), 33394, Pte., d. of w., F. & F., 2/3/17.
Miller, Andrew, b. Leeds, e. Leeds, 34377, Pte., k. in a., F. & F. 3/5/17.
Millington, Charles, b. Retford, Notts, e. Retford, Netts, 47977, Pte., k. in a., F. & F., 3/5/17.
Milner, Frederick, b. Leeds, e. Pudsey, Yorks, 33198, Pte., d. of w., F. & F., 9/5/ 17.
Milner, Herbert, b. Fagley, Bradford, e. Bradford, Yorks, 18/237, Pte., k. in a., F. & F., 1/7/16.
Milnes, Richard, b. Bradford, e. Bradford, York., 18/474, Sgt., d., Home, 29/6/15.
Millward, George, b. Sheffield, e. Sheffield, 47997, Pte., k. in a., F. & F., 3/5/17.
Minns, James, b. Whitechapel, Middlesex, e. London, 4/7904, Cpl., k. in a., F. & F., 3/5/17.
Mitchell, William, Henry, b. Bradford, e. Bradford, Yorks, 29264, Pte., d. of w., F. & F., 25/10/16.
Moffett, Henry, b. South Shields, e. Sunderland, 3/8607, Pte., d. of w., F. & F., 5/5/17.
Morris, Edwin, b. Bradford, e. Bradford, Yorks, 18/271, Pte., d. of w., F. & F., 25/5/16.
Moroney, Thomas, b., Dublin, e. Halifax, 22751, Pte., k. in a., F. & F,3/5/17, formerly 3/15433, West Riding Regt.
Mountford, William Charles, b. Rotherhithe, Kent, e. Southwark, 40792, Pte., k. in a., F. & F., 15/6/17,
       formerly 27082, K.R.R.
Murgatroyd, Arthur Edgar, b. Bradford, e. Bradford, Yorks, 18/13, Pte., k. in a., F. & F., 1/7/16.
Muscroft, Lorry, b. Bradford, e. Bradford, Yorks, 18/1112, Pte., k. in a., F. & F., 1/7/16.
Neal, Richard, b. Birmingham, e. Birmingham, 47935, Pte., k. in a., F. & F., 3/5/17.
Newsome, Joseph, b. Dewsbury, Yorks, e. Pudsey, Yorks, 27182, Pte., k. in a., F. & F., 3/5/17.
Newton, John, b. Keighley, e. Keighley, Yorks, 18/1160. Pte., k. in a., F. & F., 14/7/16.
Nicholl, Herbert Howarth, b. Bramley, e. Halifax, 22908, L/Cpl., k. in a., F. & F., 3/5/17,
       formerly 10789, 1st G.B. West Riding Regt.
Nixon, William Roland, b. Rugby, e. Nottingham, 47978, Pte., k. in a., F. & F., 3/5/17.
Norman, William, b. St. Andrews, Leicester, e. Leicester, 40492, Pte., k. in a., F. & F., 3/5/17,
       formerly 30986, Leicestershire Regt.
Normington, Arthur, b. Bradford, e. Bradford, Yorks, 18/1347, Pte, d. of w., F. & F., 1/7/16.
Normington, Joseph, b. Bradford, e. Bradford, Yorks, 18/373, Sgt, k. in a., F. & F., 1/7/16.
North, John Richard, b. Liversedge, Yorks, e. Bradford, Yorks, 18/31, Pte., k. in a., F. & F., 1/7/16.
North, Reginald, b. Liversedge, Yorks, e. Bradford, Yorks, 18/40, Pte, k. in a., F. & F., 1/7/16.
Norton, Frederick, b. Leeds, e. Leeds, 300013, Pte., k. in a., F. & F., 3/5/17.
Nowland, Walter, b. Leeds, e. Leeds, 40247, Pte., k. in a., F. & F., 29/7/17.

APPENDIX 4

Nuttall, Leonard, b. Bradford, e. Bradford, Yorks, 18/202, Pte., d. of w., F. & F, 27/4/16.
Oates, John Joseph, b. Evenwood, Durham, e. Normanton, Yorks, 40797, Pte., d. of w., F. & F, 24/11/16, formerly 28982, K.R.R.
O'Brien, James Hadcock, e. London (Huddersfield, Yorks), 40315, Pte., k. in a., F. & F, 13/11/16.
Ogley, Edwin Arthur, b. Heck, Yorks, e. Pontefract, 40799, Pte, k. in a., F. & F, 29/7/17, formerly 28983, K.R.R.
Oyston, William Wadsworth, b. Armley, Leeds, e. Bradford, 18/135, Cpl., k. in a., F. & F, 1/3/17.
Page, James William, b. Belvedere, Kent, e. Woolwich, 21443, Pte., d. of w., F. & F, 16/7/17.
Palframan, Gordon, b. Bradford, Yorks, e. Halifax, Yorks, 40246, Pte., k. in a., F. & F, 13/11/16.
Pape, Charles, b. Bradford, e. Bradford, Yorks, 18/860, Pte., k. in a., F. & F, 1/7/16.
Parkin, Charles, e. Leeds (Leeds), 40245, Pte., d. of w., F. & F, 16/11/16.
Parkin, Samuel Austin, b. Leeds, e. Leeds, 40256, Pte., k. in a., F. & F, 3/5/17.
Pass Harry b. Burslem, Staffordshire, e. Bradford, Yorks, 18/626, C.S.M., d. of w., 5/7/16.
Patchett, Herbert, b. Bradford, e. Bradford, Yorks, 18/198, Pte., d. of w., F. & F., 21/5/17.
Paterson, George Alfred, b. Forest Gate, Essex, e. East Ham, 40821, Pte., k. in a., F. & F., 1/3/17, formerly 26056, K.R.R.
Payne, Frederick George, b. Leeds, e. Leeds, 34334, Pte., k. in a., F. & F., 3/5/17.
Pearson, Samuel Benjamin, b. Hull, e. Hull, 23059, Pte., k. in a., F. & F., 3/5/17, formerly 19498, East Yorks Regt.
Pennett, William, b. Bradford, e. Bradford, Yorks, 18/358, Pte., k. in a. F. & F., 1/7/16.
Pennington, William, b. Stanningley, Yorks, e. Pudsey, Yorks, 25308, d. of w., F. & F., 1/3/17.
Phillips, Thomas, b. Windhill, Yorks, e. Bradford, Yorks, 18/1013, Pte., k. in a., F. & F., 3/5/17.
Philpotts, George, e. Leeds, 300059, Pte., k. in a., F. & F., 3/5/17.
Pinder, Harold, b. Leeds, e. Leeds, 300O32, Pte., k. in a., F. & F., 3/5/17.
Pipe, Harry, b. Bradford, e. Bradford, 27487, Pte., d., F. & F., 4/5/17, formerly 19035, West Riding Regt.
Plows, Richard, b. Tadcaster, Yorks, e. Bradford, Yorks, 18/1381, L/Cpl., d. of w., F. & F., 27/5/16.
Poole, Gilbert Edward, b. Bristol, e. Bristol, 47937, Pte., k. in a., F. & F., 3/5/17.
Poole, Harry, b. Shipley, Yorks, e. Bradford, Yorks, 18/1303, Pte., k. in a., F. & F. 15/6/17.
Powell, Albert Edward, b. Stockton, Durham. e. Sunderland, 23061, Pte., d. of w., F. & F. 9/7/16, formerly 9/14511, East Yorks Regt.
Presland, Albert Maltman, b. Bradford, e. Bradford, Yorks, 18/912, Pte., d. of w., Home, 30/11/16.
Preston, John, b. Bradford, e. Bradford, Yorks, 18/802, Sgt., k. in a., F. & F., 3/5/17.
Preston, Robert, e. Harrogate, 40307, Pte., k. in a., F. & F., 13/11/16.
Pullan, Edgar, b. Pateley Bridge, e. Keighley, Yorks, 18/619, Pte., k. in a., F. & F. 13/11/16.
Ragg, Alfred Harry, e. Leicester, 40498, Pte., k. in a., F. & F., 3/5/17, formerly 30996, Leicestershire Regt.
Redman, Harry, b. Wilsden, Yorks, e. Bradford, Yorks, 18/890, Pte., k. in a., F. & F., 1/7/16.
Reynolds, Arthur, b. Bradford, e. Bradford, Yorks, 18/1084, Pte., k. in a., F. & F., 1/7/16.
Richards, John Edward, b. Leeds, e. Leeds, 300065, Rfln., k. in a., F. & F., 29/4/17.
Richardson, Ernest, b. Leeds, e. Leeds, 300060, Pte., k. in a., F. & F., 3/5/17.
Riddiough, Ernest, b. Bradford, e. Bradford, Yorks, 18/966, Pte., k. in a., F. & F., 12/5/17.
Riley, Herbert Leonard, b. Bradford, e. Bradford, Yorks, 18/1015, Pte., k. in a., F. & F., 3/5/17.
Riley, Ralph, b. Bradford, e. Bradford, Yorks, 18/1085, Pte., d. of w., F. & F., 19/5/16.
Robinson, Frank, b. Halifax, e. Bradford, Yorks, 18/493, Pte., k. in a., F. & F., 16/9/16.
Robinson, Thomas Henry, b. Bradford, e. Bradford, Yorks, 18/195, Pte., k. in a., F. & F. 1/7/16.
Robson, Ernest, b. Bradford, e. Bradford, Yorks, 18/151, Pte., k. in a., F. & F., 1/7/16.
Rudd, Sydney, b. Leeds, e. Leeds, 36836, Pte., k. in a., F. & F., 2/3/17.
Rudstein, Solomon, b. Leeds, e. Belfast, 47940, Pte., k. in a., F. & F., 3/5/17, formerly M/2/229973, R.A.S.C.
Rumbold, William Edgar, b. Tadcaster, e, Tadcaster, Yorks, 23940, Pte., k. in a., F. & F., 27/7/16.
Rushworth. Charles, b. Bradford, e. Bradford, Yorks, 18/1205, Pte., k. in a., F. & F., 1/7/16,
Sansome, Frank, b. Bradford, e. Bradford, Yorks, 18/945, Pte., d. of w., F. & F., 4/7/16.
Saville, James William, b. Bradford, e. Bradford, Yorks, 18/776, Pte., k. in a., F. & F., 30/6/16.
Schofield, Leonard, b. Pudsey, Yorks, e. Bradford, Yorks, 18/1019, Pte., k . in a., F. & F., 15/6/17.
Schofield, Percy, b. Bradford, e. Bradford, Yorks, 18/2, L/Cpl., k. in a., F. & F., 19/5/16.
Senior, Fred., b. Leeds, e. Leeds, 25565, Pte., k. in a., F. & F., 3/5/17.

THE BRADFORD PALS

Shaw, Alfred, b. Nottingham, e. Nottingham, 47981, Pte., k. in a., F. & F., 3/5/17, formerly 68489, Sherwood Foresters.
Shaw, Charles, b. Bradford, e. Bradford, Yorks, 18/1641, Pte., d. of w., F. & F., 20/6/17.
Shaw, Fred., b. Batley, Yorks, e. Halifax, Yorks, 32534, Pte., k. in a., F. & F., 3/5/17.
Shaw, Herbert, e. Leeds (Leeds), 40238, Pte., k. in a., F. & F., 3/3/17.
Short, Ernest, e. Wainfleet, Lincolnshire, 40300, Pte., d. of w., F. & F., 12/5/17.
Shuttleworth, Thomas Whitaker, b. Kildwick, Yorks, e. Keighley, 18/1045, Pte., k. in a., F. & F., 1/5/16.
Sidebottom, Benjamin, b. Wakefield, e. Leeds, 300061, Pte. F. & F., 1/9/17.
Simpson, George, b. Leicester, e. Leicester, 40502, Pte., k. in a., F. & F., 3/5/17, formerly 31017, Leicestershire Regt.
Skirrow, Joe Forrest, b. Yeadon, Yorks, e. Bradford, Yorks, 18/1185, Pte.. k. in a. F, & F., 1/7/16.
Slater, James William, b. Bradford, e. Bradford, Yorks, 18/982, Pte., k. in a., F. & F., 3/5/17.
Smart, Bertie, b. Leeds, e. Leeds, 36966, Pte., k. in a., F. & F., 10/5/17.
Smith, Fred., b. Leeds, e. Leeds (Armley, Leeds), 25035, Pte., k. in a., F. & F., 25/10/16.
Smith, Harold Howard, b. Bradford, e. Bradford, Yorks, 18/544, Pte., k. in a., F. & F., 1/7/16.
Smith, John Edward, b. Salford, Lancs., e. Keighley (Skipton), 18/870, Pte., d. of w., Home, 7/10/16.
Spencer, Arthur, b. Leeds, e. Leeds, 300034, Pte., k. in a., F. & F., 3/5/17.
Spurr, John, b. Leeds, e. Leeds, 33114, Pte., k. in a., F. & F., 3/5/17.
Steedman, Frank, b. Leeds, e. Bradford, Yorks, 18/1291, Pte., k. in a., F.& F., 15/6/17.
Stenhouse, James Thomas, b. North Shields, e. Bradford, 18/1325, L/Cpl., k. in a., F. & F., 27/9/16.
Stott, Tom, b. Harrogate, e. Knaresborough, 23928, Pte., d. of w., Home, 22/5/17.
Sunderland, Joseph, b. Armley, Leeds, e. Bradford, Yorks, 18/385, Pte., d., F. & F., 11/10/16.
Sutcliffe, Frank, b. Bradford, e. Bradford, Yorks, 18/1196, Pte. k. in a., F. & F., 3/9/16.
Sutcliffe, Harry, b. Leeds, e. Leeds, 40255, L/Cpl., d. of w., F. & F., 3/5/17, M.M.
Swaine, George Albert, b. Bradford, e. Bradford, Yorks, 18/1333, Pte., k. in a., F. & F., 1/7/16.
Swallow, James, b. Leeds, e. Leeds, 300035, Pte., k. in a., F. & F., 3/5/17.
Sykes, Craven, b. Leeds, e. Leeds, 35295, Pte., k. in a., F. & F., 25/2/17.
Symons, Frederick William Henry, b. St. Pancras, London, e. Marylebone, 22940, Pte., k. in a., F. & F., 3/5/17, formerly 15999, West Riding Regt.
Tarran, Arthur, b. Bradford, e. Bradford, Yorks, 18/790, Pte., k. in a., F. & F., 1/7/16.
Tate, Joseph, b. Bradford, e. Bradford, Yorks, 18/89, Pte., d. of w., F. & F., 30/16/16.
Tempest, David, b. Leeds, e. Leeds, 12135, Pte., d. of w., F. & F., 2/3/17.
Tempest, John Lawson, b. Otley, e. Harrogate (Pannal), 24392, L/Cpl., k. in a., F. & F., 31/5/17.
Thomas, Frederick Edward, b. Bradford, e. Bradford, Yorks, 18/530, Pte., k. in a., F. & F., 3/5/17.
Thompson. Charles Frederick, b. Hull, e. Leeds (Hunslet), 34383, Pte., k. in. a., F. & F., 3/5/17.
Thompson, Ernest, b. Huddersfield, e. Bradford, 18/893, Pte., k. in a., F. & F., l/7/17.
Thompson, Horace, b. Bradford, e. Bradford, Yorks, 18/342, Pte., k. in a., F. & F., 1/7/16.
Thompson, James Henry, b. Bradford, e. Bradford, Yorks, 18/1434, Pte., k. in a., F. & F., 3/5/17.
Thornton, Charles Edward, b. Grimsby, Lincs, e. Richmond, 26063, Pte., k. in a., F. & F., 19/10/17.
Tidswell, Herbert Bedford, b. Sowerby Bridge, Yorks, e. Halifax, Yorks, 40233, Pte., d. of w., F. & F., 13/11/16.
Tiplady, Ronald, b. Halifax, e. Halifax, Yorks, 40237, Pte., k. in a., F. & F., 3/5/17.
Topham, George Henry, b. York, e. Bradford, Yorks, 18/984, Pte., k. in a., F. & F., 1/7/16.
Tweedale, Sam, b. Manchester, e. Bradford, Yorks, 18/99, Pte., k. in a., F. & F., 23/6/17.
Tyerman, William, e. West Hartlepool (West Hartlepool), 40314, Pte., d. of w., F. & F., 4/3/17
Upton, George Henry, b. Bermondsey, London, e. Bradford, 18/140, Sgt., k. in a., F. & F., 27/7/16.
Varlev, Herbert, b. Skipton, Yorks, e. Bradford, Yorks, 18/102, Pte., d. of w., F. & F., 17/6/17.
Vickerman, William, b. Hunmanby, Yorks, e. Scarborough, 21159, L/Cpl., d. of w., F. & F., 25/10/16.
Waddington, John, b. Bradford e. Bradford, Yorks, 18/896, Pte., k. in a., F. & F., 1/7/16, D.C.M.
Walden, Ernest, b. Bradford, e. Bradford, Yorks, 18/357, A/Cpl., k. in a., F. & F., 22/5/16.
Walker, Harry, b. Bradford, Yorks, e. York, 19559, Pte., k. in a., F. & F., l/7/16.
Walker, Stanley, b. Cleckheaton, e. Cleckheaton, Yorks, 20/191, Pte., k. in a., F. & F., 1/7/16.
Ward, John, e. Leeds, 300037, Pte., k. in a., F. & F., 3/5/17.
Watson, Donald, b. Hexham, Northumberland, e. Sunderland, 3/8787, Pte., k. in a., F. & F., 3/5/17.
Westwood, Joseph, b. Wombwell, Barnsley, e. Houghton, 22707, Pte., k. in a., F. & F., 3/5/17.

APPENDIX 4

Whitaker, Charles Gordon b. Bradford, e. Bradford, 18/245, L/Cpl., k. in a., F. & F., 27/7/16.
Whitaker, James, b. Denholme, Yorks, e. Keighley, Yorks, 18/1277, Pte., k. in a., F. & F., 1/7/16.
Whitaker, Willie, b, Wyke, Yorks, e. Bradford, Yorks, 18/596, Pte., k. in a. F. & F., 1/7/16.
Whittaker, Harold, b. Sharleston, Yorks, e. Bradford, Yorks, 18/541, Pte., k. in a., F. & F., 1/7/16.
White, Eric, b. Mendlesham, Suffolk, e. Bradford, Yorks, 18/1039, Pte., d. of w., F. & F., 8/7/16.
White, James Edward, b. Walworth, London, e. Kennington, 40816, Pte., k. in a., F. & F., 3/5/17, formerly 27031, K.R.R.
Widdop, Edwin, b. Bradford, e. Bradford, Yorks, 18/1186, Pte., k. in a., F. & F., 1/7/16.
Wild, Arthur, 18/356. Pte., k., F. & F., 5/9.16.
Wilkinson, Edgar, b. Bradford, e. Bradford, Yorks, 18/1127, Pte., k. in a., F. & F., 27/7/16.
Wilkinson, William Child, b. Bradford, e. Bradford, Yorks, 18/867, Pte., k. in a., F. & F., 3/5/17.
Wilks, Francis William, b. York, e. Bradford, Yorks, 18/467, Pte., k. in a., F. & F., 1/7/16.
Willan, John, b. Bradford, e. Bradford, Yorks, 18/1197, Pte., k. in a., F. & F., 15/8/16.
Wilson, Arthur Snowden, b. Bradford, e. Bradford, 18/1436, Cpl., d. of w., F, & F., 4/7/17, M.M.
Wilson, Fred, b. Leeds, e. Leeds, 300018, Pte., k. in a., F. & F., 3/5/17.
Wilson, Joseph, b. Leeds, e. Leeds, 36790, Pte, k. in a., F. & F., 3/5/17.
Winn, Joseph Luke, b. Nottingham, e. Nottingham, 47984, Pte., d. of w., F. & F., 5/7/17.
Wise, Thomas, b. Ripon, e. Bradford, Yorks, 18/1128, L/Sgt., k. in a., F. & F., 13/11/16.
Wood, Edward, b. Leeds, e. Leeds, 40342, Pte., k. in a., F. & F., 13/11/16.
Wood, John William, b. Middlesbrough, Yorks, e. Bradford, 18/274, Pte., d. of w., F. & F., 28/4/16.
Wood, Peter Barrett, b. Bradford, e. Bradford, Yorks, 18/564, Pte., d. of w., F. & F., 18/8/16.
Wright, Harold, b. Addingham, Yorks, e. Bradford, 18/189, L/Cpl., d. of w., Home, 15/7/16.
Yaffin, Jack, e. Leeds, 40301, Pte., k. in a., F. & F., 2/3/17.

APPENDIX 5: THE FIRST COMPLETE ROLL CALL: "A CREDIT TO THE CITY"

On Friday the 6th of November, 1914, the Bradford Daily Telegraph, as part of its "War Relief Fund" campaign, listed the first 1,000 men to enlist in what was to become the 16th Battalion. This list is reproduced here in its entirety. The inclusion of the trades and professions of the enlisted men conjures up the Bradford of the time and gives us a tantalising glimpse of the lives of these volunteers.

The Battalion's officers:

Colonel G. H. Muller, V.D. *Officer commanding the Bradford Battalion. A former commanding officer of the old Volunteer Battalion. Has shown himself to be most indefatigible in the discharge of his duties, and is extremely popular with all classes. He has the Volunteer decoration for long service. Col. Muller's father was Lieut. -Col. commanding the 2nd V.B. West Yorks (Bradford Rifles).*

Major W. Mitchell. *The veteran of the Bradford Volunteer movement, having no less than 37 years' service to his credit. Joined the 3rd West Yorks. as a private in April 1877, and promoted to lieutenant and quartermaster in 1896. Attained the rank of major in 1908. Possesses Volunteer officers' decoration and Coronation medal issued on the coronation of George V. Cashier for Messrs. Watson, Son and Smith, the well-known Bradford solicitors.*

Captain F. H. A. Gray. *Acting-Adjutant of the Battalion; hails from Dumfies. He is a most capable officer, and extremely popular with the rank and file.*

Captain James G. Crossley. *Served with the 12th Lancers, and afterwards with the 6th Lancashire Mounted Infantry. Has the Egyptian medal and star. A native of Bradford.*

Capt. Frank Holmes. *Private in 2nd V.B. West Yorks. (1896-8), and afterwards held a commission in the 3rd V.B. West Riding Regiment. Stationed at the Halifax Barracks as officer during the South African War. Retired from the 3rd V.B. West Riding with the rank of captain. Principal in the firm of Messrs. George Holmes, Son and Co., merchants, Swaine Street, and a well-known member of Ravenscliffe Golf Club. Son of the late Mr. George Holmes and Mrs. Holmes, of Cottingley Grange. His only brother, Mr. Arthur Holmes, has joined the Cameron Highlanders, and is now in Aldershot.*

Captain G. S. Blagbrough. *A native of Bradford and an old Bradford Grammar School boy. Comes from the Bridlington Grammar School Officers' Training Corps.*

Captain S. Moore. *Has served in the Civil Service Rifles. Went out to South Africa and has the medal for this campaign. Has been also in the Uganda Protectorate Service. Resides at Harden.*

Captain A. Howarth. *Bradford Battalion, West Yorkshire Regiment, eldest son of the late Mr. Thomas Howarth, of Bradford, woolcomber. Formerly of the Royal Fusiliers and Royal Marines. Has served in East, South and West Africa in various expeditions; several times wounded. Possesses the east and west Africs medals with clasps. Has a son in the same Battalion.*

Lieutenant D. L. Crabtree. *Has been in the 3rd Volunteer Battalion of the West Riding Regiment as a lieutenant. A son of the late Mr. John Crabtree, a well-known Bradford wool merchant.*

APPENDIX 5

Lieut. T. Linton Rhodes. *Served with the 2nd Battalion West Riding Regiment. A member of the well- known firm of Rhodes, Grandage and Co., merchants, Bradford.*

Lieut. A. W. Robinson. *From the Hastings School Cadets (Engineers). Lieutenant Robinson is a master at this school, and will be remembered as the well-known Bradford and Yorkshire Rugby footballer and Bradford cricketer.*

Lieut. and Quartermaster Geo. Fredk. Reynolds. *Joined the army in 1892 and served two years in the Royal Field Artillery; from 1894 to 1909 he was attached to the Mountain Artillery in India; and prior to the formation of the Bradford Battalion he was four years with the Mountain Artillery Territorial Staff for Scotland *** Aden - Operations in the interior 1 year 7 months.*

Lieutenant O. Morgan. *Son of Mr. Wm. Morgan, the well-known solicitor, of the firm of Messrs. Sam Wright, Morganand Co., of Bradford and Shipley.*

2nd Lieut. Robert Sutcliffe. *Only son of the late Mr. Tom Sutcliffe, of Idle, and a partner in the firm of Messrs. Sutcliffe and Trenholme, solicitors, Bradford. Joined the Public Schools' Battalion, 12th Middlesex Regiment, and has been training at Kempton Park. A Bradford Grammar School Old Boy and a plus golfer. Runner-up for the Yorkshire Amateur Championship, 1907.*

2nd-Lieut R. W. H. Pringle. *From the Cambridge Officers' Training Corps.*

2nd-Lieut. A. Howarth. *Bradford Battalion West Yorkshire Regiment. Son of Captain Howarth, of the same battalion. Has been a member of an Officers' Training Corps.*

2nd-Lieut. J. M. H. Hoffmann. *Bradford "Pals" Battalion. Son of the late Mr. Frank Hoffmann, of Bradford. Was articled with Messrs. Beevers and Adjie, accountants, of Leeds.*

2nd-Lieut. S. L. F. Hoffmann. *Bradford "Pals" Battalion. Son of the late Mr. Frank Hoffmann, of Bradford. Was with Mr. Henry Mason, spinner and manufacturer, learning the business.*

2nd-Lieut. F. R. B. Jowitt. *Officers' Training Corps.*

2nd-Lieut. C. H. Grimshaw. *A native of Bradford, and will be remembered by many as a member of the Ravenscliffe Golf Club.*

2nd-Lieut. F. R. Webster. *An old Artillery Volunteer and a native of Bradford.*

2nd-Lieut. B. Ryan. *Son of the chaplain of the 6th West Yorkshire Regiment.*

2nd-Lieut. J. H. Robinson. *Son of Mr. J. H. Robinson, President of the Bradford Chamber of Commerce, one of the promoters of the movement for the formation of the Battalion.*

2nd-Lieut. N . Crabtree. *A native of Bradford who has seen considerable service with volunteer forces.*

2nd-Lieut. D. Smith. *Belongs to the district, but has not yet joined the Battalion.*

Non-Commissioned Officers :

Acting Regimental Sergt. Major W. Turner
Company Sergt. Major B. Hammond
Company Sergt. Major W. Horsfield
Company Sergt. Major C. A. Watson
Quarter-Master Sergt. H. Gorman
Quarter-Master Sergt. F. Hardaker
Quarter-Master Sergt. W. W. Jenkinson
Quarter-Master Sergt. A. E. Oddy
Sergt. Cook A. Tinson
Sergt. Master Tailor W. A. McMann
Sergt. Shoemaker E. Cope
Orderly Room Sergt. H. Fearnsides
Sergt. Drummer J. S. Cooper
Sergt. F. Beaumont
Sergt. J. W. Bolton
Sergt. J. Catchpole
Sergt. D. Chambers
Sergt. J. Constable
Sergt. G. Cousins
Sergt. F. Emsley
Sergt. W. G. Evans
Sergt. W. Gillard
Sergt. B. Hanson
Sergt. H. L. Irving
Sergt. J. Lambert
Sergt. F. Lister
Sergt. J. W. Mason
Sergt. R. B. Mitchell
Sergt. W. Morgan
Sergt. B. Pratt
Sergt. J. Price
Sergt. H. Quest
Sergt. A. Redman
Sergt. A. B. Spence
Sergt. D. Wild
Lance Sergt. H. C. Dadswell
Lance Sergt. H. Edmondson
Lance Sergt. H. W. Edwards
Lance Sergt. J. Elliott
Lance Sergt. R. Lambert
Lance Sergt. H. McCulley
Lance Sergt. T. P. Quest
Lance Sergt. F. A. Swann
Corporal E. V. Appleton
Corporal F. Bancroft
Corporal F. Barber
Corporal W. Bower
Corporal N. C. Bowman
Corporal W. A. Brook
Corporal W. E. Bunclark
Corporal J. T. Burke
Corporal E. Butler
Corporal A. Chippendale
Corporal G. A. Clarke
Corporal T. A. Culling
Corporal H. Drake
Corporal T. Duckworth
Corporal N. Goodyear
Corporal T. Gorman
Corporal W. Guilfoyle
Corporal S. Hainsworth
Corporal W. Holden
Corporal J. Kilbride
Corporal H. Middleton
Corporal H. Middleton
Corporal A. H. Moulson
Corporal E. Murgatroyd
Corporal H. Newsome
Corporal H. Pearson
Corporal G. D. Pratt
Corporal L. Robinson
Corporal W. H. Sanderson
Corporal H. J. Saville
Corporal W. W. Simmond
Corporal N. A. Smith
Corporal A. H. G. Sowden
Corporal B. Sutcliffe
Corporal D. Thompson
Corporal B. K. Wallis
Corporal J. W. Wallis
Corporal F. Watson
Corporal C. F. Whittaker
Corporal W. H. Willis
Lance Corpl. P. W. Barkess
Lance Corpl. B. Bennett
Lance Corpl. A. H. Briggs
Lance Corpl. H. Cliffe
Lance Corpl. C. Clough
Lance Corpl. J. A. Dane
Lance Corpl. J. W. Dodsworth
Lance Corpl. E. Dunkley
Lance Corpl. J. C. Fishwick
Lance Corpl. E. Fletcher
Lance Corpl. W. Francis
Lance Corpl. C. H. Gledhill
Lance Corpl. G. H. Haigh
Lance Corpl. S. Hardy
Lance Corpl. H. Hartley
Lance Corpl. D. Helliwell
Lance Corpl. R. Hill
Lance Corpl. E. Hurp
Lance Corpl. W. Ingle
Lance Corpl. G. Latham
Lance Corpl. H. Metcalfe
Lance Corpl. J. Mooney
Lance Corpl. W.H. Mosley
Lance Corpl. G. H. Murphy
Lance Corpl. R. R. Oxtoby
Lance Corpl. F. Preston
Lance Corpl. L. Probert
Lance Corpl. E. Rasche
Lance Corpl. C. Stanway
Lance Corpl. J. A. Townshend
Lance Corpl. F. Walker
Lance Corpl. W. Whelan
Lance Corpl. H. C. Wilshire

APPENDIX 5

Enlisted men

A
Ackroyd, Irving, Proctor, woolsorter
Ackroyd, Willie, warehouseman
Adams, George William, engineer
Akam, James Rhodes, timber merchant
Aked, Clement, manufacturer
Aldersley, Edmund, clerk
Allcock, John William, motor lorry steerer
Allen, Percival, butcher
Allott, Frederick, barman, masseur
Ambler, Frederick, upholsterer
Ambler, John Richard, bricklayer
Ambler, Victor, spinning proofer
Anderson, James Gilchrist, clerk
Angel, Henry George Alfred, dyer's labourer
Appleton, Edward Victor, University coach
Armstrong, Gilbert, warehouseman
Arnott, Harold, clerk
Ascough, Harry, warehouseman
Ashforth, George Wheatley, bank clerk
Ashley, Albert, general dealer
Ashworth, Edward, actor
Ashworth, Harold, painter
Astbury, Reginald, mechanical engineer
Atkinson, William, seal finisher

B
Bailey, Norman, clerk
Bailey, Samuel, clerk
Balaam, George Charles, horse driver
Balme, Benjamin, woolsorter
Bancroft, Fred, solicitor's clerk
Banks, James, warehouseman
Bannister, William, dyer's labourer
Barber, Frank, mechanical engineer
Barker, Alfred, tramway messenger
Barker, Francis Albert, warehouseman
Barker, Harold, cashier
Barker, Herbert, stuff warehouseman
Barker, Walter Clarence, joiner
Barnes, Ernest Atkinson, clerk
Barnes, Ernest, clerk
Barnes, Stanley, none
Barr, Phillip Henry, yarn salesman
Barraclough, Fred, stuff presser
Barstow, William Edwin, portmanteau maker
Bartley, William, woolcomber
Barton, Charles Edward, draughtsman
Bastow, John Henry, dyer's labourer
Bastow, William, clerk
Bateman, Herbert, clerk
Batty, Herbert, labourer
Bawdon, Josiah Frederick, packer
Baxter, Fred, butcher's assistant
Beach, Frederick Charles,
Bean, Charles Edward, surveyor's assistant
Beanland, Percy, mechanic
Beanland, Robert Douglas, warehouseman
Beaumont, Fred, insurance agent
Beaumont, Jonah, woolsorter
Bebb, Harry, painter
Beesley, James, cutler
Bell, Arthur, clerk
Bell, Edward, clerk
Bell, Ralph, casemaker
Bell, William Edward, dyer's labourer
Bendall, George William, fitter
Benn, James, clerk
Benn, William Henry, manufacturer
Bennett, Benjamin, woolcomber
Bentley, George Frederick, brass finisher
Bentley, Sargent, warehouseman
Berry, Charles, pawnbroker's assistant
Berry, Frank, draughtsman
Berry, Lawrence, shuttlemaker
Binder, William Ernest, stoker
Birch, William, bricklayer
Blakeborough, Arthur, woolsorter
Blakeborough, William Herbert, professional boxer
Blakey, Frederick Archie, engineman
Blakey, Percy, warehouseman
Blaydon, Arthur, tailor's cutter
Blues, Alfred, motor mechanic
Blundell, Willie, drawing overlooker
Bogle, Clifford, dentist's traveller
Bolland, Charles Edward, warehouseman
Bolton, John William, tramway conductor
Bolton, Watson, mechanic
Bond, william, warehouseman
Booth, Allen Hodgson, architect's assistant
Booth, Herbert, draper's assistant
Booth, Joshua Myers, warehouseman
Booth, William Crane, brass finisher

Borkess, Robert, timekeeper
Bottomley, Alfred, woolsorter
Bottomley, Charles Albert, stuff merchant
Bottomley, William Ewart, joiner
Bowen, William, card grinder
Bower, Harold, mechanic
Bower, Harry, warehouseman
Bower, John Arthur, woolsorter
Bower, Thomas Edward, stuff presser
Bowes, Herbert, dyer's labourer
Bowling, William, farmer
Bowram, robert Horton, accountant
Boynton, Frank, grocer's assistant
Bradshaw, Ernest, card grinder
Breckenridge, John, traveller
Breingan, Samuel Kerr, clerk
Brennan, George Henry, brewer's storekeeper
Briggs, Albert, warehouseman
Briggs, Arthur Harold, engine driver
Brighton, Raymond, assistant overlooker
Broadbent, Joseph Foster, clerk
Broadley, Frederick William, farrier
Brodie, Martin Rutherford, accountant
Brogden, John Henry, cashier
Brook, John Croft, barman
Brook, William Arthur, engineer
Brown, George, lunatic attendant
Brown, Harry, labourer
Brown, William, waiter
Bruce, Frederick George, Labourer
Bruce, Thomas, pattern maker
Brundrett, Frank, patternroom clerk
Buckborough, James Ernest, tailor's cutter
Buckley, Albert, dyer's labourer
Buckley, Harry Holmes, clerk
Buckley, John, hairdresser
Buffham, Louis, painter
Bunclark, Walter Ernest, engineer
Burgess, James, wool merchant's apprentice
Burgoyne, John Gerald, stuff merchant
Burke, John Thomas, dyer's labourer
Burrow, Cyril Cutts, yarn tester
Burrows, frank, labourer
Burrows, John, warp dresser
Burton, Thomas, textile designer
Burton, Walter, draper's assistant
Busley, Harry, wiredrawer
Butler, Ernest Benjamin, piano tuner

Butler, Ernest, electrical jointer
Butterfield, Arthur, bank cashier
Butterfield, Gilbert Emmott, clerk
Buttery, Arthur Cecil, woolsorter
Buttrick, Hubert Ernest, draper's assistant

C

Cain, Harry, clerk
Calvert, Albert, warehouseman
Calvert, Joseph, draper's assistant
Cannon, Horace, motor engineer
Carter, Frank Benjamin, printer
Carter, Herbert Cyril, clerk
Carter, John Foster, engineer's agent
Carter, William Henry, grocer
Cartledge, Arthur, warehouseman
Cartledge, Joseph
Casemore, Harold, mechanic
Catchpole, John, motor mechanic
Cauldwell, Alfred, warp dresser
Chambers, Daniel, drayman
Child, George W.
Chilton, William, printer
Chippendale, Alred, carter
Clark, George Alfred, cashier
Clark, Joseph, driver
Clark, Leonard, card grinder
Clark, Thomas, compositor
Clayton, George, woolsorter
Clayton, John, woolsorter
Cleveland, Phillip, clerk
Cliff, Henry, wool salesman
Clough, Albert, clerk
Clough, Charlie, warehouseman
Clough, Edmund, turner
Clough, Morris, clothier's manager
Clough, Sam, clerk
Clough, Squire, clerk
Cockitt, Greenough, tram conductor
Cockitt, William Henry, tramway conductor
Cockroft, John Pearson, butcher
Coe, Frederick William, clerk
Coe, Harold Glover, draper's apprentice
Coe, Harry, piece looker-over
Coe, Tom Walter, caretaker
Colbridge, Robert Gilderdale, weaving overlooker
Collett, Joseph, dyer's labourer
Comber, John Smedley, articled pupil

APPENDIX 5

Conroy, Joseph Harold, seal finisher
Constable, Alfred, clerk
Constable, John, velvet finisher
Cook, Charles, boot salesman
Cooke, John, combing jobber
Cooper, Amos, turner
Cooper, John Samuel, musician
Cope, Edward, boot retailer
Cope, Herbert, warehouseman
Corless, Fred, clerk
Corless, Harry, groom
Corry, Egbert John, traveller
Crabtree, Herbert Bellamy, fishmonger
Crabtree, Leonard, stuff presser
Craven, Ernest, clerk
Craven, George Willie, dyer's labourer
Craven, John Milton
Craven, Sam Willie, draper
Crocker, James Norman, agricultural pupil
Croft, Harold, bookbinder
Cromwell, Garfield, barman
Crookes, Arthur John, warehouseman
Crosdale, Daniel, labourer
Crossland, Harry, clerk
Crossley, Lewis, cashier
Cryer, John Henry Ernest, carter
Culladon, Herbert, accountant
Culling, Thomas, dyer's labourer
Culling, William Alfred, warehouseman
Culloden, Edgar, warehouseman
Cussins, George, police constable

D

Dacey, William, warehouseman
Dadswell, Hugh Cecil, photographer's assistant
Dane, James Arthur, printer
Dargue, Herbert, labourer
Davies, Ernest Jones, printer's cutter
Dawson, Edwin, woolcomber
Dawson, John Ernest Jonas, clerk
Dawson, Thomas, woolcomber
Dawson, William arthur, auctioneer
Day, William George, mechanic
Daybell, Thomas, sawyer
Daykin, James William, gardener
Dean, John Percival, postman
Dearden, Ernest, plush cutter
Demaine, Harry, warehouseman

Denby, John, mechanic's labourer
Dennison, Arthur, clerk
Dennison, William, grocer
Denton, Herbert, moulder
Dickens, Ernest Victor, Jacquard harness maker
Dickenson, Charlie, engineer
Dickinson, George Hardie, clerk
Dixon, David Percival
Dixon, Farrington, clerk
Dixon, Frederick Charles, electrical engineer
Dobson, Henry, mechanic's labourer
Dobson, John, manufacturer's assistant
Dobson, Phillip Norman, assistant mill manager
Dodds, Joseph, dyer's labourer
Dodsworth, John William, seal finisher
Donohoe, Maurice, telephone engineer
Drake, Bertram, sundry business
Drake, Harry, teacher
Drake, Isaac, weaving overlooker
Driver, Leonard, stud groom
Duckworth, David, fish frier
Duckworth, Isaac, window cleaner
Duncan, Edward Manngham, labourer
Duncan, Thomas Thompson, warehouseman
Dunkley, Eppaphras, electrical engineer
Dunville, Harry, wool trade
Durrant, Sidney, exhibition attendant
Dyson, George William, lithographer
Dyson, John William, saleroom manager
Dyson, Percy, yeast dealer

E

Easterby, Albert, dyer's labourer
Edmondson, Albert, clerk
Edmondson, George, dyer's labourer
Edmondson, Harry, jewellery salesman
Edmondson, Willie, labourer
Edwards, Ernest, woolcomber
Edwards, Harry Willis, bank cashier
Edwards, Willie, warehouseman
Eldridge, Edwin Henry William
Elliott, John, night watchman
Ellis, John Cyril, assistant dyer
Ellison, Alfred. Firer
Emmens, George, warehouse clerk
Emmott, Leonard, joiner
Emsley, Fred, vanman

Emsley, Harry, tram driver
Evans, George William, steward

F

Fairfax, Frank, minister
Farley, Edward, warehouseman
Farrar, Sutcliffe, warehouseman
Farrer, Charles, traveller
Faulkner, Edmund Quincliff, yarn assistant
Fawthorpe, Harold, draper
Fawthorpe, Harry, draper's assistant
Fearnssides, Harry, clerk
Feather, Henry, spinner
Fenton, Arthur, waiter
Fenwick, Arthur, photographic assistant
Ferguson, George, fishmonger
Firth, Harry, seal finisher
Firth, Herbert, clerk
Firth, Sydney, clerk
Fishwick, George Arthur, dyer's labourer
Fishwick, John Charles, presser
Fletccher, Edward, dyer's labourer
Fletcher, John, dyer's labourer
Flood, Walter Lawrence, warehouseman
Forder, Alfred, gardener
Foster, Alfred, motor mechanic
Foster, Edwin, clerk
Foster, Howard, warpdresser
Foulds, J.
Foulds, Milford, clerk
Fowler, Crossley, clerk
Fowler, Tom, weftman
Fox, Thomas Edwin, auctioneer's clerk
France, William Henry, seal finisher
Francis, William, dyer's clerk
Freear, Thomas Wharton, woolcomber
Frost, Benjamin, cashier

G

Galloway, William Graham, traveller
Garbutt, Joseph, boots
Garlick, Louis, bookkeeper
Garnett, Tom, blacksmith
Garnham, Frederick, warehouseman
Garrett, Charles Herman, clerk
Gash, Bert, compositor
Gash, Harry, printer
Gatenby, Edgar, warehouseman
Gaunt, Frederick Matthew, carpet designer
Gee, Fred, warp twister's apprentice
German, Thomas, dyer's labourer
Gibson, John, wool buyer
Gilgan, James, spinning overlooker
Gill, William, sign writer
Gillard, Walter, mechanic
Gledhill, Charles Hiram, bookbinder
Gledhill, Ernest, tram conductor
Glover, Harry, spinning overlooker
Goldstraw, Norman, warehouseman
Gomersall, herbert, assistant salesman
Goodall, Alfred, brass moulder
Goodall, Frederick, private secretary
Goodliffe, Frank, wool apprentice
Goodyear, Norman, hatter
Gorman, Henry, shipping clerk
Gorman, Valentine, dyer's labourer
Gough, Edward, clerk
Gough, Ernest Albert, labourer
Grange, Edmund, clerk
Gransbury, George Uings, painter
Gratton, Samuel, warehouseman
Graves, Charlie, dyer's labourer
Gray, Adolphus, drayman
Gray, George Alfred, brass moulder
Gray, Gerald, shop assistant
Gray, James Henry, botanical brewer
Grayson, Arthur, photographer
Greaves, Cecil, edge gilder
Greaves, Percy, blacksmith's striker
Green, Charles, tram conductor
Green, Herbert, dyer's labourer
Green, Walter, packer
Greenwood, Arthur, hairdresser
Greenwood, Ernest, hairdresser
Greenwood, George, twister
Greenwood, Lawrence Mellor, Poor Law clerk
Gregory, Gilbert
Griffiths, Arthur Wilson, clerk
Griffiths, George Eric, dyer's chemist
Grimshaw, Harold, clerk
Groves, Fred, clerk
Grunwell, George, clerk
Guest, Benjamin, clerk
Gunyon, Cyril Paul Herbert, traveller

APPENDIX 5

H

Haddock, Percy, auctioneer
Haigh, Albert, brush maker
Haigh, George Haydn, cashier
Haigh, Joe Richard, butcher
Hainstock, Joseph Metcalfe, electrician
Hainsworth, Shepherd, tram conductor
Hainsworth, William Arthur, woolcomber
Hale, Walter, warehouseman
Haley, Charles, dyer's labourer
Haley, Henry, shopkeeper
Hall, John Alexander, warehouseman
Hall, Stanley Gaukroger, chemist
Hallett, George Thirston, engineer
Halmshaw, Hodgson, warehouseman
Halstead, Robert, wool trade
Hammond, Benjamin, curator
Hampshire, Arthur Phillips, commercial traveller
Hampson, George Edward, designer
Hancock, Fred, tramway worker
Hancock, Leonard, engineer
Hand, Edgar, wool puller
Hanson, Brinton, piece seeker-in
Hanson, Harry, clerk
Hanson, James Irwin, salesman
Hanson, Reuben, combing overlooker
Hardacre, Fred, traveller
Hardaker, Ernest Frederick, tailor
Hardaker, Harry, engraver
Hardaker, Luther, printer
Hardaker, William Richard, warehouseman
Harding, James Edwin, clerk
Hardisty, William, dyer's labourer
Hardy, Harold, clerk
Hardy, Sydney, butcher
Hardy, Sylvester, building inspector
Harper, Arthur John, photo engraver
Harper, Thomas Edward, tailor
Harris, John, fitter
Harrison, George, beamer
Harrison, Philip James, traveller
Harrison, Willie, warehouseman
Hartley, Clifford, board and casemaker
Hartley, Ernest, printer
Hartley, Harry, foreign traveller
Hartley, Harry, warehouseman
Hartley, Walter, clerk
Harvey, Ellis Ashton, pattern maker

Hasse, Oscar Waldemar, bank clerk
Hawksworth, Richard, machine ruler
Haywood, Thomas Winn, mechanic
Heaton, Harry Vaughan, wool salesman
Heaton, Joseph, twister
Heaton, William, warehouseman
Heggie, Arthur, assistant designer
Hellewell, David, yarn merchant
Hemingway, Arthur, upholsterer
Henderson, James, millhand
Heriot, James Grove, clerk
Herridge, Thomas Alfred Clegg, clerk
Hewitson, Harry, clerk
Hewitt, Frank, clerk
Hewitt, Horace, clerk
Hewitt, James Gordon, chemist
Hewitt, John Hodgson, fitter
Hey, Arthur, warehouseman
Hick, George, manufacturer
Higgins, Walter, clerk
Hill, Albert Ernest, butcher
Hill, Herbert Edward, dyer's labourer
Hill, John Robertshaw, analyst
Hill, Roland, clerk
Hinsley, William, traveller
Hirst, Oliver, clerk
Hoare, John William, patternman
Hoare, Percy, matchmaker
Hodges, Sylvester, dyer's labourer
Hodgson, Alfred, dyer's labourer
Hodgson, Harvey, cart driver
Hodgson, James Frederick, warehouseman
Hogan, John William, insurance agent
Holden, George, solicitor
Holden, Irving, kitchen porter
Holden, Walter, insurance clerk
Holdsworth, Henry Arthur, builder
Hollingdrake, Arnold John, clerk
Hollings, Hubert Arthur, draughtsman
Holmes, Charles, architect & civil engineer
Holmes, Ernest, spinning overlooker
Holmes, Herbert, warp dresser
Holmes, Wilfred, drayman
Holt, Charles Edward, dyer's labourer
Holt, Samuel, dyer's labourer
Hootan, John James, boiler fitter
Horn, Dawson, warehouseman
Horn, Ernest Briggs, clerk

Horner, Alfred William, yarn buyer
Horner, Luther, plush finisher
Horsfall, Tom, warp dresser
Horsfield, William, postman
Horsman, Harry, gardener
Howard, Ernest, dyer's labourer
Howarth, George, carter
Howe, Ernest, warehouseman
Howland, George, stoker
Hoyle, Frederick Harold, dental mechanic
Hudson, Charles Richard, painter
Hudson, Fred, woolcomber
Hughes, Frederick Caesar, apprentice to wool trade
Hughes, Sam, overlooker
Humble, James Phillip, warehouseman
Hunt, William Dennis, grocer's assistant
Hunter, Douglas, seal finisher
Hurp, Edward, plush cutter
Hurran, Thomas Burton, plasterer
Hustart, Albert, seal finisher
Hustler, Harold, warehouseman
Hutchinson, Fred, painter
Hutchinson, Norman Gwynne, clerk
Hyde, Eustace Emil, dyer

I
Illingworth, Henry, iron borer
Illingworth, Morris, clerk
Illingworth, Norman, shop assistant
Illingworth, William, cinema attendant
Ingham, Ellis, spinning overlooker
Ingham, Norman, printer
Ingle, William, card grinder
Iredale, Arthur, clerk
Irving, frank, warehouseman
Irving, Henry Leopold, commercial traveller
Isherwood, Gilbert, wastepuller
Isherwood, Wilfred, bricklayer
Iveson, Harry, warehouseman
Iveson, Ingham, brass moulder

J
Jackson, Arthur, tram conductor
Jackson, George Alfred, engineer
Jackson, James, clerk
Jackson, Joseph, woolcomber
Jackson, Walter, dyer's labourer
Jackson, Wilfred, gardener
James, Francis Montague Reynold, motor engineer

Jarman, Alfred, clerk
Jenkinson, Walter Woodhead, stuff merchant
Johnson, Alfred, clerk
Johnson, Alfred, gardener
Johnson, Henry Martin Finch, insurance manager
Johnson, Horace, blacksmith's striker
Johnson, James, clerk
Johnson, Ripley, woolsorter
Johnson, walter Shaw, millhand
Jolly, James Ernest, timber labourer
Jones, Harry, draughtsman
Jones, Llewelyn, steward

K
Kaye, Albert, warp sizer
Keating, Daniel, plush finisher
Keep, Albert, clerk
Kennedy, James, metal case maker
Kennedy, Michael Frank, shop assistant
Kenny, William, shop assistant
Kenyon, Bertram Thomas, electrician
Kershaw, Edmund, dyer
Kershaw, Frederick Percy, clerk
Kershaw, George, electrical engineer
Kilbride, John, clerk,
King, Edgar, chemical works foreman
King, Ernest Whitaker, stuff presser
King, Frederick George, mechanic
Kitchenman, Morris, newsagent
Kitson, Harry, butcher
Knight, Frederick Joshua, warehouseman
Knight, Hubert, clerk
Knight, Roland Hebden, woolsorter
Knott, Herbert, labourer
Knowles, Fred, warp dresser

L
Lambert, Arthur, draper's warehouseman
Lambert, John, innkeeper
Lambert, Robert, fruiterer
Lane, Albert Edward, music assistant
Lassey, Willie, technical student
Latham, Percy George, valuer
Lawson, Harry, warehouseman
Laycock, Charlie, driller
Laycock, Christopher, warp twister
Laycock, Francis William, clerk
Laycock, Harry, compositor

APPENDIX 5

Laycock, Richard Alfred, hairdresser
Le Grove, Joseph, clerk
Leach, Clement, cellarman
Leach, Eddy, joiner
Leach, Ernest, dyer's labourer
Leach, James Ralph, chemist's assistant
Leach, Percy, warehouseman
Leader, Sidney Ellis, clerk
Lee, Allen, dyer's labourer
Lee, Arnold, Poor Law clerk
Lee, Edward, commercial traveller
Lee, Frank, tailor
Lee, Wilfred, joiner
Leech, George Edward, butcher
Leek, Herbert, wardrobe dealer
Leeming, Fred, draper's salesman
Leeming, Harry, card grinder
Leeming, William Henry, stuff presser
Leggott, Arthur Smith, packer
Lewis, Harold, warehouseman
Leyland, Fred, warehouseman
Licence, Harry, woolsorter
Lightowler, Fred, seal finisher
Liley, William, wiredrawer
Lindow, Edwin, clerk
Linford, Joseph, newspaper organiser
Lingard, Thomas, clerk
Lister, Arthur, dyer's labourer
Lister, Frank, seal finisher
Lister, Harold, book-keeper
Little, Henry Arnold, wool buyer
Loben, John William, woolcomber
Lobley, Harry, agent
Lockett, John, seal finisher
Lofthouse, Charles Harold, yarn salesman
London, Charles cooper, clerk
Long, Arnold, millhand
Lord, Albert Edward, textile designer
Lowndes, Frederick stanley, seal finisher
Ludlam, Robert Ed., woolsorter
Lumb, Richard Arnold, schoolmaster
Lund, Tom Clough, mechanical engineer
Luty, Granville Daniel, warehouseman

M

Marshall, Harry Clifford, apprentice to wool business
Marshall, Maurice, clerk
Martin, Horace, warehouseman
Martindale, Maurice, clerk
Mason, John William, whitewasher
Massey, John, warehouseman
Matthews, Fred, civil service
McConnell, William, draper
McCormack, George Alexander, clerk
McCully, Harry, horse driver
McEvoy, Paul, florist
McFarlane, William Ward, foreman finisher
McIntyre, Arthur, clerk
McKinley, Paul, chauffeur
McMann, Frederick, tailor
McMann, William Andrew, tailor
Melville, Alexander, engineer's draughtsman
Mercer, John William, tramway employee
Middleditch, Arthur, warehouseman
Midgley, John Geoffrey, technical chemist
Midgley, Verity, drawing overlooker
Mills, Harrison, ship's cook
Mills, John William, insurance broker
Milnes, Francis Raymond, spinner's apprentice
Milnes, Harry Alexander, weaving overlooker
Milnes, Richard, clerk
Mitchell, John, bottle corker
Mitchell, Louis, warehouseman
Mitchell, Percy, law clerk
Mitchell, Robert Benjamin, clerk
Mitchell, William Garnett, stone mason
Moncaster, Herbert, postman
Monkman, Herbert, bank clerk
Monkman, John Henry, clerk
Moon, Frederick Gordon, clerk
Moon, James, clerk
Moon, Samuel Marmaduke, mechanic
Mooney, Joseph, gold blocker
Moore, Arthur, French polisher
Moore, Bernard, draughtsman
Moore, James William, labourer
Moore, Joe, warp dresser
Moorhouse, Harold, hairdresser
Morell, Franklin, professional musician
Morgan, George, clerk
Morgan, William, lodging-house keeper
Mortimer, Ernest, printer's labourer
Mortimer, Thomas Edward, warehouseman
Moseley, William Arthur, wool buyer
Moss, Robert, hairdresser's assistant

Moulson, Abraham Hirst,, waggon repairer
Moulson, Miles, bricklayer
Mountain, Thomas Statters, district manager
Murdock, Archibald Williamson, draper's manager
Murgatroyd, Ellison, traveller
Murgatroyd, Harold, engineer
Murphy, George Henry, window cleaner
Murray, Ernest, fitter
Musgrave, Frank, commercial traveller
Myers, John Arthur, gardener
Myers, Joseph, warpman
Mylrea, John Joseph, warehouseman

N
Nash, Robert Francis, beer bottler
Naylor, Joseph, dyer's labourer
Neath, John Edward, warehouseman
Nelson, Horace, warehouseman,
Nelson, Vincent, mechanic's apprentice
Newell, Francis Percival, wool trade
Newsholme, Arthur William, dyer's marketman
Newsholme, Harold, clerk
Newton, Alfred Ernest, clerk
Newton, Alfred, tailor's presser
Nicholl, Edgar, dyer's labourer
Nicholson, Arthur Brooke, apprentice engineer
Nield, George Cecil, clerk
Normanton, Frederick, poster writer
Normanton, Thomas, foreign correspondent
Normington, Robert Henry, clerk
Northrop, John, clerk
Norton, George Lofthouse, bookbinder
Norton, Verity, clerk
Norwood, George Henry, warehouseman
Nowell, James Kenworthy, wool trade
Nunns, Harold Killingbeck, clerk
Nurse, Herbert Edward, tea salesman
Nutt, Albert, warehouseman
Nutton, Lawrence Harry, overlooker

O
O'Brien, Allen, commission agent
O'Brien, William Mark, commission agent
O'Connor, Charles, packing case maker
O'Donnell, Bernard, dyer's labourer
O'Neill, John, dyer's labourer
O'Sullivan, James, French master
Oates, Walker Vernon, clerk
Oatsby, Reginald Rycroft, textile designer
Oddy, Alfred Edward, clerk
Ogden, Charles William, warp twister
Oldfield, Harry Bateman, butcher
Oswald, Harold, warehouseman
Oswald, Harold, warehouseman
Owen, George William, woolsorter

P
Packett, Donald, wool apprentice
Page, Thomas, woolcomber
Palliser, John Alfred, dyer's labourer
Parish, James Thomas Henry, warehouseman
Parker, Thomas Gladstone, manufacturer's apprentice
Parker, Willie, warp sizer
Parkinson, Edmund, clerk
Parkinson, Norman, electrical fitter
Paterson, Malcom Bruce, agricultural student
Pattison, Harold, warehouseman
Payne, Walter, silk dresser
Pearson, Ernest Stanley, clerk
Pearson, Herbert, clerk
Pearson, William, joiner
Pearson, Willie, advertising agent
Peel, Harry, warehouseman
Peel, William, waste dealer
Pennett, George Edward, warehouseman
Phillips, Vincent Alexander Andrew, clerk
Phillipson, Phillip, window cleaner
Pickering, Miles Bristow, clerk
Pickles, Ernest, engineer
Pickles, Herbert, salesman
Pickup, James Edward, printer
Pickworth, Charles, train driver
Pinder, Harry Hall, wiredrawer
Pitts, Harold, fitter
Pittsforth, Irvine, electrical engineer
Poale, Samuel, grease extractor
Pollard, Walter, warehouseman
Porter, Fred, clerk
Porter, William Hyde, warehouseman
Poustie, William, designer
Powell, Ernest, dyer's labourer
Powell, James, clerk
Pratt, Bell, printer
Pratt, Gordon Dawson, dyer
Precious, George, tramway messenger
Precious, Harold, warehouseman

APPENDIX 5

Prescott, Albert Edward, clerk
Prescott, Norman, clerk
Preston, Fred, weaver
Price, Joseph, carter
Priestley, Harry, warehouseman
Priestley, Laurie, cloth finisher
Priestley, Squire Mitchell, driver
Pritchard, Lewis Mark, ticket examiner
Probert, Lawrence, clerk
Proctor, John Whitehead, meter inspector
Proctor, Willie, engineer
Puilfoyle, William, schoolmaster
Pullen, John, machine leveller

Q

Quest, Harold, dyer
Quest, Thomas Percival, clerk

R

Raine, George, clerk
Raistrick, Albert, clerk
Ramsden, Alfred, warehouseman
Ramsden, Herbert, lithographer
Rasche, Ernest, yarn traveller
Rawnsley, Fred, clerk
Rawnsley, Gilbert Armitage, clerk
Raynard, Willie, teamer
Read, Wifred, salesman
Redman, Arthur, guide for RAC Corp
Redman, William, dyer's labourer
Renny, William
Renshaw, Ernest, labourer
Reveley, Gordon Reginald, clerk
Rhodes, Charles, accountant
Rhodes, Frederick, warehouseman
Rhodes, John, wool salesman
Rhodes, Stabley, tobacconist's assistant
Richardson, Bertie Stockdale, sizer
Ridehough, Harry, seal finisher
Riley, Thomas, canvasser
Riley, William, restaurant assistant
Roberts, Henry, butcher
Roberts, John, technical colourist
Robertshaw, George Herbert, wool buyer
Robertson, John Bright, accountant
Robinson, Ernest, warp twister
Robinson, Frederick George, salesman
Robinson, John Edward, tram cleaner
Robinson, Lewis, painter
Robinson, Ward, stuff warehouseman
Rockliff, George, clerk
Rockliff, Harry, warehouseman
Rogers, Henry Lawrence, furnaceman
Rogers, Hubert Ephraim, clerk
Rook, Herbert Frank, stuff warehouseman
Roper, Charles William, warp twister
Roper, Herbert, warehouseman
Ross, John Mackenzie, clerk
Rothwell, James Irving, clerk
Rudd, Joseph, French polisher
Rudd, Percy, clerk
Rushton, William, architect's clerk
Rushworth, William, dyer's labourer

S

Sagar, Harry, fitter
Saggers, William, fruiterer
Sanderson, William Haigh, carding overlooker
Sands, Albert Edward, brush maker
Saunders, Basil Ashby, dyer
Saunders, Harry, weftman
Saunders, James Henry, weftman
Saville, Harold Irby, mechanical engineer
Sayers, William, seal finisher
Schneider, Norman Halstead, clerk
Schofield, John James, solicitor
Schofield, Thomas Henry, clerk
Schulthess, John Ernest, technical student
Scott, Alfred, clerk
Scott, Allan, labourer
Seavers, William Henry, warehouseman
Seekings, Horace, clerk
Senior, Thomas, farm labourer
Shackleton, Ernest, iron moulder
Shackleton, john Victor, clerk
Sharman, Charles Victor, dyer's labourer
Sharp, Sam, dyer's labourer
Sharpe, Frank, borer
Sharpe, William Arthur, printer
Sharpe, William Barraclough, manufacturing stationer
Shaw, Albert, blacksmith
Shaw, Edward, woolcomber
Sheldon, John, musician
Shepherd, Albert Edward, bedstead maker
Shoesmith, Harry Lister, butcher
Shooter, James Robert, clerk
Silson, Harry Hartley, driver

Simmonds, Walter William, plumber
Simpson, Hugh Crawford Herman, electrical engineer
Sircon, Harry Innerdale, manufacturer's agent
Sives, Ernest Albert, warehouseman
Skelly, Thomas, warehouseman
Skirrow, Harry Edmondson, shop assistant
Skirrow, John Henry, weaving overlooker
Slicer, Bertram Fairfax, engineer
Slingsby, Fred, grocer
Smalley, Walter, wool buyer
Smith, Cecil Lawrence, clerk
Smith, Craven, painter
Smith, Frederick William, picture framer
Smith, Harold, warehouseman
Smith, Harry, sheet metalworker
Smith, Horace Harrison, electrical fitter
Smith, John Carr, tailor
Smith, John Joseph, warehouseman
Smith, Norman Clifford, agent
Smith, Percy Foster, stuff warehouseman
Smith, Raymond, technical student
Smith, Thomas Henry, labourer
Smith, Thomas, tripe merchant
Smith, Victor, warehouseman
Smith, Victor, weaving overlooker
Smith, Wallace Duncan, electrical engineer's apprentice
Smith, Walter, clerk
Smith, William, clerk
Smith, William, warehouseman
Soames, Ernest, spinning overlooker
Soames, Thomas, soap maker
Sowden, Albert Herbert Gilbert, clerk
Speight, William Moorhouse, chemist
Speight, Fred, mechanic
Spence, Alfred Brightrick, warehouseman
Spence, Eric, warehouseman
Spencer, Bernard, warehouseman
Spencer, Edward, clerk
Spencer, Francis William, warehouse clerk
Spencer, Jack, painter
Spiby, Walter Thomas, clerk
Spire, Henry Osborne, assistant tailor
Stables, Herbert Edward, weftman
Stageman, James William, mechanic
Standeven, Arnold, wool salesman
Stansfield, Matthew, weigh clerk
Stanway, Olando, designer
Starr, George Ernest, seal finisher
Stead, Edwin, warehouseman
Stephenson, Joe, traveller
Stevenson, Allen, clerk
Stevenson, William, engineer's fitter
Stewart, Norman, stockkeeper
Stott, Joe, draper
Strang, John William, dyer's labourer
Stretton, Arthur, metal polisher
Strothard, John, grocer's assistant
Stubbins, Herbert, salesman
Stubbs, Edgar Ernest, railway clerk
Studd, Frederick Percy, baker
Sugden, Ernest Norman, warehouseman
Sugden, Frank, contractor
Surr, William, dyer's labourer
Sutcliffe, Benjamin, decorator
Sutcliffe, Herbert, apprentice woolsorter
Sutcliffe, Herbert, overlooker
Sutton, Harry, truck builder
Sutton, Herbert, printer's apprentice
Sutton, Percy, clerk
Swain, Ernest, professional singer
Swain, Herbert, dyer's labourer
Swann, Percy Augustus, mechanic
Swettenham, Harold, meat salesman
Swift, Sam, stoker
Swift, William, case maker
Swinbank, James Allen, warehouseman
Sykes, Arthur, dyer's labourer
Sykes, James William, warehouseman

T

Tankard, Herbert, iron moulder
Tankard, Sharp, drawing overlooker
Tarrant, George, gardener
Tate, Randall Schofield, chemist
Taylor, Albert Victor, dyer's labourer
Taylor, Albert, scale maker
Taylor, George Stead, painter
Taylor, George, printer
Taylor, Herbert, tram driver
Taylor, Hubert, dyer's labourer
Telfer, David, draper
Tetley, Gilbert, cashier
Tetley, Irwin, cabinetmaker
Tetley, Walter, laboratory assistant
Thackray, Edgar, warehouseman

APPENDIX 5

Thomas, William Leonard, analytical chemist & engineer
Thompson, Harold M., warehouseman
Thompson, Louis, designer
Thompson, Malcolm, Oswold, clerk
Thomson, David, super porter
Thornton, Fred, stuff presser
Thornton, George John, carter
Thornton, John Robert, warehouseman
Thornton, Walter, assistant manager
Thorpe, Charles, car driver
Thorpe, Matthew William, warehouseman
Thorpe, Thomas, clerk
Thorton, Fred, woolcomber
Tickle, Sydney Ronald, window cleaner
Tilley, Arthur, warehouseman
Tilley, George, printer
Tilley, St Clair, coremaker
Tinson, Frederick tram driver
Tolson, Percy, clerk
Tomlin, John, weaver
Tomlinson, Dennis, bandmaker
Tordoff, Walter, dyer's labourer
Totty, Ernest Arthur, civil engineer
Townend, Herbert, blacksmith
Townend, James Edward, plumber
Townend, John arthur, traveller
Turner, John William, dyer's labourer
Turner, Walter, estate agent
Turner, William, dyer's labourer
Tuson, Thomas Wilfred George, clerk

U
Underwood, George Frederick, solicitor's clerk
Underwood, Harry, dyer's assistant

V
Varley, William Stanley, woolsorter
Vinter, Odell Norman, engineer

W
Waddilove, Norman, gentleman
Wade, Frederick Roland, weaving overlooker
Wadkin, Frank, gardener
Wainwright, Fritz, apprentice wool trade
Waite, Wilfred, labourer
Walker, Gordon, designer
Walker, Horace Robert, traveller
Walker, Percy, clerk

Walker, Peter. Woolcomber
Walker, William, clerk
Wallbank, Cyril, clerk
Wallbank, John William, lay evangelist
Waller, Frank, cloth finisher
Waller, George Arthur, engineer
Wallis, Edward Kenneth, plate-glass cutter
Wallis, John William, furnisher's salesman
Walmsley, Arthur, draper's assistant
Walsh, John, warehouseman
Warhurst, Ernest, electrician
Wasteney, George Arthur, warehouseman
Waterworth, Leslie, warehouseman
Watson, Albert John, stationer's assistant
Watson, Charles Arthur, Inspector G.P.O.
Watson, Frank, engineer's draughtsman
Watson, Lewis, draper's assistant
Watson, Lionel Cassels, assistant engineer
Watson, Maurice, clerk
Watson, Norman, butcher
Watson, William Edward, plasterer's labourer
Wedgbury, Walter, window cleaner
Weldon, Alfred, grocer
Wetherhell, Leonard, shop assistant
Whalley, James Arthur, mason
Wharram, W. Stephen, farm pupil
Wharton, Timothy, clerk
Wheelwright, Edgar, signwriter
Whelan, William, waiter
Whitaker, Charles Frederick, clerk
Whitaker, Irvin, dyer's labourer
Whitaker, Richard Edmondson, pattern room worker
Whitaker, Samuel, clerk
White, Tom, assistant surveyor
Whitehead, John, warehouseman
Whitehead, Walter, spinner's clerk
Whitehouse, George Richardson, chauffeur
Whiteley, Edgar, mechanic
Whiteside, John William, turner
Whitley, John E., insurance assistant superintendent
Whitley, William Oddy, draughtsman
Whitworth, Thomas Percy, draper's warehouseman
Wild, David, foreman wireman G.P.O.
Wildsmith, Reginald, clerk
Wilkinson, Arthur, butcher

Wilkinson, Arthur, seal finisher
Wilkinson, Clarence, traveller
Wilkinson, Harry, tramway messenger
Wilkinson, Joe, painter
Will, John William, draper
Williamson, Tom, dyer's labourer
Willis, Edgar, yarn merchant
Willis, Harold, traveller
Willis, William Henry, overlooker
Wilshire, Herbert Overend, clerk
Wilson, Edgar, chemist
Wilson, Frank, warehouseman
Wilson, George Francis, dyer's labourer
Wilson, George, window-cleaner (master)
Wilson, Gilbert Henry, warehouseman
Wilson, Leonard, wool merchant's apprentice
Wilson, Samuel, seal finisher
Wilson, William Ewart, clerk
Wise, Alfred, clerk
Womersley, Harry, iron moulder
Wood, Albert, weftman
Wood, Gordon
Wood, Herbert Morris, textile designer
Wood, John Leslie
Wood, John Thomas, warehouseman
Wood, Mark Allen Stanley, textile designer
Wood, Thomas Stanley, warehouseman
Wood, Willie Smith, upholsterer
Woodcock, Herbert William, electrical engineer
Woodhall, George Edward, driver
Woodhead, Ernest, woolcomber
Woodhead, James, warehouseman
Woodhead, Tom Ernest, draper
Woodhouse, Francis John, patternman
Woodhouse, Walter, warehouseman
Woodhouse, William Knowles, sailor
Worsnop, John William, solicitor's clerk
Wraith, Edmund, apprentice compositor
Wrigglesworth, Charles Edward, wool merchant
Wright, Louis, grocer's warehouseman
Wyld, Arthur, warehouseman

Y

Yeadon, George Stables, carpet planner
Yeadon, John, dyer's labourer

APPENDIX 6 : READING LIST

GENERAL:

Malcolm Brown: Tommy goes to War: Dent & Sons, 1978. *Based on letters, diaries and reminiscences of the ordinary soldier.*

A.G.S. Enser: A subject bibliography of the First World War. 2nd edition. Gower, 1990. *A recent guide to the thousands of books written on the First World War.*

Norman Gladden: The Somme 1916: a personal account. W.Kimber, 1971? *One man's view.*

Randel Gray: Chronicle of the First World War; 2 vols. Facts on File, 1990. *A tabulated presentation of events.*

Philip J.Haythornthwaite: The World War One source Book. Arms & Armour Press, 1992. *An excellent guide to events and sources.*

The Official History of the War. HMSO. *This multi-volume work was published over many years. The four volumes, 'Military Operations, France and Belgium, 1916,' covers the Battle of the Somme in detail.*

Terry Norman: The Hill they called High Wood. W.Kimber, 1984. *An account of a key area of the Battle of the Somme.*

Siegfried Sasson: The War Poems, Faber, 1983. *The edition from which the quotations in this book come.*

A.J.P.Taylor: The First World War: an illustrated history. H.Hamilton, 1963. Penguin, 1960. *Popular account by a leading scholar.*

The Times History of the War; 22 volumes. The Times Newspaper. *An illustrated newspaper-type chronicle of events published soon after they happened. Gives a contemporary 'feel' to the war as it progressed.*

Denis Winter: Death's Men: soldiers of the First World War, Allen Lane, 1978.

BRADFORD PALS AND THE WEST YORKSHIRE REGIMENT:

Bradford Citizens' Army League: Report of the work of the league in assisting recruiting for the Navy and Army for service in the European War from Sept.1914 to March 1916 [1916].

Fred Conquest: Brief diary of Private Fred Conquest, 18th West Yorks. Regiment. Typescript, 1915.

Fred Rawnsley: Diary of Fred Rawnsley, Signal Section, 16th West Yorks. B.E.F. Typescript, 1916.

E.V.Tempest and E.C.Gregory: History of the Sixth Battalion West Yorkshire Regiment; 2 vols. Percy Lund Humphries, 1921-3. *Appendices list those who went abroad April 1915 (1/6th) and January 1917 (2/6th), officers, casualties and honours.*

War Diaries of the 16th and 18th Battalions West Yorkshire Regiment:
  Dec.1915 - Feb. 1916   WO 95/4590
  March 1916 - Feb.1918   WO 95/2362
(At the Public Record Office, Ruskin Avenue, Kew, Richmond, London, TW9 4DU. Copies can be seen at the Prince of Wales's Own Regiment of Yorkshire Museum, 3a, Tower Street, York, YO1 1SB).

Bradford Heritage Recording Unit recorded the memories of a few Bradford men who fought in the first World War. Transcripts of the interviews can be consulted in Bradford Reference Library

Everard Wyrall: The West Yorkshire Regiment in the War 1914-1918; Vol 1: 1914-1916; Vol 2: 1917-1918. John Lane, The Bodley Head, [1928]. *Appendices list casualties.*

BRADFORD DURING WORLD WAR I:

Allerton Congregational Church: Diary issued by the Men's Own Class Feb.1916-Jan.1919. *Contains news from home and abroad.*

Bradford Khaki Club: Wonderful story of voluntary labour in the Great War, 1915-1919. 1920. *This was a social club for soldiers and sailors.*

City of Bradford: Lady Mayoress's War Guild, including the wounded soldiers' personal comforts fund: Report. 1919.

Charles Ogden: The Bradford war work souvenir. 1916. *Describes civilian work in Bradford with a list of voluntary war workers, and contains a chronological table of local war work events Aug.1914-June 1916.*

Richard I.Midgley: Attitudes towards the Great War in the City of Bradford 1914-1918. Typescript, 1987. *Huddersfield Polytechnic M.Phil thesis.*

Alan Smith: Bradford and the Great War: civilian response from Sarajevo to the Somme. Typescript, 1985? *B.A.thesis.*

COMMEMORATING AND LISTING SOLDIERS:

City of Bradford Roll of Honour Great War 1914-1918. *Lists, with brief details, most Bradford men who fought.*

The National Roll of the Great War 1914-1918. Section 9: Bradford. National Publishing Co., n.d. *Slightly fuller details of a smaller proportion of Bradford men who fought.*

Officers died in the Great War 1914-1919. HMSO, 1919. *List with very brief details and extracted in this volume.*

Soldiers died in the Great War 1914-1919. Part 19: The Prince of Wales's Own (West Yorkshire Regiment). HMSO, 1921. *List with very brief details. Sections for 16th and 18th Bns. reproduced here in full.*

Imperial War Graves Commission: The war graves of the British Empire: Great Britain and Ireland. Vol.8. 1931. *The Commission, now the Commonwealth War Graves Commission, 2, Marlow Road, Maidenhead, Berkshire, SL6 7DX, has published lists of all graves or memorial listings with brief information about each man. Includes soldiers buried in cemeteries and churchyards of Bradford.*

The unveiling of the Bradford War Memorial 1 July 1922. *Programme with a drawing of the memorial.*

Allerton and Daisy Hill War Memorial Souvenir 1914-1918, to commemorate the unveiling of the Allerton and Daisy Hill War Memorial 29 July 1922. *Details and photographs of those killed and names of those who fought.*

APPENDIX 6

The Bradford newspapers published, often some weeks after the event, lists with brief details of men killed, wounded, missing etc.: Bradford Daily Argus, Bradford Daily Telegraph, Yorkshire Observer, Bradford Weekly Telegraph, Yorkshire Observer Budget. *The only index is to a series called "Our Gallant Heroes" in the Bradford Weekly Telegraph 1915 -1918.*

OTHER POSSIBLE SOURCES OF INFORMATION:

Imperial War Museum, Lambeth Road, London, SE1 6HZ.

Liddle Collection of 1914-1918 Personal Experience Archives, University of Leeds Library, Leeds, LS2 9JT

Public Record Office, Ruskin Avenue, Kew, Richmond, London, TW9 4DU, *holds microfilm copies (WO 364) of the "Unburnt Documents", about 8 - 10% of soldiers' papers, mainly for those who received a pension after the war. The records are arranged by name. The "Burnt Documents", about 25% - 30% of soldiers' papers, are gradually being microfilmed (surnames beginning with N, O, Q, U, V and Z had been copied by June 1998) and these films (WO 363) are now available. The rest of the soldiers' papers were destroyed by bombing during the Second World War. The Public Record Office also holds microfilm copies (WO 329) of the Medal Rolls which list most soldiers with brief details including their numbers. There is an index on microfilm (WO 372). Service records for officers, of which about 90% survive, are also at the Public Record Office: Regular and Emergency Reserve officers (WO 339), with an index (WO 338) and Territorial Army officers (WO 374), arranged alphabetically.*

Ministry of Defence, CS(RM)2, Bourne Avenue, Hayes, Middlesex, UB3 1RF, *holds the rest of the "Burnt Documents" and will consult them on behalf of enquirers for a fee. It is necessary to know the soldier's number. It is hoped that these documents will also be microfilmed eventually.*

General Register Office, Myddleton Place, Myddleton street, London, EC1, *has separate indexes for the deaths of soldiers during the war.*

Simon Fowler and others: Army service records of the First World War. 2nd ed., PRO Publications, 1998.

Norman Holding has written the following booklets published by the Federation of Family History Societies:

> World War I army ancestry. 2nd ed. 1991.
> The location of British army records 1914-1918. 3rd ed. 1991.
> More sources of World War I army ancestry. 2nd ed. 1991.

INDEX OF MEN AND PLACES IN THE TEXT:

Citations use either the form of name given in the text or a fuller form if mentioned elsewhere - if it is certain that reference is to the same person. This index also includes citations for Appendix 1: *The Tyke* and Appendix 2: *The Transcripts of the Trials*, but does not reference the alphabetical sequences contained in appendices 4 and 5..

Abbeville 13
Acheville 91, 96
Ackroyd, Private W. 53
Agar, Sergeant 80
Aisne 46
Akam, Lieutenant 39
Alexandria 8
All Saints Gymnastic Club 4
Alred, Private Victor 58
Ambler, Sergeant 14
Ancre, River 59
Arleux Loop North 99
Arleux Loop South 98
Arleux Post 99
Arleux Sector 96, 102
Armitage, Captain 67
Arras 62, 73
Ashworth, 2nd Lieut. L. 74, 82
Ashworth, 2nd Lieutenant 66, 67, 86
Ashworth, Captain 74, 79, 80
Atkinson, 2nd Lieut. A. 103
Avrelle trench 85

Baker 2nd Lieut. F. G. 103
Bakes, Captain L. H. 102, 103
Ballantyne, Captain J. D. 91, 102
Bannister, Private 19
Bantock, 2nd Lieut E. G. 74, 82
Barker, 2nd Lieutenant 86
Barker, Corporal 98
Barltrop, 2nd Lieut. A. H. 74, 82
Barnes, Sergeant 67
Barraclough, Stan 104
Barrie, 2nd Lieut. W. 102
Barrow, 2nd Lieutenant 74
Barrow, Lieutenant J. M. 98, 101
Bartlett, 2nd Lieutenant 74
Basin Wood 30, 42, 43
Battishill, Captain P. H. 99, 102
Beardmore, Private 5 123

Beaumont-Hamel 14
Beauquesne 132
Becker Graben 69
Bell, Private R. 126
Bell, Private R. N. 32, 33
Bentock, 2nd Lieutenant 74, 86
Berg Graben 69
Bertrancourt 45
Bethune 54, 73
Binclark, Sergeant 14
Blagbrough, Captain G. S. 3, 8, 14, 15
Blagbrough, Major G. S. 59, 60
Bleneau trench 40
Blubberhouses Moor 4
Bond, Dickie 31
Booth, Billy 10, 29, 35, 43
Booth, Frank 49
Boweden, 2nd Lieutnant 60
Bradbury, Arthur 24
Bradford Cathedral 9, 104
Bradford City 31
Bradford Pals Old Comrades' Association 68, 104
Bradford trench 36, 37
Bradford, 2nd Lieutenant 69
Bradley, Hylda 119
Bray 85, 97, 98
Bray camp 102
Breen, Sergeant 131,133
Brickstacks 91
Brightwell, Captain A. J. 101
Brissoux trench 59
Broadhead, corporal 60, 61
Brown, 2nd Lieut. G. A. 102
Brown, 2nd Lieut. J. R. 102
Brumley, 2nd Lieut. F. O. 14
Buchanan, 2nd Lieutenant 89
Bullock, Sergeant 39
Bulow Weg 67, 68
Burgoyne, Lance Corporal 14

INDEX OF MEN AND PLACES

Burgoyne, Private C. 86
Burn, Frank 38, 49, 70, 71, 86, 104
Burton, 2nd Lieutenant 90
Burton, Lieutenant 52
Bus-les-Artois 15, 44, 131
Buttler, Sergeant 14

Calderbank, Captain J. 102
Cailloux East 53
Cailloux South 53
Calverley, Sergeant 78
Campbell, 2nd Lieut. T. S. 101
Canada trench 90
Canadian Orchard 53
Caniey, 2nd Lieutenant 90
Carter, Lieutenant-Colonel H. F. G. 47, 62, 74, 75, 80, 81, 86, 87, 92, 93, 94, 102, 132, 133
Carter, Major H. F. G. 40
Casualty Clearing Station 34, 42
Churchill, Sir Winston 104
Citerne 13
Citizens' Army League 1, 3, 6
Clarkson, 2nd Lieut. R. W. 74, 76
Claxton, 2nd Lieut. C. F. 14
Claydon, Private 90
Clements 2nd Lieut. H. J. 102
Clipstone, Nottinghamshire 5
Cloete, Stuart 42
Clough, Captain A. 14, 37, 55
Clough, Captain M. 102
Clough, Lieutenant 27, 28
Clough, Squire 10, 36
Cockenham, Lieutenant A. 103
Cockroft, Sergeant 67
Coigneux 59, 62, 68
Coles, Acting Major W. D. 101
Colincamps 15, 29, 45
Collins, Dick 31, 41
Colsterdale 5
Comerford, 2nd Lieut. A. J. 102
Condett 71
Cook, 2nd Lieutenant 74
Core, Private 126
Corless, Lance Corporal 14
Coulson, Sergeant Leslie 119
Courcellers Road 68
Courcelles 59

Cover trench 53
Cowell, 2nd Lieut. F. T. 74, 80, 82
Crabtree, 2nd Lieut. L. 102
Craven, Colonel 28
Crawshaw, Mr 4
Crimmins, Private Herbert 131, 132, 133, 136
Croix Barbes 51, 54
Cross, Lieutenant 40, 41, 52
Cross, Lieutenant R. S. 38, 51
Crossland, Corporal H. 123
Crowther, 2nd Lieut. E. 66, 82
Crowther, Lieutenant 74, 86, 122
Croxford, Captain L. H. 100, 102
Croydon, Lieutenant Colonel A. C. 60, 67, 74, 80, 81, 82, 83, 97, 98, 101
Crucifix 66, 67
Culling, Sergeant W. 53
Cussons, Company Sergeant Major 90, 100
Cussons, Private 53
Cussons, Sergeant Major G. 36, 39, 54
Cyprus 8

Dalley, Captain Harry H. 52, 55, 56, 102, 132, 135
Dalton, 2nd Lieut. r. G. 93
Dams, 2nd Lieutenant 81
Dams, Lieutenant F. D. 103
Denton, Lance Corporal 51
Dickenson, 2nd Lieut. T. E. 103
Dickes, Lieutenant A. 102
Djingjurd 8
Dodsworth, Sergeant 14
Doullens 55, 62
Doullens-Bernaville area 60
Drake, Private 37
Drake, Sergeant H. 28, 55, 128
Duckitt, Captain C. S. 29, 80
Duckworth, 2nd Lieut. C. H. 103
Dunmow trench 37, 38, 40

Ecoivres 99
Ecurie 85
Ecurie Wood 99
Edmondson, Private A. 123
Edmondson, Private G. 123
Edgware Road 51
Edward Post 51

Egypt 8, 10, 11
Empress of Britain 7, 8
Etaples 61
Euston Dump 43, 131
Euston Road Cemetery 48
Evans, Captain A. H. 99
Evans, Captain H. 102

Famechon 55
Farrar, 2nd Lieut. J. F. 102
Farrar, Sergeant 66, 67
Feather, 2nd Lieut. J. P. 102
Festubert 53
Festubert (Central) 53
Festubert (East) 53
Festubert left sub-section 54
Feuillade Barracks 73
Fir trench 62
Fletcher, Lieutenant 52
Flood, Corporal 14
Foizey, Lieutenant Harold Egbert 38, 39, 48
Fontaine-au-Pire 46
Fovant, Wiltshire 7, 135
Francis, Lance Corporal W. 98
Fraser Camp 90, 99
Fresnoy 73

Garbutt, 2nd Lieut. D. G. 102
Garde Stellung 68, 69, 70
Gaunt, Private 87
Gaverelle Trench 72
Gavrelle 73, 81, 83
Gavrelle sector 84, 86
Gavrelle-Fresnes Road 85
Gee, Lance-Corporal 10
Gertie Miller trench 90
Gezaincourt 21, 23
Gibraltar 7
Gibson, Lieutenant A. S. 53
Gill, 2nd Lieut. D. A. 57, 58
Gill, 2nd Lieut. H. 103
Givenchy Keep 54
Givenchy sector 53, 54
Goldthorpe, Corporal Norman 37, 38, 39
Gommecourt Park 63, 64, 65
Gommecourt-Hebuterne road 60
Gommmecourt saliant 62
Graham 2nd Lieut. C. P. 57

Gransbury, Private George 34
Gray, 2nd Lieut. J. 103
Greenhow, Private W. 123
Greenwood, Captain J. J. G. 101
Greville, 2nd Lieut. D. O. 74, 82
Grey trench 40
Grieg, Major McCavin 124
Guiljoyle, Pre W. 126
Guyon, Major G. S. 23, 33, 34, 49

Haig, Field-Marshall Douglas 13, 20, 25, 43, 71, 104, 133, 136
Halifax 44
Hall, Fred 49
Hallam, Private 86
Hammond, Lieutenant and Q/M B. 102
Hanson, Private Albert 84, 85
Hardaker, Private L. 128
Harris, 2nd Lieutenant 81
Harrison, Private George 10
Hartley, Frank 104
Hartley, Private Frank 37, 39, 41
Hartman, 2nd Lieutenant 63, 64
Haworth, Private J. 123
Heaton 20
Hebuterne 70
Hebuterne Keep 60
Hebuterne left sub-sector 59
Hebuterne Sector 57, 62
Hen Post 51
Herts Redoubt 54
Hewitson, Private F. 123
Hicks, Company Q.M.S. 14
Higgins, Corporal C. 60
Hilders Redoubt 54
Hill, Adrian 72, 88
Hindenburg line 62
Hodgson, Private James Frederick 16
Hodgson, Private Jimmy 15
Hoffman, 2nd Lieut. J. M .H. 14
Hoffman, Lieutenant S. L. F. 14
Hollis, 2nd Lieut. J. D. 103
Holmes, Captain F. 14
Holmes, F. 15
Holmes, Ralph 39
Holt, 2nd Lieutenant 64
Horne, Dawson 11, 29, 30, 31, 48
Horner, 2nd Lieut. W. R. 103

INDEX OF MEN AND PLACES

Horner, Captain 42
Hough, Lieutenant O. V. L. 102
Howarth, Lieutenant 41, 52
Howarth, Lieutenant A. 51
Hoyle, 2nd Lieut. F. H. 103
Hughes, Bill 21
Humphries, 2nd Lieut. W. R. 52
Hun Street 54
Hunter-Weston, Lieutenant-General Sir A. G. 21, 26, 28, 45, 46
Hustwick, Sergeant 65, 135
Hunter D. Corporal. 87
Illingworth, Captain O. 74, 79, 82
Illingworth, Private Norman 35
Ingham, private A. 21
Ingedew, Private T. W. 123
Ingles, Brigadier-General J. D. 94, 103, 133, 136
Ingram, Corporal W. 89
Isles, Gilbert 4

Jackson, 2nd Lieut. R. W. 102
Jackson, 2nd Lieut. S. S. L. 102
Jena Bart trench 59
Jewel trench 85
John Copse 26
Johnson, 2nd Lieut. J. 74. 128
Jowett, 2nd Lieut. E. 102
Jowett, Lieutenant 36, 37
Joyous trench 85

Kantara 9
Keen, Captain C. H. C. 38
Keighley, Corporal E. 66
Kellet, Private W. 86
Kennard, Lieutenant-Colonel M. N. 14, 38, 47, 50
Kennedy, Lieutenant Colonel 59
Kennedy, Major H. H. 40, 54, 133, 136
Kennington, Eric 12
Kennington, Lieutenant F. R. 102, 103
Kenny, Bill 10, 29, 44
Key-Jones, Captain 89
Kiddle, 2nd Lieut. C. F. 103
Kiddle, 2nd Lieutenant 90
King, 2nd Lieut. D. T. 57
King, Lieutenant D. T. 98, 100
King, Lieutenant J. R. 102

Kitchener Camp 91
Kitchener, Lord 1, 6, 19, 124
Knight, Lieutenant 67
Knox trench 59

L'Ecleme 50, 54
La Folie Wood 91
La Miquellerie 54
Languard trench 30, 38, 41
Lansdown Post 51
Lawson, 2nd Lieut. J. P. 102
Laxton, 2nd Lieut. C. F. 33
Laxton, Lieutenant R. E. 19
Le Plantin North 53
Lee, Corporal 51
Leeming, Private H. 123
Legend Street 40
Lehmann Graben 68
Les Lobes 50, 52
Lestram 50, 53
Ligny 46
Lillers 55
Linkburn 83
Lipton, Company Sergeant Major G. H. 52
Liverpool Docks 7
Loos, Battle of 27
Lorel, 2nd Lieut. G. R. 103
Louvencourt 45
Luke, 2nd Lieut. J. 59, 100
Lyall, 2nd Lieut. G. L. 102

MacKay, Private E. 19
MacTavish, Major 42
Maitland trench 40
Makin, 2nd Lieut. K. T. 102
Malta 8
Manley, Sergeant 14, 79
Manningham Park 3, 5
Marne 46
Maroeuil 85, 99
Marsden, 2nd Lieut. J. W. 102
Marseilles 13
Martin, Private 90
Mason, 2nd Lieut. H. R. 59
McConnel, Corporal 14
McConnel, lance Corporal 53
Meadows, Sergeant 97
Merelessart 13

MericourtAcheville Road 96
Metcalf, 2nd Lieutenant 91
Metcalf, Corporal Harry 35, 43
Midgeley, Private A. R. 123
Midgley, Private 126
Miller, Tony 4
Moat Farm 54
Moltke Graben 66
Monk trench 40
Mont St. Eloi Station 101
Mont St. Eloy 90
Montreal trench 90
Moon, Private S. M. 123
Moor, Corporal 14
Moor, Major 15
Moore, Private J. 53
Morant, Captain G. A. McK. 101
Morgan, George xii, 2, 4, 10, 11, 15, 19, 29, 30, 31, 35, 43, 44, 61, 74, 90, 91, 104
Morgan, Lieutenant 67
Morgan, Sergeant W. 14, 30
Morris, Private 86, 87
Muller, Colonel G. H. 4
Murgatroyd, Captain E. 102
Mysore Lancers 10

Neauvry 73
Neill, Major R. B. 33
Nelson, Corporal 14
Nelson, Sergeant 67, 90
Nesbitt, Captain H. S. 102
Neuve Chapelle Right Sub Sector 50
Neuve Chapelle sector 53, 54
Neuville St. Vaast 89, 90, 96
New Brunswick trench 91, 92
Newton, Corporal 14
Nicholls, 2nd Lieut. G. 59
Nicholson, Company Sergeant Major 78
North and South Monk trenches 30, 33
North, Private 126
Northern Avenue 44
Nova Scotia trench 90

O'Gowan, Major General R. Wanless 29
Oak Post 99
Oddy, Sergeant Major A. W. 126
Onam, Private C. 135
Oppy 75, 80, 81

Oppy Wood 83
Oppy-Arleux Road 98
Orchard Redoubt 54
Ottowa Camp 90
Owen, Corporal 14

Page, Private 78
Paisley Dump 42
Palestine 10
Palframan, Corporal W. 76
Parker, 2nd Lieut. N. 82
Parker, 2nd Lieut. P. C. 14
Parker, Captain P. L. 74, 75, 79, 80, 86
Parker, Lieutenant 74
Parsey, 2nd Lieut. L. 102
Patchet, Private J. 11, 51
Paus, 2nd Lieutenant O. L. 90
Peace, Captain W. 93, 94
Peace, Lieutenant 40
Pearson, 2nd Lieut. A. L. 102
Pearson, Private T. 54
Pendant Alley East 26
Pendant Copse 26
Penn, 2nd Lieut. A. S. 103
Pernes 101, 103
Picardy 14
Pioneer Graben 66
Pioneer trench 53
Platnauer, 2nd Lieut. L. M. 74, 79, 82
Ploegsteert 46
Pont Fixe South 54
Pont Remy 13
Pope & Bradley 2
Poppy Redoubt 54
Port Arthur 51, 54
Port Said 8, 13
Price, 2nd Lieut. F. de B. 102
Price, Private 37
Priday, 2nd Lieut. N. H. 63, 64, 65, 68, 78
Priestley, J. B. 15
Priestly, Sir W.E.B. 1
Pringle, Captain R. W. A. 14, 15, 34, 35, 47
Puisieux 35
Puisieux trench 26
Pullen, Sergeant 14

INDEX OF MEN AND PLACES

Quadrilateral Redoubt 15, 38
Quarries Road 96
Quarry 91, 92
Quebec 91
Quebec trench 90, 92, 93
Quigley, Sergeant G. 57, 58

Railway Avenue 44
Railway Cutting 84, 86
Ramsden, Lieutenant E. A. 103
Ransome, Lieutenant C. T. 14, 34, 40
Rawlings, Fred 29
Rawlinson, General Sir Henry 28
Rawnsley, Fred 42
Reader, Sergeant H. 131, 134
Redan 19
Redan Ridge 15
Redman, Private Harry 48
Revill, Sergeant W. H. 87
Richard, Lieutenant J. L. 102
Richmond trench 53
Riley, Batman 77
Riley, Private H. L. 51
Ripon 5, 6
Robb, 2nd Lieutenant 89
Robinson, Lieutenant 3, 78
Robinson, Major A. W. 62, 67, 69, 70, 102, 103
Roche, Captain 42
Roche, Captain C. 102, 110, 123
Rockliff, George 36
Roclincourt 85, 91
Rossignol farm 60
Rossignol Wood 65, 66, 67, 68, 70
Rue de L'Epinette 53
Russell, Captain H. 14, 19

Sackville Street 29, 30, 40
Sailly aux Bois 59, 60
Salmon Glucksteins 4
Salmons, 2nd Lieut. H. 103
Sands, Sergeant Albert E. xi, 5, 71
Saville, Sergeant 14
Scott, 2nd Lieut. P. H. 103
Scott, Alfred 4
Scott, Sergeant Major H. 4, 87
Serre 21, 26, 41, 59
Serre Cemetery 104

Serre Church steeple 33
Serre Road 15, 38
Severn, Private Harry 34
Shackleton, Lance Corporal 14
Shetland trench 53
Skipton 3
Slack, Yorkshire 47
Sleigh, Lieutenant 63, 64
Slingsby, Private F. 19, 22
Smith, 2nd Lieut. E. 103
Smith, 2nd Lieut. G. W. 103
Smith, Captain 31
Smith, Captain D. 34, 36
Smith, Captain Donald C. 47
Smith, Captain Donald G. 11
Smith, Private 19, 39
Southern Avenue 29
Souza, Captain L. L. de 99, 102
Sowden, Sergeant 14
St. Catherine, near Arras 84
Staff, 2nd Lieut. O. H. 63, 64, 86, 87
Stanley, 2nd Lieut. J. L. 74, 80, 82, 86, 97, 98
Steal, Private E. 123
Steele, Sergeant 86
Stephenson, 2nd Lieutenant 41
Stephenson, Captain A. D. 38, 39
Stewart, Brigadier-General Ian 94, 95
Stubbs, Private W. 123
Stump Alley 66, 67
Sucrerie 19, 99
Suez Canal 9
Sunken Road 78, 79
Sutcliff, Lieutenant R. 29
Sutcliffe, Lieutenant R. 14, 34, 47, 48
Sutcliffe, Private H. 57, 58
Symonds, 2nd Lieut. Frank 35, 47, 100

Tankard, Private H. 123
Tarran, Private 78
Taylor, George 14, 104
Tempest, Captain E. V. 42, 50
Tetlow, Cyril 20
Thiepval 24, 41
Thiepval Memorial 47
Thievres 55, 59
Thornton, 2nd Lieut. C. A. F. 103

Thornton, 2nd Lieutenant 41, 131, 132, 133, 135
Thornton, Captain J. R. 63, 64, 70, 71
Thornton, Private F. 123
Thornton, Reverend 9
Tidmarsh, Sergeant 7.8
Tilly, Major C. W. 62
Tired Alley 96
Tommy Post 99
Tooke, Captain B. 51
Topham, Private T. 123
Totnes trench 90, 91, 92, 93
Tucker, 2nd Lieut. G. L. 66, 67, 74, 82, 86
Tweedale, Private S. 86

Vailly 62
Vercingetorix trench 59
Verdun 25
Vignacourt 131, 132
Village Line 53
Vimy 91
Vimy Ridge 73

Waddilove, Private Norman 35
Waddington, Abe 43
Wadsworth, Arthur 2
Walton, 2nd Lieut. J. J. 102
Walton, 2nd Lieutenant 52
Watson, Lieutenant 52
Watson, Sergeant 14
Whitaker, 2nd Lieutenant 41
Whitaker, Lieutenant 40
Whitaker, Private William 48
White House 95
Whithead, 2nd Lieut. J. 103
Whitley, Thomas 4
Whittacker, Captain F. W. 102
Wilcock, Dudley 5
Wild, private Arthur 131, 132, 133, 134, 135, 136
Wilkinson, Company Sergeant Major 67, 120
Will, John 10
Willerval 99
Williams, Captain F. T. 38
Williams, Lieutenant E. 103
Wilson, 2nd Lieut. E. 55, 91, 102

Wilson, Ernest 38
Windmill 83
Windy Corner 54
Wise, Corporal T. 131, 132, 134, 135
Woman Street 57, 65, 68
Wood trench 80
Wood, Corporal W. S. 123
Wood, 2nd Lieut. A. B. P. 102
Wood, 2nd Lieut. J. L. 51, 103
Wood, Lieutenant J. L. 102
Woodhouse, Lance Corporal 14
Woodroofe, Doctor 4
Worsnop, 2nd Lieut. J. W. 28
Wright, 2nd Lieut. R. B. 103

Yankee Street 57
Yellow Street 57
Yiddish Street 64
Yorke, Captain H. E. 133, 136
Ypres 46

ADDENDUM

FASCIMILE OF

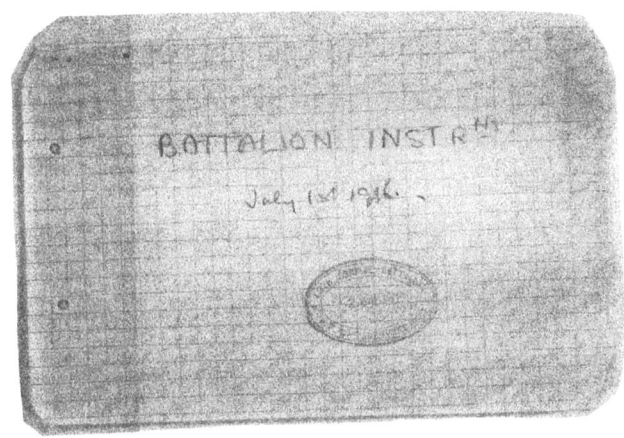

*BATTLE ORDER OF
THE 93rd INFANTRY BRIGADE
1/7/1916*

THE BRADFORD PALS

S E C R E T.   Copy No.

Refer'ence
1:20,000 Map.

93rd Infantry Brigade Order No. 37

22-6-16.

1. The Brigade will be disposed on Y day as follows:-

Brigade Headquarters	BUS
18th Durham L.I.	COURCELLES
15th West Yorks Regt.	BUS
16th "	"
18th W "	"
93rd Machine Gun Coy	"
93rd Bde. Trench Mortar	"

2. Troops will march to their positions of assembly on Y/Z night in accordance with attached March Table.
   Head of the Column to cross SAILL AU BOIS - MAILLY Road at 10 p.m.
   All Units will be in positions of assembly by 1-30 a.m. Z day.

3. 93rd Brigade Machine Gun Company and 93rd Brigade Trench Mortar Battery will be in position by 9 p.m. Y night.
   The same route as the remainder of the Brigade will be used

4. The route to be used will be reconnoitred both by day and night by one officer and one N.C.O. per platoon.

5. Strict orders will be issued to all ranks that :-
   a. Perfect silence must be maintained on the march and in the trenches.
   b. No smoking or lights will be permitted after leaving billets.
   c. Ranks <u>must</u> be well closed up on the march.

6. The three Companies of the Battalion of the 92nd Infantry Brigade holding the line will be withdrawn at 1-30 a.m. Z day.

7. Officers Commanding Units will report at once to Brigade Headquarters when they are in position in their assembly trenches.

8. Reports on the march will be sent to the head of the Column till reaching COLINCAMPS - afterwards to Brigade Headquarters LEGEND STREET.

ADDENDUM

SECRET.

INSTRUCTIONS FOR THE ATTACK.   Copy No.

19/6/16.

1) The attack of the 31st Division will be carried out by the 93rd and 94th Brigade; the 93rd Bde on the right and the 94th Bdeon the left. One Company 12th K.O.Y.L.I. will be attached to each Bde. 92nd Bde less one Battalion will form the Divisional reserve. The remaining battalion will hold our present line of trenches.

2. The dividing line between the 93rd and 94th Bde will be a line drawn from the northern point of LA SIGNY FARM orchard, thru K.28.c.1d and the southern point of MATTHEW COPSE, K.29.c.59. The division between the two Forward Brigades and the Bde in Divisional Reserve will be SACKVILLE ST.

3. The 93rd Bde completes its task in four "bounds." The ground occupied by each bound will be consolidated by the troops told off to capture it.

The actual attack on each line will be carried out by successive waves of troops at distances varying from 50 to 200 yds between each wave.

4. For the attack the dividing line between the 93rd and 94th Bde will be:- Junction of trenches K.29.c.8p.-S. corner of SERRE Village (inclusive to 94th) - thence along hedge forming S.E. boundary

2.

of SERRE to K.30.b.62 (incl. to 94th) - thence along hedge to where it cuts trench at L.25.a.26 (inclusive to 94th).

5. OBJECTIVE OF 1ST BOUND:-
German trench K.30.c.26 to junction of trenches K.36.a.19. This will be consolidated and garrisoned by two companies of 15th W. Yorks, and will be known as the GREEN LINE.

2nd OBJECTIVE:
German trench from Southern corner of SERRE tocross tracks at K.36.a.87. This will be taken by the 16th W. Yorks and consolidated and garrisoned by the remaining two companies of the 15th W. YIorks, and will be known as the RED LINE.

3rd OBJECTIVE:-
German trench from S.E. corner of orchard at L.25.a.26 to L.25.a.74, thencethence to PENDANT COPSE (incl).This line will be taken by the 16th W. Yorks, with one Company of the 18th D.L.I. on the right to take PENDANT COPSE. It will be consolidated and garrisoned by the 16th W. Yorks,with one Company of 18th D.L.I., and will be known as the BROWN LINE.

4th OBJECTIVE.-
German trench from point L.25.a.74 to cross roads L.26.c.56, and thence to junction of PENDANT ALLEY EAST and PUISIEUX TRENCH at L.26.c.3555. This line will be consolidated & garrisoned by 18th W. Yks and known as the BLE LINE.

ADDENDUM

6. When the final objective has been reached the line will be held as follows:-

93rd Bde on the right - from Cross roads L.26.o.56 exclusive to corner of fence L.25.a.26 exclusive.
94th Bde on the left from corner of fence L.25.a.26 inclusive to our own trenches at K.23.d.32.

The line must be strongly entrenched and all preparations made for putting up wire as soon as possible.

Battalions are to be prepared to hold this line against heavy counter-attacks.

The dividing line between the Brigades will be the same as for the attack.

7. Strong points (garrisoned by 1 officer, 2 NCOs and 25 O.R. rxxiix and 1 Machine Gun) will be established and lettered as below:-

```
GREEN LINE   -   "O"   K.36.a.19
RED LINE     -   "P"   K.36.a.79.
BROWN LINE   -   "Q"   100 yds W. of PENDANT COPSE.
    do.      -   "N"   L.25.b.93.
    do.      -   "K"   L.25.c.59.
    do.      -   "R"   L.25.a.74.
BLUE LINE    -   "F"   L.25.b.41
    do.      -   "G"   L.26.b.47.
```

4.

8. The following deep sapes will be run out towards the enemy's lines, with a view to being opened up afterwards near the enemy's trenches on the day of the attack and afterwards used for communications.

"A".Sap - From junction of trenches K.29.c.84 towards German communication trench at K.29.d.13.

"B" Sap - From trench K.29.c.86 towards German communication trench at K.29.d.18.

These are under construction by the 13th York & Lancs, under the supervision of O.C. 252nd Tunnelling Company.

9. The German communication trenches up to GREEN LINE will be cleared by 12th JH.O.L.L.I.(2 Companies).

The clearing and construction of communication trenches forward of these will be carried out by the Battalions concerned.

10. Four main communication trenches will run from the GREEN LINE of defens up to SACKVILLE STREET. A fifth trench will take over from PYLON AVENUE and then continue to SACKVILLE STREET. The two Northern and two centre HOMEWARD BOUND. the one most southern of these will be OUTWAR BOUND trenches; the

11. From SACKVILLE ST. forward to the front line there will be two outward and two homeward main communication trenches. The

ADDENDUM

5)

two outward will be WARLEY AVENUE and FLAG AVENUE, and the two homeward GREY and BLENBAU

? The outward trenches are:- WAGRAM - NORTHERN AVENUE - SOUTHERN AVENUE - NAIRNE - EXCEMA - WARLEY - FLAG *summed*
The Homeward trenches are:- CENTRAL AVENUE - RAILWAY AVENUE - JORDAN - CARAU - GREY - BLENBAU. *[initialled]*

12. Dumps will be formed and numbered in accordance with sketch issued to Company Commanders. For Very pistols, cartridges and ammunition, No. 3 will be the dump for this Battn and the 18th D.L.I. For rations No. 2 will be the Battn dump, i/c of 2/Lt. Thornton and 6 men of the band. Each dump will contain 2,000 food and water rations and 50,000 rds S.A.A.

13. The Battalion will issue from its assembly trenches into the open by means of ladders or steps in the traverses.. A stake driven in over top of parapet is also necessary in order to assist men in getting out.

14. Infantry marking fans coloured Yellow above and red below will be issued at the rate of 4 per Company. These discs must be waved during the attack and not kept still, the object being to show the gunners the position of the front line of the infantry.

6.

15. A system of runners in relays will be organised by Companies to keep in touch with Battalion H.Q., and approximate casualty reports will be rendered on passing over each objective and on reaching final line. These casualty reports need only state the number of Officers and of O.R., without specifying whether killed, wounded, or missing. Too much stress cannot be laid on the rendering of these casualty reports, as the rapidity with which reinforcements come up depends entirely on the speed with which Coy Commanders render casualty reports to Battn H.Q.

A detailed casualty report for record purposes (giving date on which they occurred), must be rendered as soon as possible. In this report accuracy is essential.

Company Commanders are reminded that it is of the utmost importance to keep Battn H.Q. informed at frequent intervals of the state of affairs, in order that higher authority may be informed accordingly.

16. If any screens are found in captured trenches they should not be pulled down, as they are a sign to German artillery not to fire on the trenches in which they are placed.

All men should also be warned against the probable misuse of white flags and signs of surrender by the enemy. The enemy have been known to sham death and then fire into the back of our assault.

ADDENDUM

If any prisoners are taken, 2 men provide a sufficiently large escort.

17. Wire cutters will be carried by each section according to the numbers available. They will be attached to the shoulder strap by lanyards and carried in the belt. Men carrying wire cutters will wear a yellow band round the right arm.

Two mallets per platoon will also be carried in a similar manner, as these are indispensable for removing enemy entanglements in order to use them for our own purpose.

Six coils of concertina barbed wire will be carried by each platoon. These can be carried between two men on stakes, which will be used for wiring.

18. No orders and only the specially issued maps of the German trenches will be taken into the attack.

19. Trench police will be detailed to regulate the traffic in the trenches by the Brigade, who will see that the outward and homeward trenches are only used as such, with the exception of staff officers, R.O.O.'s, telephone linesmen, or R.B. and Pioneers engaged on maintenance of trenches.

20. All ranks are to be warned to keep well down in the trenches during the bombardment and wirecutting. The strictest discipline will be maintained previous to the assault.

21. Tools to be carried by the men will be issued to Battn Commanders

8.

by the Brigade. Mobilization tools of units will be kept intact and packed in vehicles.

22 Troops will be allotted distinguishing pieces of cloth, of the same colour as the line they will occupy. This Battn will wear blue strips of cloth tied to their right shoulder strap.

It is the duty of all ranks to see that no men belonging to forward bounds are allowed to stay behind the bound allotted to them.

Bridges:

23 If bridges are not placed over the trenches, the easiest way to cross is at the traverses, where the trench generally narrows.

24 O.C. 15th W. Yorks will arrange for a tape or pin line of pickets to be placed in "No Man's Land" 50 yds out the night before the assault takes place, parallel to the line of attack. All unit commanders will have compass bearings of the points on which they are directed to march.

25 All officers surplus to 22, together with 75 other ranks, will be left with first-line transport as reinforcements.

One NCO and 20 men will be detailed to act as carriers for Trench Mortar Batteries.

Two NCOs and 60 men will be detailed as carriers for water, rations, ammunition, R.B. material, etc.

One NCO and 2 men per Battn will be detailed as battle police, and 2 NCOs and 4 O.R. to act as trench police.

ADDENDUM

9.

50 per cent of Coy and H.Q. signallers will be left behind with the transport and be called for as required to replace casualties. All articles to be carried will be made up into one-man lots, and the men actually tested in carrying them before the attack.

DRESS.- F.S. order, without packs or greatcoats, as per sketch issued. The following will be carried:-

Waterproof sheet and cardigan. } By all NCOs
3 sandbags   } and men.
2 Mills grenades
170 rds ammunition

1 pick or shovel, in the proportion of } By all men.
2 shovels to 1 pick.   }

Four flares will be carried by every officer and NCO. These flares will be used for showing the position of the front line to contact patrol aeroplane.

The packs and greatcoats will be stored under Battn arrangements.

Two gas helmets will be carried by all ranks. One of these will be worn with the front rolled up over the face. A 2nd case troops should have to enter trenches or localities where there is gas. All ranks should be warned that cellars may be full of gas and should not be entered without smoke helmets being lowered.

Signallers, Lewis gunners, and others issued with P.H.G. helmets will wear the P.H.G. helmet and carry the P.H. in the satchel.

10.

Every officer, NCO, and map will start for the attack with full water bottle, iron ration, and one complete day's ration in his haversack. A hotmeal will be given before proceeding to assembly trenches. Vickers gunners attached to Battalions will be fed by those batns.

The following positions will be used in each bound for dumping S.A.A., tools, wirecutters, etc., collected from dead and wounded:-

First Bound - Strong Point O.
Second   do.   M.P.
Third   do.   Q.M.R.B.
Fourth   do.   P. & D.

Special parties will be detailed by Battns to deal with any Germans passed over between the brown and blue line which are not being consolidated.

Particular attention will be paid to tunnels, which it is

ADDENDUM

11.

believed the enemy constructs to support front trenches.

Company Commanders will impress on their men the necessity of pushing forward to their objective regardless of the progress of units on either flank. By doing so they will help these units if they are in any way held up.

They will also make it known to all ranks that the care of wounded is not in their province, and special men are detailed for this purpose. In addition to the 4 stretcher bearers per Company, 4 extra per Company of the band will also be detailed.

The day on which the preliminary bombardment commences will be known as U, and the day of the assault as Z.

In order to enable patrols to examine the enemy's wire, there will be no artillery fire on the enemy's front line between the hours named below:-

V night - 11 pm - 12 midnight.
W night - 10.30 pm - 11.30 pm.
X night - 12 midnight to 1 am
Y night - 11.30 pm to 12.30 am.

During the remainder of these nights the enemy's wire will be kept under fire.

The 92nd Brigade will carry out a raid on one of the nights

12.

preliminary bombardment. Advantage will be taken of one of the lulls mentioned in the above paragraph for this purpose.

On the day of the attack the actual hour of attack will be known as zero. Saps A and B will be opened up one hour before zero. The openings will be about 30 or 40 yards distant from the German first line.

Communication trenches required to join these sap-heads to the German front line will be dug by 12th KO.Y.L.I. as soon as the first objective is captured.

The Battalion will take up its position of assembly under cover of darkness the night before the assault takes place, as per attached sketch.

The Battalion of the 92nd Brigade holding the line during the preliminary bombardment will leave one company in our trenches and march to its place of assembly as soon as the 93rd and 94th Bdes have occupied the front line. The Company of the 92nd Bde left in the front line will be distributed equally in each assaulting Bde section, the object being to always keep a few men in the front trench after the attack has gone forward in case it is unsuccessful, and to rally any of our men who may be driven back and ensure that they do not retire further than the original front line.

ADDENDUM

13.

Heavy artillery lifts as follows:-

9.20 Lifts from GREEN line for 93rd Bde.
0.40

{ Set Thought attack life

If it be found necessary to re-bombard some locality during the assault with heavy artillery, the bombardment will last for 30 minutes, the last 5 of which will be intense.

Every commander, Company commander, or section commander will keep in touch throughout with the commander of the similar formation on his flanks. They must know the dispositions and action being taken by their neighbours, more particularly so when the units on their extreme flanks belong to another Division.

There will be a smoke bombardment during the preliminary bombardment along the whole of our front for 15 minutes, to take place at the following times, which have been arranged to coincide with special artillery bombardments to take place each day. (check these)

V   4.10 to 4.25 am
W   9.10 am - 9.25 am
X   4.40 am - 4.55 am
Y   5.50 am - 6.15 am

14.

Y. 6.10 – 6.25 am
6.10 – 4.25 p.m.
During the assault the smoke barrage will be as under:-
0.0 to 1.0 – JOHN COPSE to SERRE-PUISIEUX road.

The sketches of the various types of strong points issued must be thoroughly explained to all men, and if possible practice in their construction carried out.

One battery of Stokes mortars will be in Sap A and one in Sap B. Emplacements will be 100 yds forward of the front line trenches and be opened up one hour before zero.
Ammunition dumps are also being constructed near the batteries Before the assault there will be 10 minutes hurricane bombardment by the Stokes batteries all along the line. For this bombardment six batteries will be detached from the Brigades and placed under the orders of the Divisional Bombing Officer, who will make all necessary arrangements for the bombardment.

The remaining 3 batteries will not come into action and will remain under the orders of their respective Brigadiers.
During the period 10 minutes before zero to zero, the attacking troops will issue from their trenches and form up on their assaulting line.

15.

Runners will be on the usual scale of 4 per Company and 12 at Battn H.Q., who will wear their distinctive badge. They will wear service dress, rifle, single bandolier, and gas helmet. They must have an intimate knowledge of our trenches, the position of Battn and Brigade H.Q., dumps, water pipes, etc. They will be given instruction in the ground they are likely to work over in advance by means of maps and visits to Batn. O.Ps, and will be shown likely positions battalions will take up. They must be worked in relays, and dugouts must be constructed for them at suitable intervals.

In the event of any guns being captured they will be removed by the artillery as soon as possible. Teams will be told off ready for this purpose.

When pushing forward signallers, machine guns, or trench mortars, it is advisable to send forward two parties a second by another route to make sure of one reaching the required point.

No. 1 platoon will provide the garrison for a strong point, and No. 14 will be detailed to help consolidate and man it.

16.

No. 8 Platoon will detail a garrison for F strong point, as will aos No. 16 platoon, who will be told off to consolidate it. This will ensure, in the event of casualties, that the garrison will consist of one officer, 2 NCOS, and 25 men when the forward blue line is taken.

For the purpose of ensuring Vickers guns reaching their destination, one will be attached to No. 16 platoon, but will remain at Q in the Brown line. The Platoon Commander will give all possible help to ensure the gun getting there .... 2 Vickers guns will go with HH.Q. .... to its position on N. the other going to H. The two Vickers will be attached to No. 16 platoon. .... 1K ...... will go to K .... to These, together with one from H.Q., will go to K .... to form the garrison there, the other two remaining there until the Brown line is taken. They will then work along the communication trench into the point B, and one go to strong point F and the other to G.